THE COMPLETE IDIOT'S GUIDE® TO

Golf

Second Edition

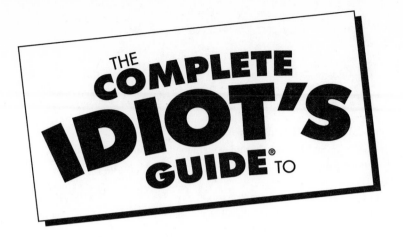

Golf

Second Edition

by Michelle McGann with Matthew Rudy

ALPHA

A member of Penguin Group (USA) Inc.

ALPHA BOOKS

Published by the Penguin Group

Penguin Group (USA) Inc., 375 Hudson Street, New York, New York 10014, U.S.A.

Penguin Group (Canada), 10 Alcorn Avenue, Toronto, Ontario, Canada M4V 3B2 (a division of Pearson Penguin Canada Inc.)

Penguin Books Ltd, 80 Strand, London WC2R 0RL, England

Penguin Ireland, 25 St Stephen's Green, Dublin 2, Ireland (a division of Penguin Books Ltd)

Penguin Group (Australia), 250 Camberwell Road, Camberwell, Victoria 3124, Australia (a division of Pearson Australia Group Pty Ltd)

Penguin Books India Pvt Ltd, 11 Community Centre, Panchsheel Park, New Delhi—110 017, India

Penguin Group (NZ), cnr Airborne and Rosedale Roads, Albany, Auckland 1310, New Zealand (a division of Pearson New Zealand Ltd)

Penguin Books (South Africa) (Pty) Ltd, 24 Sturdee Avenue, Rosebank, Johannesburg 2196, South Africa

Penguin Books Ltd, Registered Offices: 80 Strand, London WC2R 0RL, England

International Standard Book Number: 1-59257-309-6
Library of Congress Catalog Card Number: 2004115919

07 06 05   8 7 6 5 4 3 2

Interpretation of the printing code: The rightmost number of the first series of numbers is the year of the book's printing; the rightmost number of the second series of numbers is the number of the book's printing. For example, a printing code of 05-1 shows that the first printing occurred in 2005.

Printed in the United States of America

Note: This publication contains the opinions and ideas of its authors. It is intended to provide helpful and informative material on the subject matter covered. It is sold with the understanding that the authors and publisher are not engaged in rendering professional services in the book. If the reader requires personal assistance or advice, a competent professional should be consulted.

The authors and publisher specifically disclaim any responsibility for any liability, loss, or risk, personal or otherwise, which is incurred as a consequence, directly or indirectly, of the use and application of any of the contents of this book.

Most Alpha books are available at special quantity discounts for bulk purchases for sales promotions, premiums, fundraising, or educational use. Special books, or book excerpts, can also be created to fit specific needs.

For details, write: Special Markets, Alpha Books, 375 Hudson Street, New York, NY 10014.

Publisher: *Marie Butler-Knight*
Product Manager: *Phil Kitchel*
Senior Managing Editor: *Jennifer Bowles*
Senior Acquisitions Editor: *Renee Wilmeth*
Development Editor: *Jennifer Moore*
Senior Production Editor: *Billy Fields*

Copy Editor: *Kelly Henthorne*
Cartoonist: *Richard King*
Cover/Book Designer: *Trina Wurst*
Indexer: *Tonya Heard*
Layout: *Becky Harmon*
Proofreading: *Donna Martin*

Contents at a Glance

Appendixes

Contents

Foreword

I first met Michelle at an American Junior Golf Association tournament when she was just 16 years old. Michelle was standing there on the range behind another girl. Even though she was young, she was so tall (with a presence), and she was just killing the ball!

The next year, she made it through qualifying for the U.S. Women's Open, and I happened to be there doing corporate work. I had an extended conversation with her parents about Michelle turning professional right out of high school. It was the same situation as a lot of those kids who are going to the NBA early. She had the length and the strength, and she had great command of her abilities and her emotions. But she would be giving up four years of fun in college, and nobody likes to have fun more than Michelle. Once she decided to turn pro, I asked her to spend lots of time with Donna Caponi (a veteran and two-time, back-to-back U.S. Women's Open champion) to learn the ropes. Luckily, Michelle's parents found time to travel with her those first few years, and she blossomed into a star. I'm pleased with the level she's reached. People probably know her more for her hats than her talent, but she has the opportunity to go down in history as one of the dominant players on the women's tour.

No matter what happens on the golf course, attitude is the most important thing. And that is one of the key reasons why Michelle is so good. She's a competitor, and she has a great attitude. If she gets down, she doesn't stay down for long. And she's a wonderful student, with an ability to catch on to new techniques and concepts very quickly. She's a very knowledgeable person, and she understands the golf swing.

But it's her attitude that makes Michelle such a great person to teach beginners about golf. When you decide to play this game, you need to have a sense of humor, and she has one of the greatest. As I'm sure you'll find out as you read *The Complete Idiot's Guide to Golf, Second Edition*, Michelle is interested in teaching you the basics of the golf swing, but her first goal is to help you enjoy yourself out on the golf course.

So have fun. Golf is the hardest game in the world to play. Professionals make mistakes on half of their shots, to a certain degree. A beginner is going to be lucky to hit one good shot out of ten. Understand that the game is about enjoyment. So many things in life go fast. Fortunately, golf isn't one of them. Golf gives you a chance to get away from the day-to-day hassles, the incessant ringing of the telephone, and the always-overflowing e-mail inbox. And with the different sets of tees and handicaps, it is the one game the whole family can play together, outside.

Let me leave you with a final piece of advice. Michelle covers a lot of ground in this book, and she's giving you great information. But the golf swing is a complex thing, and you'll struggle if you try to focus on 12 different things at once. Focus on one thing and work on that, then move on to the next thing. You'll get more out of this book, and more out of your game.

Dave Stockton
winner of 11 PGA Tour and 14 Champions Tour tournaments

Introduction

When I'm playing in a big golf tournament, with bleachers, television cameras, corporate signs, and huge crowds, it's easy to forget how solitary this game really is.

When I was a kid, my favorite part of playing golf was walking out on the course with my father. Once we got away from the parking lot and the clubhouse, it seemed like we were all by ourselves, just the two of us, miles away from the rest of the world. Playing golf meant getting away and doing something I loved with my dad. And when I got to my ball, everything was quiet, and the only one who could make it fly was me.

By picking up this book and making the commitment to learn to play golf, you've made a great decision. Not only are you going to discover how to play a wonderful, strategic, challenging game, but golf gives you a chance to get away—either alone, with old friends, or with new ones whom you meet at the course. It doesn't hurt that some golf courses are the most beautiful places on Earth.

The game isn't easy. You'll miss more shots than you hit well, but if you love a challenge, you've picked the right sport. No matter how skilled you become, golf is always a demanding test. I play for a living, and I'm still challenged every day. The excitement comes from the different obstacles you're presented with every time out. I'll try to get you ready for them.

What You'll Find in This Book

I'm going to do the best I can to give you a straightforward tour of the game of golf, from its terminology and equipment to the swing, and through your first trip to the driving range and the golf course. Even though this book is called *The Complete Idiot's Guide to Golf, Second Edition*, I know you aren't really an idiot. You just need a little help getting started. Or, if you've played a few times but need some advice on the basics of the game, you can start from there. I've broken the book into five parts, which makes it easy for you to skim through and find the information you need.

Part 1, "The Hole Truth: Explaining the Game," is completely devoted to the nuts and bolts of golf—definitions, descriptions, and terminology. As you'll soon discover, this sport has some strange lingo that can be tough for a rookie to decipher. Understanding what's going on out there and what equipment you need is half the battle.

We'll move on in Parts 2 and 3 to the swing. Starting with the grip, I'll show you how to get the ball moving in **Part 2, "Swing, Swing, Swing: Getting Airborne,"** along with some simple drills that will help you get the feel of the swing. **Part 3, "The Next Step: Some More Advanced Techniques,"** will deal with some more advanced drills and techniques, once you've got a good working idea of the golf swing.

In **Part 4, "Hitting the Links, or at Least the Driving Range,"** we'll make the jump from the "classroom" (most likely your backyard, where you practice) to the golf course. I'll set you up at the driving range for some practice shots, then give you directions for playing for real on the course. I'll go over some rules and courtesies you should always follow while playing, along with some practical advice that will take some of the mystery out of the game.

Part 5, "Beyond the Basics," deals with the final touches: golf organizations you can join to play with other beginners, golf and business, how to deal with cheaters, and even a little gambling. I want you to have the complete picture!

You won't become a great golfer overnight. I would never make a promise like that. But I can promise you that you'll enjoy yourself more by using the advice I've got to offer in this book. If you enjoy yourself, you'll play more often. Play more often, and believe me, you'll get better. Hit 'em straight!

Bonus Beacons

You'll notice the following sidebars throughout this book. They highlight certain points I want to be sure you catch.

Double Bogey

To learn how to avoid certain mistakes, look in these boxes. (In golf, a *double bogey* means scoring two strokes above par on a hole.)

Caddie's Advice

Check these boxes to find tips that will help you improve your technique and strategy.

Par Primer

I'll reinforce the definitions of important terms in these boxes.

Extra Swings

These boxes will give you some extra information or little-known facts.

Acknowledgments

I would like to thank my parents and my brother, J. C., for all their love and support.

Trademarks

All terms mentioned in this book that are known to be or are suspected of being trademarks or service marks have been appropriately capitalized. Alpha Books and Penguin Group (USA) Inc. cannot attest to the accuracy of this information. Use of a term in this book should not be regarded as affecting the validity of any trademark or service mark.

Part 1

The Hole Truth: Explaining the Game

I know you're excited and anxious to get outside and start hitting balls, but we need to take care of some other things first. You'll be glad we did.

If you were learning how to fly a plane, you would start out in ground school before getting in the plane. Then you would have a better idea of what to expect when you got up in the air. Part 1 of this book is ground school for golf. I'll build your golf vocabulary and go through the game's basics in Chapters 1 and 2. You'll soon be able to talk a good game, even if your swing isn't perfect.

In Chapter 3, I'll introduce you to the different kinds of equipment you're going to need to play this game. That way, when we get down to the business of the swing in Part 2, we'll be on the same page—literally and figuratively.

Let's Get Started: The Basics

In This Chapter

- The bare essentials: What you're supposed to do out there
- From Scotland to Scottsdale: A little history of the game
- The anatomy of your golf club
- Bare essentials: The different clubs and their uses
- Balls, tees, and the other great stuff you'll need to play

You've got this book open on your lap. Maybe you have a borrowed set of clubs spread out in front of you, and outside the sun is shining. You're ready to start swinging. I know the feeling. But just bear with me a few minutes. In this chapter, we're going to go over some of the basics of the game and take a quick look at the equipment you'll need to get your golf game off on the right foot.

Golf: A Primer

Chances are, you know what you've gotten yourself into. Friends, family, or business associates play this game, and you want to get in on it. You aren't alone. The previous decade was one big golf course construction boom, and now you can find at least one shiny new driving range in the middle of most big cities. In Japan, golfers hit practice balls from multistoried driving ranges into giant nets. There's no space to build golf courses, and the courses they do have are quite expensive, so for some Japanese players, hitting practice balls into the net is the only golf they know. Now that's dedication!

Here in the United States, it's a little easier to get into the game. The goal is very simple: getting the ball in the hole in as few shots as possible. But I think you'll discover many different ways to achieve that goal, and it isn't as simple as it sounds. For every different golf course you play, the obstacles are different. Some have lots of water, damp golf-ball cemeteries just waiting for you to make a mistake. Others have trees blocking your path, or hills and valleys that affect your stance when you try to hit the ball. If you play the same course day in and day out, you get to know its contours, but conditions change. Wind changes your shots, as does hot or cold weather. Rain makes the course softer (so shots don't roll very far), and summer heat bakes the grass and makes it as hard as your driveway.

Before I convince you that this game is impossible, let me tell you that all of these conditions, which seem to be plotting against you, are what make the game so enjoyable.

When I was a kid growing up in Boca Raton, Florida, my dad sent me out with six clubs and a little bag. I played the same course nearly every day for six years. I didn't get bored because I was playing a different golf course every time, thanks to the windy conditions on Florida's east coast and the inconsistency of my golf game. I was hitting shots I hadn't had to hit before, from new and foreign locations (like behind that big palm tree on the 16th fairway!).

You'll find that after you start playing this game, it will be just as much fun to recount a woeful "if I only hit it 5 yards farther …" tale about a water ball as it is to gloat about that snaking 20-footer that dropped into the hole. It's like a fisherman talking about the big one that got away: The stories are half the fun!

Back in the Dark Ages

Historians are sketchy about just when golf was invented, but King George of England made a proclamation in 1245 that his subjects weren't practicing their archery enough because they were spending too much time on the golf course. (Many a golf widow or widower has felt the same thing.) Scottish shepherds were knocking stones into rabbit holes in the late 1100s on the site where the famous St. Andrews Golf Club sits now, so the game is very old. The first set of official rules was ratified in 1744. They were very simple, and most of them still apply today.

The key rule in golf is the same as it was back then: Play it where it lies. That means hit from where you find it.

Golf first came to the United States just before the turn of the century. A few organizations started up in the East and Midwest, and in 1895, they got together to form the United States Golf Association, which is still the sport's governing body. Developers really started to build courses in the first two decades of the twentieth century. By 1940, the first men's professional tour, the forerunner of today's PGA (Professional Golfers Association) Tour, had started, followed by the women's pro tour, the LPGA (Ladies Professional Golf Association), in 1950. Now, nearly 50 million Americans play golf every year, and golf is a $40 billion industry.

Stars like Tiger Woods, Phil Mickelson, and Annika Sorenstam have turned golf into an incredibly popular spectator and television sport. More people are watching the game—and deciding to give it a try—than ever. It's truly cool to be a golfer now, and it doesn't matter if you're male or female, young or old. Teenager Michelle Wie is making history competing in both LPGA and PGA Tour events. I'll bet you she doesn't get teased about being a golfer when she's back at high school in Hawaii.

Club Anatomy

Along with the ball (more on that later in this chapter), the golf club is the primary piece of equipment you'll need. Clubs come in a variety of styles, but they all have the following characteristics:

- The **grip** is where you hold the club. It's usually made out of some kind of rubber, but some clubs still have a leather grip. The grip covers the top part of the shaft, which is the club's engine.

- The **shaft,** which usually is made of either steel or graphite, provides the leverage and kick that makes your ball fly. Generally, the longer the shaft, the longer you'll hit a shot with that club. One way to think about shafts on golf clubs is to compare them to the handle of a broom. Think about how much dirt you can brush away with a long-handled broom compared to how much you could move with a short-handled broom. The longer handle gives you more leverage, and you can move more dirt. Shafts come in all kinds of different flexes, which is a fancy way to describe how much a shaft bends when you swing, but I'll talk about those specifics in Chapter 3.

- Connected to the end of the shaft is the **clubhead.** If you're doing things correctly, this is the part of the club that will hit the ball. If you can imagine the club as a metal representation of your leg, you can quickly see why the part of the club attached to the shaft is called the **heel** and the other end of the head is called the **toe**. (The only way to get a "knee" on your club would be to wrap it around a tree, and I don't want to encourage any bad behavior.)

This is a standard 5-iron. The end of the head closest to the shaft is called the heel. The other end is called the toe.

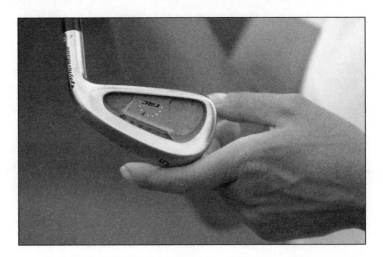

On the clubhead are four distinct regions—the clubface, the sole, the hosel, and top of the club. Let's look at each of these in more detail:

- The **clubface** is the area with which you're trying to hit the ball. Look closely and you'll notice a set of horizontal grooves. These grooves help put spin on the ball. Spin makes the ball fly farther (by imparting backspin—more on that later) and stop when it lands on the green (the closely mown area holding the hole in which you're trying to put your golf ball).

- The **sole** is the part of the clubhead that rests on the ground, like the sole of your shoe. The way the sole is designed depends on what the club is used for. On a driver or a wood (types of clubs designed to help you hit long shots), the sole is broad and flat, so it skims over the ground. On an iron (on the steel-headed clubs in your bag), it's designed to cut through grass and dirt.

- The **hosel** is the opening where the shaft connects to the clubhead. Back in the old days, shafts were made of hickory and had to be lashed to the clubhead with thin, strong string. Now, club makers use a strong glue and cover up the seam with a piece of plastic called a **fairing.** Irons don't have much of a top, but on the top of most woods, manufacturers place a small arrow or line that helps you align the ball in the center of the club before you swing.

> ### Extra Swings
>
> If you're left-handed, don't worry. Clubs are made for you, too. They're the same as clubs righties use, just mirror-images.

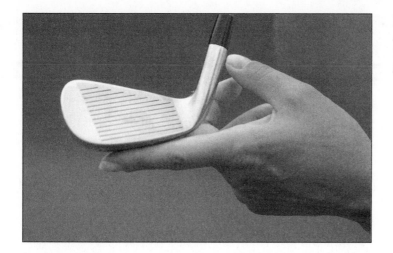

The lines on the front of the clubhead are called grooves. The bottom of the club is called the sole.

The Basic Bag

The rules specify that you can't carry more than 14 clubs in your bag while playing golf. It's up to you to decide what clubs you want to carry, but a standard set of clubs includes three *woods* (driver, 3-wood, and 5-wood), nine *irons* (3-iron, 4-iron, 5-iron, 6-iron, 7-iron, 8-iron, 9-iron, pitching wedge, and sand wedge), and a *putter*.

My bag includes three woods—a driver, 3-wood, and 5-wood—two hybrid clubs, seven irons, and a putter.

Extra Swings

Advanced players usually use longer irons like the 1-iron, 2-iron, and 3-iron, and beginners or other players who don't swing very hard substitute those clubs for more woods, like a 7-wood and 9-wood. You can also use new clubs called *hybrids*, which blend the qualities of irons and woods. They also replace long clubs like the 3- and 4-irons.

Woods

The woods have the longest shafts of any club in the bag. Their head is designed to hit the ball either from a small wooden peg called a *tee*, which elevates the ball slightly (you can only use a tee, appropriately enough, in the *tee-box*), or from a relatively flat surface like the fairway, which I'll talk about in the next chapter. These clubs are designed to hit the ball a long way, sometimes at the expense of accuracy. Woods are numbered from 1 (the driver) to 11, and the smaller the number on the club, the less loft it has. That means a driver will hit the ball longer and lower than a 7-wood or a 9-wood will. Clubs like 9-woods and 11-woods replace longer irons like the 4- and 5-irons in the bag.

Par Primer _____

The **tee box** is the flat, nicely groomed place where you start to play a hole. In the tee box, you hit your first shot from between different colored markers that indicate the difficulty and length of the hole—from black (most difficult) to red or green (easiest).

Woods are called woods because they used to be made from the wood of persimmon trees. A few companies still make woods out of persimmon, but the vast majority of all new woods sold today are made from either steel or titanium.

Generally, as a beginner you'll have more luck with metal woods, because the clubheads are bigger, which gives you more area to hit the ball. The titanium driver I use has a head that is more than twice as big as the clubhead on the driver I used when I first turned pro.

Extra Swings

Titanium is a much stronger metal than steel at a fraction of the weight. By making the clubhead with titanium, the designer can make it much bigger, stronger, and lighter. Using a titanium clubhead doesn't necessarily mean your shots will go farther, but the bigger heads are supposed to have a bigger *sweetspot*, which means you can hit the ball a little bit off the center of the club and still have a good shot.

As newer, lighter metals have been developed, driver clubheads have gotten much bigger. That gives you more room on the face to hit the ball. My driver (left) is more than twice as big as a club from 1998 (right).

Irons

After you've hit your longer shots with the woods, your irons help you get the ball onto the green. They come in lots of different lofts, which helps you hit shots of different lengths and heights. Just like woods, the irons are misnamed. They aren't really made of iron, but mostly of steel. A few companies are making irons out of titanium, but that's only important if you've got thousands of dollars to spend for clubs.

Irons with the smallest numbers, like the 3-iron or the 4-iron (1- and 2-irons exist, but only terrific players usually have them in their bags), have the longest shafts and are designed to hit the ball lower and farther, and, like the woods, you give up some accuracy in exchange for distance with these clubs.

Shafts get shorter as the numbers printed on the sole get bigger, until you get to the sand wedge, the shortest club in the bag. A standard sand wedge has a 34-inch shaft, which is 8 inches shorter than a standard driver shaft. The shortest clubs, like the 9-iron, pitching wedge, and sand wedge, are designed for accuracy, not distance. An optimum shot with a pitching wedge flies high in the air and lands softly, without much roll. That way, you can aim right at the hole.

Because their shafts are so much shorter and they are designed to get the ball in the air, in the beginning you'll have the most success with your 9-iron and pitching wedge. These are good clubs to practice with when you first start out, because they will help you discover what a great shot is supposed to feel like.

Extra Swings

Professionals call their wedges "money clubs," because you can't win a pro tournament unless you can hit the ball close to the hole and make a few putts.

Keep practicing with those two clubs, because when you finally make it to the course, they'll be the ones that will save you quite a few shots.

The Putter

Some people say the putter is the most important club in the bag. If you look at professional golf statistics, this is probably true. Of the 70 or so shots the average pro takes in a round, almost half, or about 29, are putts. The putter is also the club that's easiest to change—and the most subject to whim. Most regular players have three or four putters they rotate in and out of their bag. If they feel like one's having a "cold streak," they play with a different one.

Putters come in all different shapes and sizes. The two main types are mallet and blade putters. A mallet putter has a rounded back and a large, flat sole. The weight is distributed across the face of the putter, making it more forgiving on off-center putts. A blade putter has more right angles, making it easier for some players to align with the ball.

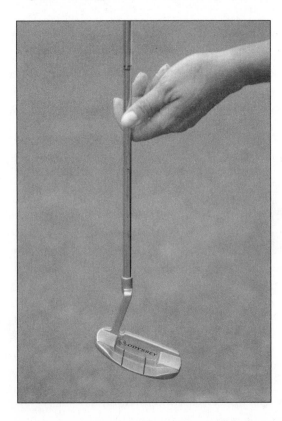

A mallet-headed putter has a rounded back and is more forgiving if you miss the center of the clubface with your stroke.

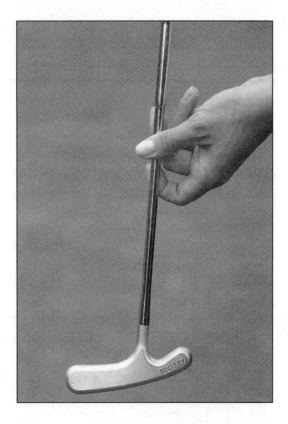

A blade putter has more right angles and is easier for some players to align.

Walk into any golf shop or sporting-goods store, and you'll probably see hundreds of putters lined up for sale. They have different shapes, weights, and lengths, but the one thing they have in common is a clubface that lines up perfectly perpendicular to the target. When you hold a putter properly, with the sole resting on the ground, the face should be pointed straight at where you're aiming. Sometimes, if your golf bag is dropped on the ground or jostled, the putter, which is usually made of a softer metal than the rest of your clubs, can get bent. Nothing makes it tougher to putt than having a putter that isn't square to the target. Not only do you then have to worry about hitting the ball in the right direction, you have to think about making small adjustments in how the face of the putter is pointed before you start. That's more trouble than you need.

A relatively new development in putters is the extended shaft. Several professional players who were experiencing the *yips* experimented with different shaft lengths to try to

Par Primer

The **yips** are a mysterious condition that impact the motor movements of the hands. A person with the yips gets an involuntary spasm while hitting the ball and loses control of the putt.

find some relief. With a long shaft, you can brace the top of the club on the chest and use the big muscles of the arms and shoulders to make the stroke. The long putters have caught on, and quite a few players, both pro and amateur, use them. Aside from having a long shaft and two grips, they are the same as regular putters.

Loft Lessons

Shafts are only part of the equation that determines how high and how far your shots will travel. All the woods and irons in your bag have different lofts. *Loft* is the angle the clubface sits in relation to the ground when the sole is lying flat on the ground.

Can you tell the difference in loft between a driver (left), sand wedge (center), and 3-iron (right)? The driver has 10 degrees, the sand wedge has 56 degrees, and the 3-iron has 21 degrees of loft.

Caddie's Advice

It might not look like it, but even your putter has loft. Most are built with 2 or 3 degrees of loft. If it had no loft, your putter would cause the ball to skid when you hit it, making it hop off target.

Your sand wedge has about 56 degrees of loft, compared to 9 or 10 degrees of loft on a driver. You can almost scoop up a quarter from the carpeting with a sand wedge, while a driver's face is almost perpendicular to the ground. The more loft a club has, the higher it helps you hit the ball in the air and the shorter the ball travels in distance. A long shaft and a little bit of loft promotes a long, low shot that rolls quite a bit. Lots of loft makes the ball fly high and land soft (stay in place without rolling very much).

As you can imagine, it's much harder to get the ball in the air with a club that doesn't have as much loft. So a 3- or 4-iron probably wouldn't be good choices if you have a little stream or creek in front of you and are worried about hitting a ball into the water.

Loft and shaft length are the two primary factors that make up the differences between the irons in your set. After you've hit enough of each club at the driving range, you'll have a rough estimate of about how far you hit the ball using each club. Of course, hitting out of thick grass or sand means having to make some adjustments.

Extra Swings

Some players get so fed up with trying to hit their 3- and 4-irons that they switch to 7- and 9-woods—clubs with bigger clubheads, longer shafts, and lots of loft. They say it's the best of both worlds. Seven-, 9- and even 11-woods have become popular with many LPGA players because they are both easier to hit than long irons and they make the ball fly higher. They're great for beginners, too.

What Are All Those Pockets in the Golf Bag For?

Of course, clubs aren't the only things you're going to need to play this game. Golf has more stuff than almost any other sport. If you wanted to, you could fill a whole shopping cart with golf gadgets. (If you did cram all that stuff into your golf bag, you would get a very dirty look from your *caddie!*) After all, the 2004 Professional Golf Association Trade Show in Orlando took up almost a million square feet of space. They had to fill it up with something.

For now, I'll concentrate on the most common and most important accessories you're going to need to play. The most important, obviously, is the ball. Dozens of companies sell hundreds of different kinds of balls (and we'll sort through them in Chapter 3), but a standard golf ball must be 1.62 inches in diameter, weigh no more than 1.68 ounces, and be approved by the *United States Golf Association* (*USGA*) for play. If you aren't playing in any tournaments, then it doesn't really matter if your ball is approved by the

Par Primer

A **caddie** is someone you hire to carry your clubs for you during your round. He or she not only keeps your clubs clean and organized, but also knows the ins and outs of the course and helps you decide what clubs to use for various shots.

USGA, but if I played in a USGA event with a ball that hadn't been approved, I would be disqualified. Fortunately, you don't have to worry too much about unapproved balls.

Par Primer

The United States Golf Association (USGA), which is based in Far Hills, New Jersey, is the rule-making organization for golf in the United States. The USGA sets the rules that both amateurs and professionals play by, approves equipment used in the game, and runs national tournaments like the U.S. Open, U.S. Women's Open, and U.S. Amateurs.

All of the balls sold by the major manufacturers at golf courses or sporting goods stores have been approved.

Aside from balls, the two other items you will be using the most are tees and a divot-repair tool. When you hit your first shot on a hole, you're allowed to place it on a wooden peg, or *tee*, to elevate it a bit so you can get a nice, clean swing at it. That's the only time you can use a tee. Tees come in packages of 20 or 30, and sell for less than a dollar. You use a divot-repair tool to repair dents made in the green, the closely-mown area where the hole is, when your shot lands. I'll teach you the technique in Chapter 22, and I'll go into more detail about accessories in Chapter 20.

The Least You Need to Know

◆ Golf's goal is simple: Hit the ball into the hole. But most of all, your goal should be to have fun.

◆ Golf started in the 1100s in Scotland and England.

◆ The three main parts of the club are the grip (where you hold the club), the shaft (the club's engine), and the clubhead (what you hit the ball with).

◆ The four main parts of the clubhead are the face, sole, hosel, and fairing.

◆ The basic set of golf clubs includes three woods (driver, 3-wood, and 5-wood), nine irons (irons numbered 3 through 9, a pitching wedge, and a sand wedge), and a putter.

◆ The main accessories you need are balls, tees, and a divot-repair tool.

2

Golf Jargon: Getting It Down

In This Chapter

- ◆ Finding your way around the golf course
- ◆ Expanding your golf vocabulary
- ◆ Using a scorecard to keep track of your game
- ◆ Figuring out your golf handicap

If you're just picking up the game, you may find the wide open spaces of a golf course a bit overwhelming. And all that golf lingo—birdies, eagles, shanks, slices, and so on—can be pretty confusing. Sometimes amateurs I play with in pro-ams come up with golf terms even I've never heard of.

Don't be intimidated. After this quick lesson in how a golf course is organized, the process of playing and scoring a hole, and golf terminology, not only will you get more out of this book, but you'll be able to understand what those television commentators are talking about when they say Tiger Woods needs to get up and down from the bunker to make a birdie. Trust me, they aren't talking about a parakeet.

Your Golf Course Road Map

Before you even take a swing on the golf course, it helps to know a little bit about the playing field. You wouldn't drive around in a strange city without a map, would you? The course is made up of several different parts. All courses are broken down into holes. Most have either 18 or 9. Each hole is made up of a few other parts—the tee, fairway, and green. On each green is the actual hole where your last shot will wind up, the "finish line," so to speak.

The *tee*, which is sometimes called the tee-box (it's usually shaped like a square or rectangle), is where you begin playing each hole. (A tee is also the peg you use to hit the ball from the tee-box.) Looking out from the tee, the goal is to hit the ball to the closely cut area called the *fairway*. Take my word for it, it's much easier to play from the manicured grass on the fairway than it is to play from the *rough*, which is the grass to the sides of the fairway that looks like your lawn would if you went three or four weeks without mowing it. The rough is designed to be more difficult to play from—a penalty for missing the fairway. Usually, the farther you are from the fairway, the deeper and thicker the rough becomes. *Primary rough* is intermediate-depth grass just off the edge of the fairway. *Secondary rough* is unkempt, long grass outside of the primary rough. Secondary rough is bad news.

Par Primer

The word **tee** is one of several words that has two meanings in golf. A tee is the peg you use to hit the ball from the tee-box. It's also a shorthand name for the tee-box itself.

Think of the fairway as an expressway toward your ultimate goal, the *green*. Like any expressway, the fairway has curves, which are called *doglegs*. A dogleg is just like it sounds—a hole that curves to the right or left, like the shape of a dog's leg. The green is a small patch of grass that should be even more manicured than the fairway. Surrounding the green is a ring of grass cut just a little bit higher, called the *fringe* or *collar*. As you play toward the green, a flag sits in the hole as an aiming guide. At some courses, the flag is color-coordinated. For example, a red flag might mean the hole is on the front part of the green (closest to the tee), a white flag might mean the hole is in the middle, and a blue flag might mean the hole is toward the back. When you make it to the green and can see the hole, you remove the flag and try to hit your ball into the hole. Accomplish that, and you start again at the next tee with some new challenges.

Of course, avoiding the rough isn't the only difficult part about this game. You also need to avoid bunkers, hazards, and out-of-bounds. *Bunkers* are pits of sand situated throughout the course, usually in spots close to where you meant to hit the ball (that sounds pretty mean of the course designer, but later in the book, I'll teach you how to get out of one of those pits). You don't have to add a stroke to your score for hitting into a bunker. You just have to worry about blasting your ball out. But if you hit into a *hazard*, which could be a pond, stream, lake, swamp, or even an ocean if you live on the coast, you're automatically penalized one shot. The same is true if you hit the ball *out of bounds*. That means you've hit past the edge of the field of play, and usually into somebody's backyard. Try not to trample any of their flowers when you go to retrieve your ball. Out-of-bounds is marked with rows of white stakes. Hazards are marked with red stakes.

Criss-crossing many courses are little cement or gravel roads called *cart paths*. If you're riding in a cart as you play, you should try to keep your cart on the paths as much as possible to prevent wear and tear on the grass. The paths usually run parallel to and off to the side of each hole. It's important to keep the cart as close to the path as you can. Never, ever drive a cart any closer than 15 yards from the green. You'll look like a rookie, and worse, you'll damage the course.

There's more to a golf course than just the holes. Most have a building near the first hole called the *clubhouse*. In the clubhouse are usually locker rooms, restrooms, a snack bar or dining room, and the *pro shop* or *golf shop*. In the shop, you can make an appointment called a *tee time* to play, pay for your round, and buy any extra equipment you need. At most courses, you must check in at the shop before you play.

Par Primer

Each time you swing at or hit the ball, it counts as a **stroke** or **shot**. In some situations, you have to add a **penalty stroke** to your score; more on that later.

Double Bogey

Cart paths aren't like the roads you drive your car on—they aren't wide enough for two carts. Watch out for oncoming traffic. If another cart is coming, slow down and let it by, and keep your feet and legs inside!

Eagles, Birdies, Pars, and Bogies

Now that you can find your way around, let's move on to some other basic terms that have to do with the score you make on a given hole. After all, knocking the ball into the hole with the least number of shots is the basic goal of the game! Most golf courses have three different kinds of holes: par-threes, par-fours, and par-fives. (Some courses have just par-threes.) *Par* is the score an expert golfer would expect to make on the hole if he or she played it properly. Add the par scores for each hole and you get a par value for the course itself. Most 18-hole courses have a par of 72 shots. (A few have pars of 69, 70, or 71.) As a professional, I'm supposed to take no more than three shots on a par-three, four on a par-four, and five on a par-five. Of course, you'll be setting some different goals in the beginning, but believe me, making your first par or birdie will be exciting!

Par-threes are the shortest holes, usually between 90 and 230 yards. In a best-case scenario, it should take one shot to hit the ball onto the green of a par-three hole.

Par Primer

When you play an actual game of golf, you'll play either an 18- or 9-hole round. It's called a **round** because at most courses, you return near the clubhouse both when you finish the ninth hole and the 18th hole.

Par-fours are medium-length holes, between 240 and 470 yards. Here, it should take two shots to reach the green. Par-fives are the longest, usually between 480 and 600 yards. Depending on length, players will take two or three shots to hit it on the green on a par-five. What term you use to describe your score for a given hole depends on whether it takes you more shots than par or fewer. In this case, less is more—the lower your total score and the more it's below par for the whole course, the better.

Every time you swing the club with the intent of hitting the ball, it's called a stroke or shot—even if you swing and miss. So, starting with your shot from the tee, if you finish a hole in the same number of strokes as par, that's what you've made, a *par*. Take one stroke less than par, and you've made a *birdie*. If it takes you two strokes less than par, drinks are on you, because you made an *eagle*. If you need one more stroke than par on the hole, you have a *bogey*. Two shots over is a *double-bogey* and three over is a *triple-bogey*. Any more than that I don't even want to think about, and you shouldn't either. Then it's time to pick up the ball and start again on the next hole.

Extra Swings

Nobody is really sure how the terms birdie, eagle, and par came into use on the golf course. Most likely, somebody realized it was too cumbersome to keep answering "one over par" or "two over par" when asked about his or her score on a hole, so something quicker came into practice. The rarest of all scores, the albatross or double-eagle, is a score of three under on one hole, which only happens on a par-five. Gene Sarazen had the most famous double-eagle in golf history when he knocked a 3-wood into the hole from 240 yards away on the 15th hole of the last round of the 1935 Masters tournament. The shot tied him with Craig Wood, and Sarazen went on to win.

Holes: What All Those Numbers Mean

A blank scorecard can tell you everything you need to know about a golf course. Most of them even have a little map on the back that will help you formulate a strategy for playing a hole. But even for some experienced golfers, some of the numbers on the card mean little more than an advanced calculus problem on the blackboard did for the typical ninth grader.

As a beginner, the most important pieces of information you need to know about on a scorecard are the number of the hole, par for that hole, and distance of the hole.

The sample scorecard shown here lists the hole number, the hole distances from each set of tees, and par. Write your score for each hole on one of the blank lines below the distances. (Do it when you get to the next tee, never on the green! You don't want to hold up play behind you!)

A sample scorecard. For each hole, it lists the hole distance for different sets of tees, provides blank lines for writing scores, and indicates par for each hole.

We've already talked about what par means, so we'll move right to distance. This can sometimes be a misleading number. As you can see on the sample scorecard, several different yardage figures are given for each hole. The distance depends on what tees you play from. Most courses have at least three sets of color-coded tees—championship tees, regular tees, and women's tees. Playing from the championship tees, or "playing from the tips," means you are making each hole as long and difficult as possible. Don't worry about these tees, which are usually set off by blue or black markers, until you get some more experience. At a lot of courses, playing from these tees is too hard for all but the best golfers. Most men and the best female golfers play from the regular tees. These tees, which usually have white markers, make the course an average distance.

The red tees are for average female players and young or beginning players of either sex. From the red tees, each hole will play the shortest.

The distance on your scorecard will vary depending on the set of tees from which you are playing. This card has two different sets of distances—the championship tees (or blue tees), and the standard tees (yellow on this card). The distances for two other sets of tees are on the other side. Also, keep in mind that the distance on the card is to the exact center of the green, not to the specific place where the hole is. You see, the people who run golf courses are pretty crafty. They change the location of the holes on the greens every day. (As if the game wasn't hard enough!)

The handicap number appears along the bottom row of the example scorecard. We'll talk about individual handicaps later in this chapter, but in this case, the handicap number ranks the hole's difficulty out of the 18 on the course. If the handicap number for the fourth hole is "1," that means the fourth hole is rated the most difficult hole on the course. This system is used to balance golfers of different skill levels. If, on average, I play a round in 15 fewer shots than you, we could subtract one shot from your score on the 15 hardest holes out of the 18 we play and make our match an even contest. Golf is one of the few sports in which players of all skill levels can compete on the same course on fair terms.

At the top of some scorecards, you'll see two numbers you won't have to worry about very much. One is the *slope*; the other is the *course rating*. A course rating is the score a theoretical player who parred every hole on an average course would shoot at the particular course you're playing. A standard, average course has a course rating of 72. So if on a scorecard from your local course you notice a course rating of 68 or 69, that means your course is relatively easy, compared to the average. Some courses have ratings as high as 78 or 79. Shinnecock Hills, the course in Long Island where the 2004 U.S. Open was played, has a course rating of 79.2!

Slope is just another way to determine the relative difficulty of a course. A higher slope rating means the course is more difficult—it has more water hazards and elevation changes. This number can range between 55 and 155. According to the United States Golf Association, the sport's governing body, the average slope rating is 113. It helps to know about these numbers so you can pick an easier course to practice on until you improve, but after you're out playing, you don't need to worry about them.

Calling All the Shots

You know what the green is and how to keep score. Now, let's run through the names of the shots you need to get to the green.

A shot from the tee-box of a par-four or par-five is called the *drive* or *tee-shot*. On a par-three, it's just called a *tee-shot*. When you're getting ready to hit onto the green from at least 100 yards away, you're hitting an *approach shot*. An intermediate-length shot (from, say, 40 to 90 yards) is called a *pitch*. That's where the name "pitching wedge" comes from. Little bump and run shots around the green are called *chips*. Once on the green, you'll be putting with, guess what? The putter.

Golf's most colorful language probably comes in the few seconds after a person finishes his or her swing. Aside from a few moans, groans, and profanities, this is the time you'll hear your partner talk about chili-dips, tops, fats, fades, hooks, shanks, and chunks. Let's run through a list of descriptions along with some quick definitions:

> **CAUTION**
>
> **Double Bogey**
>
> Nothing exposes a rookie golfer quicker than calling chips and pitches by the wrong name. Remember, pitches are longer shots. Chips come around the green.

- **Slice.** As they learn to play the game, most beginners put quite a bit of sidespin on the ball. Instead of hitting it square with the face of the club, the club hits with a glancing blow. Usually, this glancing blow is "outside in," which means the club approaches the ball from the ball's right to its left (for a right-hander—lefties should reverse all the directions here). This makes the ball spin the opposite way, from left to right. A severe left-to-right curving shot is a slice, and if you have one, we'll work to try to fix it.

- **Fade.** A fade is the little sister of the slice. A gentle left-to-right curving shot, a fade is generally intentional, usually to follow the contour of a hole that curves from left to right.

- **Hook.** A hook is the opposite of a slice. If the club hits the ball on a sharp "inside out" path, it puts the opposite, right-to-left spin on. These shots curve sharply left. Shots with hook spin tend to roll quite a bit more than shots hit with slice spin. You generally want to work to eliminate a hook, as you would a slice.

- **Draw.** A draw is generally the most desirable ball flight in golf. A slight right-to-left spin, a draw shot is more under control than a hook and still rolls more than a shot with no slice spin or hook spin.

- **Push.** When you hit a shot that flies on a straight path, but right of the target, you've pushed it.

- **Pull.** As you might guess, a pull is the opposite of a push. When your shot flies on a straight path, but left of the target, you've pulled it.

◆ **Fat.** Hitting a shot fat means you've hit more of the ground and less of the ball. The club hits the grass and dirt too soon, slows down, and then doesn't have enough steam to get the ball where you want it to go. This kind of shot usually pops up in the air and then falls to the ground quickly, or, worse yet, just dribbles out in front of you. Some people call it hitting a shot "chunky" or "thick."

◆ **Top.** Topping the ball is just like it sounds—it means hitting the ball on its top half. This shot turns into a "worm-burner," which means it never gets airborne and skitters along the ground.

◆ **Shank.** A shanked shot is one hit off the side of the club instead of the face. This one is the most physically dangerous miss-hits of them all, because a shank goes screaming off almost at a right angle to the person who hits it. If you're standing off to the side, you might not be ready.

Caddie's Advice _____

Don't fret if you hit a slice or a fade. Because of your body makeup and flexibility, you will have either a natural draw or natural fade. Lots of pros hit a draw, but quite a few hit a fade. I do, and so does Jack Nicklaus, and we're getting along just fine.

◆ **Chili-dip.** A chili-dip is a fat shot hit around the green. It usually happens when somebody is trying to bump the ball onto the green and hits the ground too far in front of the ball.

◆ **Stiff.** Golf's nirvana! To knock it stiff means to hit a pure, perfect shot. One of these a round will always keep you coming back.

In This Game, Handicaps Are Good

Earlier in the chapter, I briefly touched on the handicap system for golf holes. The handicap system I'll be talking about now is related, but a little different. This system, set up and maintained by the United States Golf Association, also levels the playing field for golfers of all different skill levels. But instead of ranking holes on a course, this system assigns each golfer a number, the *handicap*, based on the scores he or she usually shoots for an 18-hole round. The number, at least theoretically, is an accurate indicator of what that golfer's skill level is. Then you should be able to compare your handicap with your opponent's and figure out how to make an even match by subtracting the correct number of strokes from the weaker player's score. Got that?

After you've got a handicap, it's all pretty simple. Going back to the original example I used when discussing hole handicaps, if my handicap is 0, which means I usually shoot even-par 72,) and yours is 15, which means you usually shoot 72 + 15, or 87, we should subtract a shot from your score on the 15 hardest holes on the course to get a more accurate comparison of our scores. The handicap number simply points out how many shots a person is expected to shoot over an even-par 72. It's figuring out the handicap that gets a little tricky. Good thing most clubs have computers that do all the work. In a nutshell, you take the 10 best scores of the last 20 rounds you played (you turn in your scorecard at the pro shop when you've finished, or, at some courses, enter the information into a computer in the locker room). Average those 10 scores and subtract 72. That's your handicap. You've got some time before you have to worry about it.

The Least You Need to Know

- ◆ A golf hole's three main parts are the tee (where you start), the fairway (how you get there), and the green (the finish-line).

- ◆ Par is the number of shots it should take an expert golfer to finish a hole. Two below par is called an eagle, one below par is called a birdie, and one over par is called a bogey.

- ◆ Course rating and slope show how hard a course is. The bigger the number, the harder the course.

- ◆ A handicap is the number of shots a person is expected to shoot over an even-par score of 72. The higher the handicap, the weaker the player.

Sticks and Stones: Your Equipment

In This Chapter

◆ How do you find the perfect fit?

◆ What are the best club bets for women, seniors, and kids?

◆ How do you get your money's worth in the used-club market?

◆ Which wood is right for you?

◆ Which putter is right for you?

◆ Which golf ball is right for you?

It's all fine and good to know the difference between a 3-iron and a 5-wood, but if you've ever watched a professional golf tournament on television, you've probably noticed that we play with dozens of different kinds of clubs. This is partly due to money—we get paid to play with and endorse certain kinds of clubs. But after all, this is our livelihood, so if I can't hit the ball well with the kind of clubs I'm playing with, either something is wrong with my swing or I need to find some clubs that work better.

Although your livelihood doesn't depend on whether or not you can hit with a 3-iron straight down the fairway, finding the right clubs and other equipment is important if you want to enjoy yourself. I'll help you make some of those decisions in this chapter.

The Perfect Fit: Sizing Clubs

Many golf companies make solid, high-quality, low-priced clubs built for the average-sized golfer. The industry has general loft and shaft-length standards, so for most of the clubs you buy from your local sporting-goods store or golf shop, these factors will be similar. If you're going to be playing only occasionally, these clubs will work just fine, especially if you learn from the beginning with one of these new sets. Then, the way you develop your swing will fit the qualities of the club in your hand. If you're going to be buying the clubs right off the shelf, you can skip to the next section and learn about "feel."

If you have more money to spend, or you're planning to play a lot of golf, you might want to consider customized clubs. Virtually all of the same companies that offer standard sets off the shelf will also tailor clubs to fit your body and swing. Customized clubs are probably only a good idea if you have some playing experience, because the club fitter needs to watch you swing and gauge what kind of specialized shafts to put in your clubs. If you're still learning, it might be hard to get an accurate reading.

Caddie's Advice

If you do decide to get fitted for clubs, be aware that many club fitters have an affiliation with a certain club company. They'll obviously be interested in getting you to use that brand of club. If you're interested in that brand, great. Just be sure to try a few different kinds of clubs before you decide on one brand.

But if you are interested in customized clubs, remember: Shop around. Check your local phone book and look for a larger sporting-goods or golf shop—someplace you can try quite a few sets. Also, a larger store will be more likely to have sales people who can accurately measure you for your set. If you belong to a private club, your club's pro shop probably has someone who is experienced in club fitting.

The major factors in club fitting are your height, arm length, and swing speed. Let's take a look at each of these individually:

◆ **Height.** If you're tall, like me, you probably have a more upright swing (we'll talk more about upright and flat swings in the next section). If you have an upright swing, the lie of your clubs needs to be adjusted. A club's *lie* is determined by the angle the clubhead extends from the shaft. On a clock's face, the shafts of clubs with an upright lie come into the clubhead from 11 o'clock. Normal or flat-lie clubs come in at 9 or 10. If you think of yourself in profile, holding a golf club at rest on the ground, where the shaft connects to the clubhead is like a hinge. For a taller golfer with an upright swing, that hinge needs to be closed a little bit. For a shorter golfer, it needs to be opened.

♦ **Arm length.** Arm length is the major factor that determines how long your shafts need to be. You never want to feel like your clubs require you to reach unnaturally toward the ground. You shouldn't be crouching to hit the ball, and you shouldn't have to choke up on the club for it to fit comfortably. A club fitter will measure your arm length much like a tailor or dressmaker would. With your arms at your sides, the distance between the tip of your middle finger and the ground determines how long or short your shafts should be.

Caddie's Advice

Usually, you can tell a graphite shaft's flexibility just by swinging it a few times. A regular-flex shaft will visibly bend as you finish your swing. Stiff shafts won't move.

♦ **Swing speed.** If you're a younger, stronger person, you probably have more swing speed than someone who is a little older or a little smaller. How hard you swing the club determines what kind of shafts your clubs should have. Most PGA and LPGA pros play with steel shafts that are designated stiff or extra-stiff. These are the most rigid shafts, which means they have the least flexibility or whip as you swing. A pro golfer usually swings plenty hard enough to hit the ball a long way, so he or she doesn't need the extra whip of a flexible shaft, because that extra flexibility comes at the expense of some accuracy. Average golfers are most likely to use steel or graphite shafts with regular, senior, or women's flex (in order of flexibility). If you have a slower swing, more flexible shafts will help you get more distance.

It's All About the Feel

Clubs can be impeccably fitted to your body and swing and can cost a thousand dollars, but if they don't feel right, you won't enjoy playing with them, and you won't enjoy golfing. Feel is a very personal thing, and the only advice I have for you is to try as many different clubs as you can. Everyone has a different body and a different swing, so a club that feels great in your hand and is comfortable to swing and hit with may be worthless to someone else.

For example, most pros use *forged* blade irons. These irons are hammered out from a piece of metal and have a very thin profile. Most clubs used by the average golfer are *cast*—hot metal is poured into a club-shaped die, and the finished product is popped out like a cookie from a cookie cutter. Forged blades are much more difficult to play with because the mass of the head is located low and behind the ball, not around to the sides of the ball, so a shot hit just slightly off-center won't fly very far. But when a shot is hit properly with a forged club, it is easier to control. Cast clubs are larger and more forgiving, but most pros feel they can't *work* the ball as well, which means it's harder for them to curve the ball left or right intentionally. Thankfully, working the ball isn't something you need to worry about right now.

The club on the left is a forged blade. The one on the right is a cavity-backed, perimeter cast iron.

The irons Tiger Woods uses would feel horrible in your hands. Every time you miss-hit a ball just a little bit, it would skitter off to the side. Put your larger, cast irons in Tiger's hands, and he would still be a wonderful golfer, but he wouldn't be able to do some of the things he does as well as he could with his own clubs.

It's even possible to experience significant differences in feel between irons made the same way. You might be far more comfortable with a conventional-looking set of cast irons instead of a radical-looking set. You won't know until you try a few shots. And remember, just because your favorite pro on television plays a certain kind of iron, it doesn't mean you'll like them or play well with them. All the top companies produce nice equipment, so a set of any of those brands is a good investment. But you should pick the ones that feel comfortable in your hands.

Par Primer

Forged irons are hammered from an individual piece of metal. Cast irons are made from hot metal poured into a club-shaped die.

Perimeter Weighting Is Your Friend

Most new cast irons have some kind of perimeter weighting in the clubhead. A club with perimeter weighting has extra weight distributed around the outside edges of the clubface, which helps you out when you miss-hit a shot (refer to the previous photo for a look at a club with a cast, perimeter-weighted club). The extra weight on the outside diminishes the shock of a miss-hit and keeps more of the weight of the clubhead behind the ball, so your shots fly straighter and farther.

If you're a beginner and are considering buying new clubs, perimeter weighting is a must. Manufacturers are making it harder and harder for you to make a mistake, because almost all new clubs have perimeter weighting.

 **Caddie's Advice**

When you're considering a new set of clubs, be sure to compare the perimeter weighting. Different companies move this weight around to promote higher or lower shots.

Irons, Like Clothes, Should Always Match

It's very common to have a different brand of driver and 3-wood or different brand of woods than irons, but in most cases, your 3-, 4-, 5-, 6-, 7-, 8-, and 9-irons should be the same brand. Different kinds of irons have different characteristics and hit the ball different distances and heights. Your goal should be to have a set of clubs that will allow you to hit the ball a graduated set of distances. If you have a mismatched set, you'll probably have distance gaps. For example, if you have a 5-iron from one manufacturer that goes 170 yards, a 6-iron from a different manufacturer that goes 165, and then a 7-iron that goes 140, you have too much of a gap between clubs. To avoid having to accommodate a gap like that, it's better to keep things simple by sticking with the same brand. All together, you can get a good matched set of irons for less than $300.

Wedges are a different story. Many people buy wedges made by equipment companies that specialize in making just those clubs. Also, some players decide to carry a third wedge, called an L-wedge or lob wedge, which has more loft than a sand wedge. It's designed to hit the ball very high in the air. Some companies that make regular sets of irons don't make a lob wedge, so if you find one you like from a different company, you can just add it to your set.

CAUTION **Double Bogey**

Most companies make more than one model of club with the same brand name. The different models can have different characteristics. Make sure that all of your models match!

A Forest of Woods

Imagine your set of clubs laid out on the floor in a row, from the longest (the driver) to the shortest (the putter). Starting from the middle, the closer you get to each end, the more you can tinker around. Irons are a big investment, and when you buy them, they come in a set. Drivers and other woods, you can buy one at a time. They don't usually cost as much as a set of irons (although some cost as much as $600!), and most regular players have a few different ones they rotate in and out of their bags.

I'm going to talk mostly about the driver here, but my comments apply just as well to the other woods. When you're considering drivers, you have to look at several factors. We'll go over the most important: length, clubhead size, shaft, loft, and feel.

Extra Swings

A new kind of club called a hybrid has become popular on the professional tours in the last few years. It's called a hybrid because it has a small, dense head like an iron, but a wider, flatter sole like a wood. They're easier to hit than long irons, and they also work great out of the rough. Try one, and it just might replace your 3- or 4-iron.

- **Length.** Just like the rest of your clubs, the length of the shaft determines how far you can hit the ball. A driver with an extra-long shaft can give you more distance but is much harder to control. Most pros try to find a happy medium. I use a standard-length driver and still hit the ball as far as I need to. Tiger Woods actually uses a driver with a shaft that's about an inch shorter than standard, for more control.

- **Clubhead size.** The lighter the metal a driver head is made of, the larger the clubhead tends to be. A larger head usually means a bigger sweetspot or prime hitting area. That gives you a reduced margin for error. Again, however, some people don't think they have as much control with a giant clubhead.

- **Shaft.** Like your irons, drivers offer shafts made with many different types of materials. Some professionals still use drivers with steel shafts, which tend to be the stiffest choice. You can buy drivers with a variety of different graphite shafts, which give you different levels of that whip we talked about at the beginning of the chapter. As a beginner, you're probably better off with a graphite shaft that has "regular" flex. Then the shaft will help you do some of the work.

◆ **Loft.** If you usually hit the ball low, then you might want to get a little more air under your shots with a driver that has more loft. Most new drivers come in a variety of different lofts, as I described in "Loft Lessons" in Chapter 1. Pros use 8 or 9 degrees of loft (we generate more clubhead speed, which produces more backspin and makes the ball fly higher). Average players should use drivers that have 11 or 12 degrees of loft.

◆ **Feel.** As I've said over and over in this chapter, perhaps the most important element is feel. Try as many drivers as you can. If you're with a friend who has a new one, ask to give it a test run. Out on the professional tour, word of mouth is the single biggest factor that gets people to change drivers. If I hear that somebody is having a lot of success with a new driver, I get my hands on one and try it in practice. If it works, I put it in my bag.

Men's	Shaft Length (in Inches)	Degrees of Loft
3-iron	39	21
4-iron	38.5	24
5-iron	38	27
6-iron	37.5	31
7-iron	37	35
8-iron	36.5	39
9-iron	36	43
PW	35.7	47
SW	35.5	53

Women's	Shaft Length (in Inches)	Degrees of Loft
3-iron	38	24
4-iron	37.5	27
5-iron	37	30
6-iron	36.5	34
7-iron	36	38
8-iron	35.5	42
9-iron	35	46
PW	34.7	50
SW	34.5	56

The Putter: Ultimate Vanity Club

Professional golfers change putters even more frequently than they change drivers. After you've played a few times, I think you'll find that to be true for yourself as well. The putter is the easiest club to practice with—your living-room carpeting and a drinking glass tipped on its side can serve as a practice green. There might be 3 feet of snow on the ground outside, but you can always practice with your putter. Because putters are relatively inexpensive, usually less than $100, it's easy to have two or three with which to practice.

Some people are very loyal to one putter. Champions Tour player Ben Crenshaw used only one putter for about 15 years of his career. Most people, however, go through streaks and slumps and get some kind of psychological comfort from changing putters. Arnold Palmer had so many putters in his garage that a few years ago, he donated 1,000 of them to charity. I have two or three that I rotate in and out of my bag, and like drivers, when I see someone doing well with a certain brand of putter, I take one to the practice green and try it.

A typical amateur player will take at least 35 shots with the putter during an 18-hole round of golf. That's more swings with the putter than with any other club in the bag. So it's important to have a putter that feels right for you, and most importantly, makes the ball go where you want it to. That means more than anything else, even how it looks.

Extra Swings
Some putters are made with an insert in the face, made out of a different material than the rest of the head. The insert is designed to give a softer feel at impact. Some players like to use a putter with a softer face on fast greens. It's really just a matter of taste.

I have a close friend I often play with for fun. She uses a 20-year-old putter her father gave her. It was part of a cigarette promotion, and it looks like a chunky brown cigarette on a stick. But she makes putts and feels confident with it. We tease her over and over, at least until she makes a 20-footer. If you asked any pro whether he or she would use a wooden table leg (if that were legal, which it isn't) to putt with if it made the ball go into the hole, the answer would be unanimous: Where do I get one, and how much does it cost?

Clubs for Women, Seniors, and Kids

Equipment companies have become a lot more accommodating to women, seniors, and kids in the last few years. I grew up in the early 1980s, a time when quite a few golf companies started to take women's golf seriously. Thirty years ago, only a few companies offered decent sets of women's clubs, and many of those weren't designed specifically for women—they were just knock-offs of men's clubs painted different colors. Even professional players sometimes had to buy men's clubs and modify them to get a good fit. Now, with the women's pro golf tour (the LPGA, or Ladies Professional Golf Association) gaining in popularity and more women than ever playing the game, almost all of the major companies offer great women's sets at good prices. The same holds true for seniors. The Baby Boomer generation is full of 50-somethings now, so all the major manufacturers have responded by producing sets that come with more flexible shafts and hybrid clubs instead of long irons.

Good women's clubs are designed proportionally smaller than men's sets. That means they don't just have shorter shafts, but proportionally smaller clubheads. Using the correct size clubs makes it easier for you to keep control of the clubhead and hit more accurate shots.

The kids' club market used to consist of Dad cutting the shaft down on his (or Mom's) old set. We now know that that's the worst thing you can do for your growing golfer. Cutting the shaft down creates an extra, extra stiff club—one that's way harder for Junior to hit than necessary. The major club companies now offer great kids' sets pegged to both age and height, and they've kept the cost low enough that you won't have a heart attack when your child grows 3 inches over the summer.

Buying Used Clubs

The main advantage in buying used clubs is that you'll likely save yourself quite a bit of money. Because new sets of clubs are coming out in bunches year after year, and hard-core golfers tend to trade up to them, you can sometimes buy the hot clubs of last year at a fraction of the price they were new. Optimally, you should be able to try out the clubs before you commit to buying them. Here are some other things to look for when buying a used set:

◆ **Rust.** You don't want any. Many irons are made from a stainless steel alloy. If the person who had the clubs before you didn't dry them off after they got wet, the clubs will have rust specks on them. Once the specks appear, it's much easier for the rust to spread. Rust doesn't really hurt the performance of the club, but it doesn't look too great in your bag. It gives people the impression you don't take care of your equipment.

◆ **Wear.** Like anything else, golf clubs do wear out. The grooves on the face get shallower and shallower, and if the clubs are made out of a softer metal, the sole starts to wear out from all those little nicks and bumps caused by rocks and other hard objects just below the surface of the ground. Unless they are really taken care of, irons don't last much longer than 10 years. I was heartbroken when I had to give up my first set of adult-sized irons after 12 years, but they just wore out. Some companies do offer to refurbish irons they sell.

◆ **Cost versus utility.** If you plan only to play a few times a summer, you don't need to spend hundreds of dollars on a used set. You can find a very nice set of used golf clubs for around $100, bag included. Of course, I'm not guaranteeing the bag won't be huge, green, and ugly …

> **Extra Swings**
>
> Auction sites like eBay offer everything from hard-to-find antique putters to a stiff-shafted 2-iron to go with the set you already have. Better yet, there's usually more than one of the same club to choose from, so you can compare prices.

The Internet, newspaper classified ads, used–sporting-goods stores, and the golf shop at your local public course are all great places to look for used clubs. If you aren't sure about judging wear on clubs, stick with clubs you find at used–sporting-goods stores or in a pro shop. The proprietors of these places buy the clubs from someone else with the intention of reselling them, so they usually make sure to get decent-quality equipment.

Balls: It's All About Spin

The first time you wander into the golf shop of your local course to play a round, the first thing you'll see when you get up to the counter is a giant display filled with dozens of different kinds of golf balls. They all have different names and marks, and all of them claim they will make you a better player. You'll hit the ball farther; you'll make more putts; you'll walk across water hazards without getting your feet wet—all that good stuff. Well, to a certain extent, those claims are true. If you know what kind of swing you have and what qualities you are looking for in a golf ball, the claims on a lot of the boxes are true. (Of course, walking across water is the topic of a whole different *Idiot's Guide!*) The two biggest differences in golf balls are what their covers are made of and how fast they spin when you hit them. We'll deal with the different kinds of covers later in this chapter. For now, we'll go over what spin means to you, the beginning golfer.

As we talked about in the previous chapter, a slice or a hook comes from putting too much sidespin on the ball during the swing. As a rookie, if you're putting a lot of sidespin on the ball, the last thing you want is a ball that promotes spin. Your slices will slice more, and your hooks will hook more. It will be even harder for you to control your shots, and you'll spend quite a bit of time in the trees or someone's backyard. And since you don't need to worry yet about putting a lot of backspin on the ball, playing with a high-spin ball just doesn't make sense.

What makes balls spin more or less is a complex question. It has to do with the construction materials of the cover and core of the ball. State-of-the-art tour balls like the Titleist Pro-V1 are made with multiple layers, which make the ball spin a little bit when hit hard with a driver and a lot when hit with a wedge. That's the best of both worlds for tour players, who don't want to lose control of a tee shot but want to make the ball stop on fast greens. Average players don't generate enough clubhead speed to get the ball to back up on the green anyway, so a high-performance, high-spin ball isn't really necessary.

As you can imagine, when it comes to ball technology, you get what you pay for. Premium balls cost more than $50 a dozen, and you're paying for that variable spin performance I just described. For the average player, lots of great balls are in the $15 to $20 per dozen range. They are made with fewer layers than a premium ball, and they aren't quite as versatile as the premium balls. But for 95 percent of the players in the world, they'll work just great.

Caddie's Advice

You can buy new balls in packages of three, or a box of four packages, which makes a dozen.

> **Extra Swings**
>
> As a beginner, you might want to consider buying X-Out balls. These balls have some minor defect that does not affect performance—usually a bad paint job. Most of the time, you won't even be able to tell what's wrong. X-Outs don't pass quality-control tests, so the companies that make them cross out the name, box them, and sell them as seconds at a fraction of the price. You get good-quality golf balls for cheap. Besides, nobody but you will see them, unless you blast one into somebody's yard.

The Least You Need to Know

- The main factors in getting clubs fitted are height, arm length, and swing speed.

- If you are buying a new set of irons, your best bet as a beginner is a set of perimeter-weighted cast irons.

- When buying drivers, irons, and putters, the most important factor is how they feel in your hands and when you swing, not what they look like.

- The Internet, newspaper classified ads, used–sporting-goods stores, and the pro shop of your local public course are all good places to look for used clubs.

- Tour-caliber golf balls change their spin characteristics depending on the kind of shot you're hitting. That's great, but it's expensive. Average players will do just fine with a mid-price ball.

Part 2

Swing, Swing, Swing: Getting Airborne

It's time to take the jargon you picked up in Part 1 and put it to use with a club in your hand. This part is devoted to the basics of the golf swing.

In Chapter 4, we'll make sure that you're holding the club correctly. Learning a good grip from the beginning will spare you quite a few troubles down the road. Chapter 5 covers the moment of truth—the actual swing. I'll go over alignment, the backswing, and contact—the moment you've been waiting for. After you've hit a few balls, knowing the physics of how a good golf swing works will help you develop one yourself. You'll do that in Chapter 6.

Chances are, if you've never swung a golf club before, hitting that little white ball will feel pretty foreign. Chapter 7 offers you some of the best tips I've learned over the years. I'll give you some practice drills in Chapter 8 that should make you feel a little better. If something goes wrong, the troubleshooting tips in Chapter 9 will help you make a quick fix.

Chapter 4

Get a Grip

In This Chapter

◆ Getting a grip on terminology

◆ The three most common grips: overlapping, interlocking, and baseball

◆ Putting grips

◆ Tips for setting your grip the right way

Your grip might seem insignificant at first, but the way you hold onto the golf club determines quite a bit about the way you swing and the way you hit the ball. Some professionals and top amateurs have self-taught or unconventional grips and swings, but they are the exceptions, rather than the rule. Learning to hit a golf ball consistently with a bad grip is certainly possible, but why make the job harder than it needs to be? This chapter will help you get a grip—on the club, that is.

Which Grip Should You Use?

The perfect grip should allow you to comfortably keep control of the club and help you feel the relationship between your hands and the clubhead.

After all, your grip is the only thing that connects you to the club during the swing. Set up the grip incorrectly, and you have some major difficulties to overcome to make the ball do what you want. Harvey Penick, the Texas teaching pro who taught Ben Crenshaw and Tom Kite as kids, said he could tell what kind of golfer a person was just by looking at his or her grip.

For a right-handed golfer, no matter what grip variation you decide to use, your left hand should grip the club closest to your body, and the right hand just below, closer to the clubhead. In a right-handed swing, the left hand serves as the swing's "steering wheel," directing the club, and the right hand provides the leverage and power. For left-handers, the right hand should be highest on the grip, closest to the body, and the left hand just below, nearer the clubhead. The functions are opposite as well—a lefty's right hand steers the swing and the left provides the power.

With the sole of the club resting flat on the ground and the shaft pointing at your belly button, grasp the top of the club, near the butt end of the grip, with your left hand. The shaft should rest in the crease where your fingers attach to your palm.

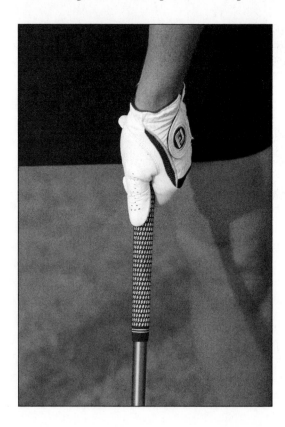

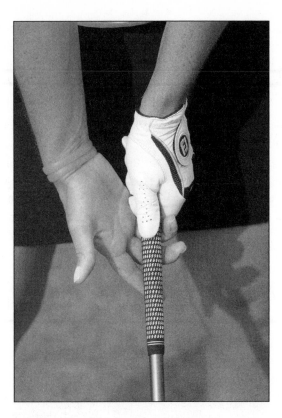

When your left hand is in place, slide your right hand onto the grip below your left. Connect your hands together in the grip you prefer—overlapping or interlocking, or leave them as two separate entities.

The three most common grips—overlapping, interlocking, and baseball—are variations of one another. Which one you choose should depend on the size and strength of your hands and the thickness of your fingers. Also, the different grips promote certain kinds of ball flight. Let's go over the three kinds of grips, and I'll explain why they promote different kinds of shots. Remember to reverse my instructions if you're a lefty. Here's how to position your hands for each of the grips:

- ◆ **Overlapping.** This grip is often referred to as the Vardon grip, after turn-of-the-century player and instructor Harry Vardon, who popularized it. To make an overlapping grip, grab the club with your left (top) hand. The tip of the club should rest near the spot where the fleshy edge of your palm meets the base of your pinkie finger, as shown in the accompanying photo. The shaft should cross near where your ring and middle fingers connect to your hand, then across the middle joint of your index finger. Curl the fingers of your left hand loosely around the club. Place your right hand on the club's grip, with your right pinkie finger nestled in the groove between the index and middle fingers of your left hand. The shaft should rest comfortably in the channel created by curling the fingers of your right hand around the grip. The thumb of your right hand should rest almost directly on top of the shaft, pointing straight down at the clubhead. Your left thumb should rest just next to the right thumb, also pointing straight down the shaft.

In the overlapping grip, the pinkie of my right hand rests in the groove between the index and middle fingers of my left hand.

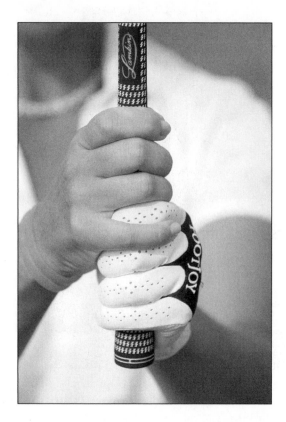

Now, lie the clubhead, with the sole flat, on the ground and take a look at it. The palm of your right hand should be perpendicular to the ground. This grip promotes the feeling that your hands are working together as a unit during the swing. You need to have fairly strong hands and fingers to use this grip, because fewer of your fingers are actually grasping the club and helping control it. Most professionals use the overlapping grip.

◆ **Interlocking.** This grip is a variation of the overlapping grip. Take the same beginning steps as the overlapping grip, but instead of resting your right pinkie in the groove between your left index and middle fingers, interlock the right pinkie and left index fingers, as shown in the following photo. This grip even more strongly promotes keeping the hands connected during the swing, and requires a little bit less hand and finger strength than the overlapping grip. This grip is better for people with small hands or short fingers; many women and young players might benefit by starting out with this grip. Tiger Woods and

Jack Nicklaus started out with this grip and never changed it, so it certainly works for players at all levels.

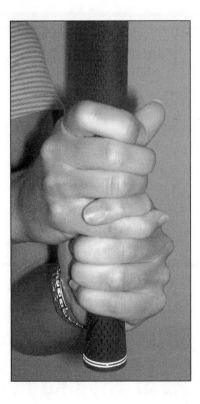

In the interlocking grip, the pinkie of my right hand curls around the index finger of my left hand.

◆ **Baseball.** This is also called the 10-fingered grip. The least conventional of the three, the baseball grip allows you to keep all 10 fingers holding the club. Grab the club with the left hand closest to the body and then slide the right hand onto the grip. Your hands should be touching, with all eight knuckles lined up on the underside of the shaft, as shown in the later photo. If you don't have strong hands, this might be a good grip for you. It's easier to keep hold of the club when you have all 10 fingers on it. If you have trouble swinging hard enough to get the ball airborne, the 10-finger grip lets you release, or uncock, your wrists more easily into a shot (more on that in the next chapter). You can get a little more power this way, but it's tougher to control the clubhead.

Par Primer _____

In the **interlocking grip,** the pinkie of the right hand curls around the index finger of the left hand. In the **Vardon** or **overlapping grip,** that pinkie rests in the slot between the index and middle fingers of the left hand.

In the baseball grip, all 10 of my fingers are holding the grip.

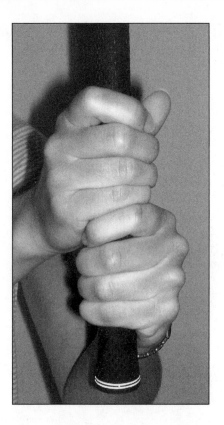

The Long and Short of Gripping a Putter

The standard putting grip looks very much like the overlapping grip, with one major difference. Instead of placing the right pinkie finger in the groove of the index and middle fingers of the left hand, you do just the opposite. Place your left index finger directly over the pinkie of your right hand. This is called an overlap grip. A majority of professional players putt this way. Some switch positions with their hands and use a cross-handed putting grip, as seen in the following photo. To make a cross-handed putting grip (for a right-hander), place your right hand on the top part of the grip. Your right pinkie should grasp the grip a quarter of an inch from the end of the club. Then place your left hand below your right, with the heel of your left hand touching the side of your right index finger.

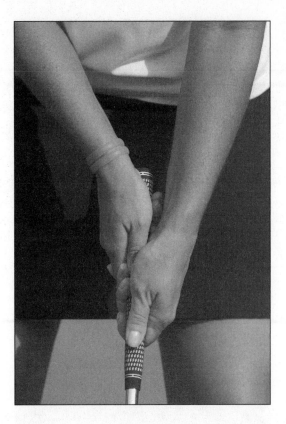

The cross-handed putting grip, where the left hand is below the right on the grip, helps keep your left wrist more stable.

Some players like putting cross-handed because it makes it tougher for the left wrist to move during the swing. If you get any kind of shake or twist in your left wrist during the putting stroke, the face of the putter will not stay on your aiming line, and you'll miss. With the cross-handed grip, your left wrist is partially braced by resting against the extended shaft. With a standard grip, the left wrist is floating above the shaft, and you have to rely on your muscles to keep it stationary.

If you decide to use a *long-shafted putter*, you will have to modify your grip. Most long putters have two separate but identical grips, one at the end of the shaft and another a few inches below where the first grip ends. To grip this club, you first need to grab the upper grip. Simply close your left hand around the grip and make sure it rests on the pad just below where your fingers connect to your hand. Then with your left hand around the top grip, brace the knuckles of your left hand against the center of your chest. Don't push too hard. Just rest the top of the club there and use that spot as the lever for your

Par Primer

A long-shafted putter has a shaft about as long as your driver. You brace the top of the shaft on your chest when you putt.

swing. Think of your left hand as the top of a long pendulum. The right hand (lower) grip should be in your normal putting grip (see Chapter 10) with the palm of your right hand facing the target and perpendicular to the ground.

If you have a lot of nervous twitches in your hands and wrists (the yips), the long putter is a great choice because it takes your hands and wrists completely out of the swing. You're using the big muscles of your arms and shoulders to make the putting stroke. The long putter will feel a little bit clumsy at first if you have any experience with a traditional-length model, but if you're just starting out, feel free to try it. You won't have any ingrained habits or preconceived notions. Try a long putter as well as lots of different standard putters and pick the one that feels the best when you swing.

> ### Extra Swings
>
> Some people think that anchoring a putter to your body as you putt, as you would with a long putter, should be illegal. It's something the USGA (the rules organization for golf) is considering. Keep that in mind before you invest in a long putter.

Other kinds of grips, like this claw grip, help keep your hands more stable through impact. PGA Tour player Mark O'Meara used this grip to fix his problem with the yips.

Caress, Don't Strangle

Sam Snead, one of pro golf's legends, said that the best piece of advice he ever got about the golf swing concerned the grip. He said that you need to grip the club as if it were a little bird—firm enough that it wouldn't fly away, but not hard enough to squash it. That might be hard to visualize, so try to think of it this way: Grip the club only as tightly as is necessary to keep it in your hands and under control.

If you grip the club too tightly, the tension in your hands and lower arms keeps you from being as flexible through your shoulders as you need to be. As a result, you can't turn as well, which translates into less distance. Don't worry about losing your grip on the club. As you start your downswing, your grip will automatically tighten. You won't even notice it.

Caddie's Advice _____

It's important to remember to grip the club more in your fingers than your palms. This allows your wrists to hinge freely.

Pressure Points

You can tell whether you're gripping the club too tightly in two ways. The first is a little bit painful, and the second is a little bit expensive.

If you're gripping the club with too much force, you'll give yourself some blisters on the heel of your left hand, where the butt of the grip hits your hand, and on the middle joint of your index finger of your right hand, the last finger at the bottom of the shaft. Of course, if you're wearing a golf glove on your left hand, you'll see a worn spot before you get that blister on the heel of your hand. You'll also see holes start to develop on the fingertips of the glove if you're gripping the club too hard. Take these cues and make some changes before it gets painful.

Extra Swings

One of the most painful things that can happen to you while you're out on the course is to get a blister. That's especially the case when you're out there without anything to cover the sore. The club is rubbing on a raw wound every time you swing—something that's hardly conducive to playing good golf. It is crucial to carry two or three bandages in your golf bag for such emergencies. The best kind are the cloth strips, which are more flexible than the plastic kind. Be sure to get the bigger-sized variety, so that the blister is fully covered. Bandages are also handy for blisters you might develop on your feet. I also carry an extra pair of socks, just in case.

How Grip Affects the Flight of Your Shots

With a totally neutral grip—that is, one with each hand on one side of the grip—the placement of your hands has the least to do with the flight of the ball. But because people have different body and swing shapes, it's often necessary to manipulate the position of the hands on the grip to promote a certain kind of ball flight. Minor modifications in the standard grips I talked about earlier in this chapter are perfectly acceptable, but try not to stray far. A fundamental grip is one of the biggest factors in a solid swing. The less conventional your grip becomes, the more trouble you'll have repeating it, and the harder it will be for you to get advice from an instructor. He or she wouldn't really know what to do with you.

In general, how you shift your hands on the shaft will exaggerate your ball flight in the given direction. For example, take a club and make a standard overlapping grip. Your hands should be basically neutral—your left hand is on the left side of the grip, facing away from your target, while your right hand is on the right side of the grip, facing the target.

Strong Grip

For this example, the side of the grip closest to the hole is the front. The opposite side is the back. The top of the grip is the side facing skyward. If you rotate your left hand toward the top of the grip, so that if you look down, you can see two knuckles (on the left hand) instead of just the one for the index finger, then you've made a stronger grip. A *strong grip* makes it easier for the clubhead to come through the hitting area with the face closed, or pointed to the left of the target. That angle will cause the ball to have right-to-left, or hook, spin.

> **Par Primer**
>
> Rotate your left hand more toward the top of the grip, so you can see the knuckles of your left hand's first and middle fingers. You've created a **strong grip**.

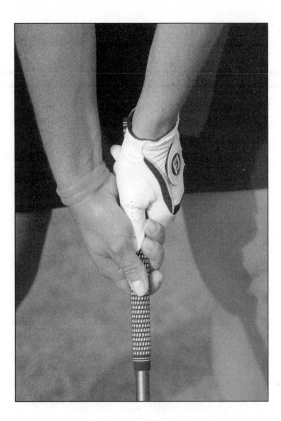

A "stronger" grip. Notice the left hand has rotated more toward the top of the club.

Weak Grip

If you rotate your right hand toward the top of the club, again so you can see two knuckles on your right hand instead of one, then you've created a weaker grip. As you might guess, the weaker grip is the opposite of a stronger grip. With a *weak grip*, it's easier for the clubhead to come through the hitting zone with the face open, or pointed to the right of the target. An open clubface will cause the ball to have left-to-right, or slice, spin.

Par Primer

Rotate your right hand more toward the top of the grip, so you can see the knuckles of your right hand's first and middle fingers. You've created a **weak grip**.

You don't have to move your hands very far on the grip to notice a big difference in the flight of your ball. It isn't necessary to make radical changes. Experiment on the practice range and make only the minimum change necessary to get the results you're looking for. Changing the grip should only be a last resort, after you've determined that you can't fix the problem by changing a part of your swing. I'll cover more details about the swing in Chapter 6.

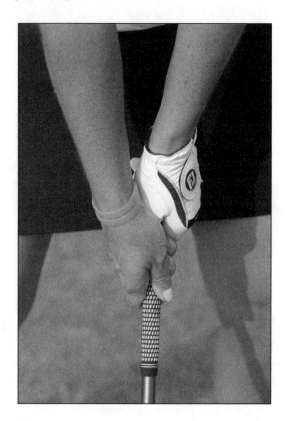

A weaker grip. Notice the right hand has rotated more toward the top of the club.

Grip Size

The size of the grips that are on your clubs can also affect the way you hit the ball. Logically, your grips should fit your hands, but because most companies sell their clubs with standard-sized grips, most people don't realize that they can decide for themselves how big or small they want their grips to be.

If you do have small hands, you'll find it much easier to get your fingers around the shaft of the club if it has smaller grips. Be prepared, however, for increased vibration in your hands and wrists when you make an off-center hit. Some people like to feel that, because it tells them just what kind of bad swing they made. Others hate it. Champions Tour player Jim Thorpe has the grips stretched so thin on his clubs, he might as well be grasping bare shafts.

If you have larger hands, or you're experiencing arthritis symptoms in your hands or wrists, oversize grips can really help you. I have larger than average hands. If I played with standard-sized grips, I wouldn't have enough room on the shaft to get a good grip. My fingers would go around the grip with a whole lot of finger left over, and my fingertips would bang into the palm of my hand. A slightly oversized grip allows me to hold the club comfortably. If you have arthritis in your hands, a larger grip makes it easier for you to keep hold of the club, and you don't have to close your fingers quite as far around the grip.

Double Bogey

On the other hand, using grips too large for your hands can hurt your game. If you have small hands and a big grip, you lose that crucial feel between grip and clubhead. The club becomes unwieldy in your hands, making you feel like you don't quite have control.

Grip Material

Because the grips are the only connection your hands have with your clubs, you need to choose the type of grip material that gives you the best connection. Here are some of the different kinds of grips, and their gripping characteristics:

- **Natural leather.** The most expensive and hardest to care for, natural leather grips are not very resistant to water but are very easy on the hands. Unless you're a pro and you're planning to hit 500 balls a day, they aren't for you.

- **Synthetic leather.** With most of the features of natural leather but not so much of the cost, synthetic leather grips are very popular. They wear out a little bit faster than rubber grips.

- **Rubber.** The most resistant to water, rubber grips are good, general-purpose grips for the beginning player. They are also the least expensive and easiest to install.

- **Cord.** Some players like a very rough grip surface that provides great traction through rain, sweat, or snow. Cord is the answer for that kind of player, but you pay a price. You need tough hands, because corded grips feel like rough-grade sandpaper.

Caddie's Advice

To save yourself the aggravation of constantly taking clubs in to be regripped, if one club needs a new grip, get them all taken care of.

After you've found a grip that works for you, be very diligent about keeping them in good condition. You should also replace your grips when they become worn. Most grips have dimples or lines in them. Much like the tires of your car, when the marks start to fade, it's time to start thinking about new grips. If you play once or twice a month, you'll only have to replace them once a year. (Chapter 20 covers replacing your grips.) It doesn't cost much—no more than four or five bucks a club.

The Least You Need to Know

- ◆ The three main grip types for regular shots are the interlocking, overlapping, and 10-finger grips.

- ◆ For the interlocking grip, link your hands together by wrapping the pinkie of your right hand around the index finger of your left hand. Reverse the process if you're a lefty. This grip is the best for people with small hands or short fingers.

- ◆ For the overlapping grip, which is the most common, place your right pinkie in the groove between the index and middle fingers of your left hand. Reverse if you're a lefty.

- ◆ The 10-finger, or baseball, grip is the simplest of the three grips. All 10 fingers grasp the club, and the side of the left index finger rests against the side of the right pinkie.

- ◆ The most common putting grip is the reverse overlap. Place your left index finger in the groove between the pinkie and ring fingers of your right hand.

- ◆ Shifting your hands in the grip affects the flight of your shots. If you turn your left hand so that it is more on top of the club, you've created a strong grip. This promotes right-to-left shots. A weak grip, where the right hand turns more on top of the shaft, promotes a left-to-right flight.

- ◆ Be sure to play with the right-sized grips on your clubs.

Chapter 5

The Moment of Truth

In This Chapter

- ◆ Starting off with the right stance
- ◆ Alignment: Pointing in the right direction
- ◆ Swing thoughts: Keeping your pre-shot thoughts simple
- ◆ Taking the club back
- ◆ Judging your progress

Golf is different than many other sports. In basketball or baseball, the ball comes to you, and you have to react to it by bouncing it, throwing it, hitting it, or catching it. In golf, the ball just sits there, waiting for you to walk up and do something to it. Hall of Fame baseball player Ted Williams once told golf legend Sam Snead that baseball was much harder than golf because the golf ball doesn't move when you're trying to hit it. Snead's response was classic. "But Ted, we have to play our foul balls!"

If you're just starting out in golf, I'm sure you've felt that sinking feeling in your stomach when you stood in front of the ball, that what-am-I-supposed-to-do-now feeling. Where do I put my feet? Okay, I think I'm ready. What do I do now?

It's perfectly normal to worry about your swing. If you've never done it before, a golf swing is a very strange movement indeed. You're turning your upper body and swinging your arms, all of which has to be coordinated with shifting your weight back and then forward again. It's a tough thing to do perfectly time after time. In fact, it's so hard that even people who hit hundreds of golf balls a day—as professionals like me often do—don't get it right every time. Becoming a good golfer isn't about eliminating all of your bad shots. As I'm sure you know, nobody's perfect, and no matter how hard you try, you won't be able to hit every shot exactly right. Your goal, then, should be to hit as few bad shots as possible, and when you do hit a bad one, to make sure that the mistake is in the right place (away from water and the out-of-bounds stakes).

If you keep this principle in mind and judge yourself by your improvement and not your score, it will be so much easier to stay motivated and enjoy yourself. When you first start out, you're going to struggle. That's true with learning any complicated process. But if you learn the fundamentals I'm going to go over in the next few chapters, you'll have a solid foundation to build on, and not only will your scores get better, but your game will improve. Those two goals go together.

Stance: Stand and Deliver

Before you consider trying to swing the golf club and hitting the ball, you need to think about two things. I went over the first thing—your grip—in Chapter 4. When you have a good grip, the next thing you need to worry about is how you set up for your shot. No matter how good your swing is, and no matter how far you hit the ball, if you don't set up properly, you'll have bad aim. What good is a huge, 300-yard drive if you accidentally aim for the parking lot 50 yards left of the fairway? You'll be able to brag to your friends that you really crushed one, but you'll also spend the rest of the afternoon apologizing to the owner of the car with the window cracked by your wild shot.

Let's talk first about your stance. Place your feet shoulder-width apart and gently flex your knees. Bend slightly at the waist, until your arms hang freely in front of you. Try this without a club. Let your arms drop almost straight from your shoulders. Without turning your shoulders, sweep your arms back and forth a few times. They should be moving about a foot in front of your belt buckle—if they're any farther away, you're hunched over too far. Your stance should feel like you're ready to catch a fragile object someone in front of you has tossed. Your weight should be on the balls of your feet, but your heels should stay on the ground.

> **CAUTION**
>
> **Double Bogey**
>
> It's important to keep your feet shoulder-width apart in the setup. Any wider, and you'll restrict how far your shoulders can turn. Any narrower, and you might have trouble keeping your balance.

Here, I'm in the proper stance. My feet are shoulder-width apart, I have a light flex in my knees, and I'm bending lightly at the waist, but my back is straight.

In this picture, my back is hunched too far forward, as if I'm reaching for the ball.

In this picture, my back is too stiff and upright. This isn't a natural, athletic position.

Now that you have your feet planted, shoulder-width apart, and your arms hanging loosely in front of you, look straight down. I like to rotate my left toe out, toward the target, slightly, because it helps me make a more complete turn on my backswing. It also helps me feel looser and more athletic.

This photograph shows my setup with a 5-iron. The ball is in the middle of my stance. My feet are shoulder-width apart. My arms are hanging naturally from my shoulders, not pushed out in an exaggerated move. Notice how my hands are slightly ahead of the ball—toward the target.

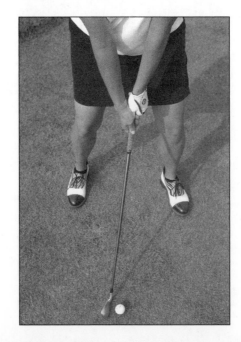

Now that you have your feet in the right position, you're ready to grab the club. Keeping your feet in the set-up position, grip your 5-iron in the grip you learned in Chapter 4. With your arms hanging loosely in front of you and your hands on the grip, the sole of the club should rest flat on the ground. Obviously, for a longer club, you need to stand a little farther from the ball than you do with a short club like a wedge, so make those little adjustments for each club. But the key here is to get into a natural, athletic position. You aren't artificially holding your arms in any position. They hang down from your shoulders. The club should rest comfortably in your hands and on the ground. Now you're ready to take the next step—aiming your shot.

To make sure you're in the correct stance, refer to this checklist:

- ❏ Are your feet shoulder-width apart?
- ❏ Is the toe of the foot closest to the target rotated 3 inches toward the target?
- ❏ Is the toe of your back foot, the one farthest from the target, pointed to a spot perpendicular to the target?
- ❏ Do you have a shallow, athletic knee-bend?
- ❏ With your arms hanging in front of you, does the sole of the club rest flat on the ground?
- ❏ Is your weight resting lightly on the balls of your feet?

Alignment: Are You Going My Way?

I've been on the practice tee with hundreds of amateur players who have come to me for advice on their golf swings. I always ask them to set up as they normally would and hit a few balls, so I can get an idea of their skill level. Easily 75 percent of the amateurs I see make the job of hitting a golf ball much harder than it has to be by setting up incorrectly. Many of them just flat out aim at the wrong point in the distance. Two major factors influence your aim for a shot: where your feet are pointed and where the clubface is pointed. The way your golf club is designed, with a sloped top edge, it sometimes gives the optical illusion of being pointed straight at the target, but in reality, it is pointed to the left of the target. Many beginners make the mistake of aiming at the target with the top edge of the club; the approach that yields a more accurate shot is to aim the bottom groove of the club at the target.

Par Primer

When you're in your stance and ready to start your swing, you're **at address.**

The other issue is the way you position your feet in relation to your target *at address.* If you place a club on the ground in front of your feet, the club on the ground should point directly at your target. The three main aiming problems I see with amateurs are alignment, closing the stance, and opening the stance. Let's talk a little bit about each.

◆ **Alignment.** This is simply where your feet and your clubhead are aimed before the shot. If a line drawn in front of your feet points to the left, you're going to hit the ball to the left. If that line points straight at the target, but the clubhead is pointed toward the left, the ball will still go left. In order to hit the ball consistently to the target you're aiming for, your feet need to be aligned straight at the target, and the bottom groove on the face of the club should be perpendicular to the imaginary line that runs just in front of your feet. This is called a square stance. Remember the club we laid on the ground to show where your feet were pointed? That's the imaginary line I'm talking about.

◆ **Closing the stance.** If you're hitting from a closed stance, your right foot (the one furthest away from the target) is moved back from the imaginary line—the one drawn in front of your toes that should point to the target. The closed stance looks a little like you're just aiming to the right, but with one big difference. If you aim to the right, both your shoulders and your feet are in line with the target in the setup. With a closed stance, your shoulders are pointed straight ahead, and the imaginary line in front of your feet is pointed to the right of the target. Closing your stance will move the pivot point of your swing forward. It forces you to swing across the ball from your body out, or inside-out. You'll put lots of right-to-left spin on the ball but will have trouble aiming your shots.

Caddie's Advice

You might be tempted to close your stance if you hit a lot of slice shots. Resist the temptation. Fix the problem in your swing. If you just close your stance, you're adding the problem of a bad setup to the problem that's causing your slice.

◆ **Opening the stance.** In an open stance, the foot closest to the target is pulled away from the imaginary line, while the shoulders are still in line with the target. The opposite of the closed stance, an open stance promotes a swing that comes across the ball from the outside in. As you learned in Chapter 3, this will make the ball spin from left to right. Unless you really want to fade or slice the ball, stay away from an open stance when you're hitting long irons or woods. There are some situations for which an open stance is good, like for chip shots. I'll talk about those later in this chapter.

If I drew a line in front of my toes, it would point to the left of where I really wanted to hit the ball. My stance here is open.

Draw that line again here and you would see it pointing to the right of where I want to hit it. My stance is closed.

To recap, let's go over what will happen to your ball because of your stance and alignment. If the imaginary lines in front of your shoulders and feet both point straight at your target, and the bottom groove of your clubface is perpendicular to those lines, you have perfect alignment. If your shoulders and feet are aligned properly, but the bottom groove of your clubface is pointed to the left or to the right, your ball will fly in the direction the clubface is pointed.

If the imaginary line in front of your feet points to the right or left of the target, while the line in front of your shoulders still points straight at it, you have a closed or open stance. A closed stance will generally cause the ball to curve from right to left, while an open stance will do the opposite. I know this is a lot to digest right now, so don't worry about it too much. We'll go over it again in Chapter 9, so you can match whatever specific problems you're having to a good solution.

Caddie's Advice

On the practice range, lay a club down in front of your toes. Where does the shaft point? It should point at your target.

What's a Swing Thought, and Should I Have One?

Some coaches say that you should be thinking about certain things as you go through your golf swing, like "Back and slow, through and fast," or "Slow, slow, slow; quick, quick, quick." On a simple level, some swing thoughts are good, because they can be catchy ways to remember what you should be doing. My favorite is one I still use every time I play. I've found a melody from a song that is the same tempo as one of my really good swings. Do you know the Beatles' song "Help"? The song starts, "Help, I need somebody." I begin my swing on "Help," hit the ball on "need," and make my follow-through on "somebody."

Although simple swing thoughts can be useful, avoid trying to think about several parts of your shot as you take your swing. For example, if you read a book full of golf tips, like this one, and try to keep all of them in your mind during your swing, you'll experience paralysis by analysis. You'll have so much on your mind, you won't be able to just let it go and swing the club.

When it comes to the golf swing, my advice is to take one swing thought at a time and work on it until it becomes second nature. For example, when you're working on your backswing, which I'll be talking about in just a second, you can think to yourself each time, "Back and slow, back and slow, back and slow." But after you've practiced a slow backswing enough times, it should become second nature, and you won't even have to think about it anymore. Then you can move on to the next thing, like "turn, turn, turn," or something to that effect. My dad took me to a teaching professional when I was eight to learn the fundamentals of the game, and my first teacher taught me this way, focusing on one thought at a time.

Caddie's Advice

In the beginning, keep things simple. Practice one or two principles at a time. Any more and your brain won't be able to process them all.

Even today, I like to make my swing as uncomplicated as possible. The less I'm thinking about the whole process, the better I'm generally hitting the ball. Of course, because you're still learning, you're going to have to study the basics of the swing. But after you've learned those, repetition through practice and playing is what *grooves your swing*. Learning the proper fundamentals means the swing you do groove will be a good one that you will repeat over and over again with predictable results, even under pressure.

Par Primer

Grooving your swing means practicing it enough that the whole process becomes second nature. You aren't thinking about its parts, just the whole unit.

Before We Start

I know you must be looking forward to actually hitting golf balls by now, but bear with me a little bit longer. Before you go out and bang it around, I want to give you a few things to think about. That way, the first habits you develop will be good ones.

Certain mechanics and movements will make you hit the golf ball long and straight. That's no secret. But these mechanics and movements are pretty much limited to the 6 inches in front of and behind the ball during the swing. Which means, no matter what you do to get the club back away from the ball and then down toward it again, as long as you keep the clubface in a good position at impact and you are shifting your weight properly at the time, you're going to hit a good shot.

Of course, many of the positions and movements I'm going to describe to you in the next couple of chapters are the optimum way to get the job done. But the tips and drills I'm giving you will just make it easier for you to get the result you want, which is to hit the ball long and straight. If you're getting good results with an unorthodox method, then by all means, keep doing what you're doing. If you've ever watched a professional golf tournament, I'm sure you've noticed that the golfers don't have identical swings. Each person has his or her own idiosyncrasies that come from how he or she learned and how his or her body is built. Lee Trevino swings around his body on a very flat trajectory. He learned to swing that way because he grew up in a part of Texas that was very windy. His flat swing keeps the ball lower to the ground and out of the wind. Kelly Robbins of the LPGA Tour has a very upright swing. She's tall, and uses that height to get great leverage and hit long, high shots. As far as swings go, mine is comparatively simple—no loose movements and a straightforward pivot through the ball. I played softball as a kid and a teenager, and I think when I got seriously involved in golf, my swing evolved from the athletic motion of throwing a softball.

You'll have your own idiosyncrasies as well. Don't be disappointed if you can't exactly duplicate some of the things I'm going to be talking about. You won't be able to, and you don't need to. Try to understand the principles behind the movements. Then it will be easier for you to figure out why things are going wrong and what you need to do to fix them. Look at PGA Tour player Jim Furyk, who won the U.S. Open in 2003. His swing looks like nothing I could even describe, but I'll try. He picks the club straight up off the ground in his backswing and then drops it almost straight down in his follow-through. Many people have said he looks like he's swinging inside of a phone booth. But he was a great college player and he's one of the best players on the PGA Tour. It works for him.

You'll also tailor your swing to the various strengths and weaknesses of your body. If you're extremely flexible, you'll probably have a big shoulder turn. If you're more muscular and less flexible, you'll probably use more leg drive than shoulder turn. If you have a bad back, you'll use your arms and shoulders to generate clubhead speed. There is such a thing as an ideal swing, but few people have one that looks like it. We all just do the best we can to come close!

Playing Catch

The beginning of your backswing, the move you make bringing the club away from the ball and on its way behind you, is the one that sets the tone for your whole swing. Remember how I said the 6 inches behind and in front of the ball are the most important in the swing? The first part of your backswing covers that 6-inch distance behind the ball.

The best advice I ever got for starting the swing came from my dad when I was a kid. I would get into my regular stance and address the ball with my 5-iron. Six inches behind my back foot, on the same line as the ball I was trying to hit, my dad teed up another golf ball. When I took my backswing, my goal was to keep the backswing low and slow enough to nick the top of the teed-up ball and brush it off the tee. If I kept my backswing artificially low, then I would blast the other ball off the tee. That was some immediate feedback that I was doing something wrong. If I snatched the club up in the air too quickly on the backswing, I'd miss the ball behind me completely. Even today, when I'm having trouble with my tempo, I can tee a ball up behind me like my dad did when I was little, and it still works. I'll give you some more details about that drill in Chapter 8.

Another image that may help give you the right idea for the beginning of the backswing is to think of yourself as being in a baseball or softball batter's box. You're setting up for your shot and aiming where the pitcher would be standing. The catcher is in a crouch behind you. Take your club back slowly so that the catcher can stick out the glove and *catch* your clubhead during the backswing.

Fundamentally, the beginning of the backswing is one of the easier parts of the swing to master. Your tempo is the most important factor. Physically, think about keeping your arms just rigid enough so that they don't bend, and move both arms and the club back (away from the target) in a one-piece motion, like the pendulum of a clock. When your arms swing as far back as they can naturally, they will tug at your shoulders and try to get them to follow along. Go with that feeling and allow your shoulders to turn, like the beginning of a baseball swing, but on a different plane. You've just made the first step in your new golf swing.

Caddie's Advice

Making a fast backswing doesn't help you hit the ball farther. Expend your energy on the way down.

Little Victories

After you've mastered this simple combination of moves—bringing the club back low and slow from the ball and beginning to turn your shoulders—and before you move on to take some full swings, try a few little swings.

Take a pile of practice balls and find a secluded spot on the driving range. Take a 5-iron or a 6-iron and get into your regular stance, with the ball equidistant between each foot. Then, taking the club back 2 feet or so, just until your shoulders start to turn and bringing it no higher than your shins, practice making contact with the ball. Even if you've never swung a golf club before, you should be able to make contact most of the time in this drill. Your goal is to make the ball pop into the air and roll about 15 yards. You're going to flub some, but that's no big deal. Nobody's videotaping it.

The idea is to get used to the feeling of the club hitting the ball and the position the club needs to be in at impact to make the ball travel straight, whatever the trajectory. You'll easily be able to tell when you've gotten good contact with the ball. Solid shots don't feel like anything. If you hit the ball on the *sweetspot* of the clubface, you won't feel anything in your hands. If you hit the ball with some other part of the clubface, you'll feel a distinct vibration, and you'll also hear a different, more hollow sound. A good shot will "clack," like a plastic case snapping shut. A poor shot will sound like a softball coming off of an aluminum bat, more of a "thunk." These small swings are the beginning steps in creating muscle memory. Believe it or not, one day, you'll step up to the ball and hit it without even thinking about it!

Par Primer

The **sweetspot** of a club is the optimum area on the clubface on which to make contact with the ball. If you hit a ball on this spot, all of the weight in the clubhead is behind the ball, and you'll get the most distance and accuracy.

Each time you hit a ball solidly with one of these one-quarter swings, you've earned a little victory. Practice this drill until you can make solid contact seven or eight times out of ten. Then you'll be ready to take on the next challenge, a full golf swing.

Ball Position

Many coaches will tell you to change where you position the ball in your stance for the different kinds of shots. In general, this is true, but it's something you don't need to worry about until you're a little more advanced. In general, the longer the club, the more forward (toward the target) you should move the ball in your stance. For a short-iron shot, the ball should be in the middle of your stance, an equal distance from each foot. As your clubs get longer, you should inch the ball forward in the stance. For the driver, the ball should be lined up with the heel of your front foot, the one closest to the target.

I advise amateurs to start by playing the ball in the middle of their stances and then adjust according to how the ball is flying. If you have trouble getting the ball up in the air, move the ball forward (toward your target) in your stance. If you're popping a lot of shots up in the air, move the ball back in your stance a little bit. No matter where the ball is in the stance, it should never be more than 4 inches, or the length of a dollar bill, from the midpoint between your feet.

With an iron (I'm using a 5-iron), the ball should be near the middle of your stance. You can draw a line down from your belt buckle to the ball.

As the club in your hand gets longer, your ball position should move forward. With a driver, the ball is two inches behind my left heel, more toward the front of my stance.

The Least You Need to Know

◆ Before you hit your first golf ball, it's crucial to have a good stance and alignment.

◆ Draw an imaginary line in front of your feet in your stance. That line will point where your shot is aimed.

◆ If that imaginary line in front of your feet is pointing in a different direction than the imaginary line in front of your shoulders, you'll hit balls with side spin.

◆ A closed stance, where your back foot is pulled back from the imaginary line, will cause your ball to curve to the left. An open stance, where your front foot is pulled away, will cause you to hit shots that curve to the right.

◆ The most important parts of the swing are the 6 inches just before and after you hit the ball.

◆ Begin your backswing low and slow. Imagine a baseball catcher behind you reaching out and catching your clubhead.

◆ Earn little victories. Practice with small, one-quarter swings to get the feel of the club hitting the ball solidly.

Chapter 6

Swing Mechanics: How It All Works

In This Chapter

◆ Keeping on your toes: Good balance

◆ Weight and see: Moving in the right direction

◆ Breaking the swing into parts

◆ Pulling it all together

In this chapter, I'm going to be throwing a lot at you. I'll go over the meat and bones of your golf swing—how to start it, keep it on the right track, and finish it. Because of all the different parts and positions in it, the swing isn't such a simple thing to perfect, but with some good advice, you can build one with a minimum amount of suffering and frustration.

Are you ready? Let's get started!

Getting Some Balance in Your Golf Diet

If you tried some of the techniques I talked about in Chapter 5, like taking some small swings at the ball to get the feel of what solid impact is like, then you've made the first step in building your swing. But before you can unleash your shoulders, arms, hands, and the club on the ball to make it fly, you have to build a good foundation. Getting your feet in the right stance is part of that good foundation, but you have to admit, it's pretty easy to look at a diagram and put your feet in the place it says is correct. It gets a little harder when you add the force and movement of a swing.

Golf would be such an easy game if we could get set up in a perfect stance, weight perfectly balanced in the center and slightly forward over the toes, and just stop everything right there. But alas, you have to move. The adventures are in the movements.

Your feet are anchoring you to the ground, but before you can make a good golf swing, you have to be able to distribute your body weight effectively over those anchors. Where that weight settles changes through the swing, and being sensitive to these changes and when they should happen, is critical to making a good swing.

Before we start talking about those weight shifts, let's talk about where your weight should be before you start to swing. Let's talk about balance. Imagine yourself standing on a crowded train, facing the side of the car. You're in a normal, relaxed position, with your feet about 6 inches apart and your hands at your sides. The train suddenly slows down. What happens to your body weight? It pitches in the same direction the train is moving, and you lose your balance. Now imagine the same situation, but this time, your feet are spread shoulder-width apart and your knees are slightly flexed. You're ready for that change in the train's speed. Then what happens? You probably don't even lose your balance. Your legs act as shock absorbers and naturally offset the difference in the train's momentum.

Caddie's Advice

For the golf swing, your center of gravity is an axis that runs in a straight line from your head down your spine and to a point in between your feet (when you're in a golf stance).

In the golf swing, like on that train, your goal is to always keep your balance. In order to hit the ball with any kind of force and accuracy, you're going to have to shift your weight several times during the swing. If you can keep your balance before, during, and after this process, your probability of success increases dramatically. Picture yourself on that train again. You have a narrow base (your feet are only 6 inches apart). You've got a pencil in your hand. The train slows down, and as it does, you have to take that pencil and make a mark in one of those bubbles on a standardized test form that's stuck on the wall. That's a tough thing to do as you're losing your balance and staggering to recover. It's no easy feat to do from a wide, solid base, either, but you've got a much better chance than you do if you're flying down to the other end of the car and apologizing to the woman whose hat you knocked off.

In the remainder of this chapter, I'm going to go into more detail about the different parts of the swing, but all through those tips and discussions, it is important that you remember this one constant: No matter where you are in the swing, you have to keep control of your body and stay in balance. When you lose your balance, you lose your chance to hit the ball with any kind of consistency.

The best piece of advice I ever got about balance was pretty simple. When you take your stance, and your feet are set up at shoulder width, imagine two brick walls rising from the ground right at your sides, next to each foot. No matter what happens in the swing—no matter what kind of weight shift or turn you try—no part of your body should touch those brick walls. For this drill, you have to stay "inside," even if it's a sunny day! If your shoulders or hips stray and bump the brick walls, that means you're tipping or tilting instead of turning or shifting. Tipping or tilting can happen only if you're out of balance.

Balance is such a feeling concept that it's hard for me to give you ways to work on it. Visualization is the technique I use. Imagine walking across a narrow wooden beam that's only 12 inches wide. You would have to pay special attention to keeping your weight balanced directly over the beam so you wouldn't fall off. Now imagine that the beam is 4 feet wide, and you can spread your feet apart. You have a much wider base to balance your weight up. A golf swing is built on the same principles.

No matter what, you want to keep your body inside imaginary walls that come straight up from the outside edges of your feet. If you do, you'll keep your balance and make better, more consistent contact.

I like to think of my stance as a pyramid, with a wide, stable base. I also think consciously about keeping my shoulders centered over my hips. Whether it's golf or carrying a shopping bag or trying to lug a mattress up the steps, if your shoulders shift off center from your hips, you're going to lose your balance and have to shift some other part of your body to compensate. In a golf swing, it's these compensating movements that give you trouble. You'll understand what I'm talking about when you get to the section on reverse pivoting a bit later in this chapter.

The All-Important Weight Shift

Just when you figured out good balance, now you have to start shifting your weight around! I've gone over how important balance is in the golf swing. The next most important thing, even more important than the technique you use to get the club through your backswing and back to the ball, is shifting your weight the right way during the swing. Golf isn't an arm game. We aren't out here shooting pool. If you stand over the ball, keep the entire rest of your body still, and swing the club just with your arms, you won't be able to hit it very far. By themselves, your arms can't do much. The muscles there aren't very large compared to, say, the big muscles across your back and in your thighs (of course, guys like Arnold Schwarzenegger are exceptions). To hit a golf ball any significant distance, you need to get those big muscles, as well as the natural momentum of your body weight, into your swing. That's why two weight shifts are crucial to the swing—the one to the back foot during the backswing, and the other to the front foot just before impact.

In any golf swing, no matter how you get the club into the backswing with your arms and shoulders, as you draw the club away from the ball, you have to shift your body weight from a centered position over the ball to a position almost directly over your back foot (the one farthest from the target). The feeling of the weight shift is difficult to explain but easy to describe. Imagine you have a big blister on the heel of your left foot. The blister would really hurt if you put any weight on that foot, but some glue that mysteriously appeared on the bottom of your shoe prevents you from lifting the injured foot off the ground.

That feeling, that your foot is on the ground but you aren't putting any weight on it, is the one you're looking for when you shift your weight during the swing. It is important—crucial, actually—that when you shift your weight you don't shift your whole body. In plain English, that means don't tip over. You want your weight to shift with as little rocking as

Double Bogey _____

The toughest thing to learn about shifting your weight during the swing is to avoid swaying—letting your weight move outside of your feet—as you shift. Try to keep your shoulders as level as possible during your shifts.

possible in your shoulders and hips. If we drew an imaginary line across the tops of your shoulders, that line should stay as close to parallel to the ground as possible during the swing. Again, think of that big blister. Don't put pressure on it, but don't take that foot off the ground.

Let's go over the system of weight transfer you'll need for your swing. After that, we'll talk about getting your arms and shoulders into the act. We'll put the two together, and you'll be out doing some grass damage in no time!

When you're in the ready position, knees slightly flexed, feet shoulder-width apart, and front foot pointed slightly at the target, your weight should be distributed evenly over both feet. Imagine that someone on a bike is coming right at you, and you have to be ready to move in either direction to get out of the way. Luckily, golf is a nonviolent sport. As you take the club back and away from the ball, you should start feeling that imaginary blister on the heel of your front foot (the one closest to the target—left for righties and right for lefties!). By easing your weight onto your back foot (don't sway or tip!) you're *loading* power into your swing.

Par Primer

Shifting your weight to your back foot as you take the club back from the ball is called **loading**.

Your body weight is all set up to slam forward and give you some extra force to put into the shot. When you've finished taking the club back and are starting to bring it down toward the ball, it's time to do the slamming. You then shift the weight forward onto your front foot (ouch! imaginary blister on my back heel!) just before your arms and hands get to the ball. Like a whip, your hands and the club get a boost from the body weight that's coming through the hitting zone like a freight train. Make sure all innocent bystanders are out of the way, because the train's coming through!

When you finish, all of your weight should be squarely over your front foot. You should almost be balancing on it, with your back foot acting as a stabilizer. That's the goal. Lots of practice will help you get there!

Reverse Pivoting: The Graveyard Shift

Now that you understand the concept of using your body weight to help propel the ball, it should be easy to see why a *reverse pivot*, when your weight shifts the wrong way during the swing, is one of the worst things that can happen to you.

The most common cause of the reverse pivot is the desire to "scoop" the ball with the club. Many rookies don't trust that their swing and the loft of the club are enough to get the ball airborne. They try to somehow get the edge of the club under the ball and lift it into the air. Imagine digging sand out of a ditch with a shovel. As you scoop out the sand, you pitch your shoulders back to hurl it to the side. If you do that in your golf swing with hopes of scooping the ball up into the air, you'll throw your body weight against the direction your arms, hands, and the club are going. So instead of getting that boost from your weight shift, your arms and hands are swimming against the current upstream. The club slows down, and as you scoop, the ball does just what the sand did when you got it out of the ditch: It gets tossed off high and to the side.

> **Par Primer** _____
>
> When you shift your weight to the back foot instead of the front foot during the downswing, you're making a **reverse pivot.**

> **Caddie's Advice** _____
>
> Don't feel bad if you develop a reverse pivot. Believe it or not, Spain's Jose Maria Olazabal developed one just after he won The Masters in 1994, one of pro golf's most prestigious titles.

The easiest way to get rid of a reverse pivot is to make sure that you make that first weight transfer to the back foot during the backswing. After you've got your weight over your back foot, there are only two things that can happen as you swing toward the ball. Either your weight can stay back there, which feels very awkward, or it can shift forward as you bring your shoulders and arms down toward the ball. (For advice on how to fix a reverse pivot, see Chapter 9.)

Breaking Down the Swing

After you've developed the fundamentals of shifting your weight during the swing, it's time to worry about the mechanics of getting the clubhead back and through to the ball in the best possible position. The three main parts of the swing are the *backswing*, which is the movement of the club back away from the ball; the *downswing*, which starts right where the backswing ends and lasts through impact with the ball; and the *follow-through* (also called *takeaway*), which is the chunk of the swing from just after impact until you're finished.

> **Par Primer** _____
>
> When you take the club back away from the ball, you're making a **backswing**. The **downswing** is the move from the end of the backswing to actual contact. The **follow-through** is the finish after contact. The **takeaway** is another name for the follow-through.

I've already talked a little bit about the actual moment of impact in the last chapter. This feeling is relatively easy to duplicate over and over if you're just taking small, one-quarter swings on the practice range. The challenge is to build a swing that lets you make a full backswing and swing through the ball with the most power you can keep under control. Let's start with the backswing.

The Backswing: Potential Energy

The elements of the backswing are summarized in the following steps:

1. Take the club back from the ball low and slow.

2. Keep the clubhead on the imaginary line through the ball to the target for as long as possible.

3. Fold your right elbow (left elbow for lefties) into your side while keeping your left arm (right arm for lefties) reasonably straight.

4. Turn your shoulders away from the target.

5. Coil your shoulders as much as is comfortable.

The first 6 inches of the swing are a simple, slow move away from the ball with a one-piece combination of the hands and arms. After that, the general principle you want to follow is like a chain reaction—arms, shoulders, hips. Picture a straight line that runs from the center of the golf ball to the target for which you're aiming. Now imagine that the line extends from the back of the ball in the opposite direction as well. For as long as you can in the beginning of your backswing, you want to keep the clubhead moving back from the ball on that line.

About a foot and a half behind the ball, you won't be able to keep the club moving back on that straight line. If you did, you would tip over, and by now you know that any tipping is bad news. So when you can't move the club back along the line any more, you start to wrap it around your body. The coiling action that starts at this point is relatively easy, and almost reflexive. Keep your right elbow as tight to your side as you can. As you can see in the following photo, as you raise your hands, the right arm will fold into place almost automatically. When your hands reach hip level, start to turn your shoulders away from your target. Keep that right arm folded near your body and your left arm as straight as possible, and you'll be in good position.

Caddie's Advice

Don't forget to reverse instructions if you're a lefty!

Keep turning your shoulders and moving your hands back until your hands reach shoulder height. Don't force them any further—just as close as you can get them to shoulder height without straining. At this point, you should have your back turned toward your target as much as you can. Unless you're extremely flexible, you won't be able to get your back to completely turn to the target, but you should turn as far as you can without straining.

I'm in the middle of my backswing. As my shoulders turn, my right arm folds close to my side, and my left arm is relatively straight.

When you reach the top of the backswing, you need to cock your wrists to get ready. This is a fairly simple maneuver, but if you forget to do it, you'll lose a lot of power. With your right hand, stick your thumb out as you would if you were hitchhiking. Now, bend your wrist so that your thumb is moving backward toward you. You won't be able to bend it very far. Your wrists were designed to move much further the other way. But you should be able to cock your right wrist about two inches. Remember that feeling. With your hands on the club, try to duplicate that cock when you get to the top of the backswing.

If we took a picture of you at this juncture, called the top of the swing, it should look like the following photo. My left arm is relatively straight, and my right elbow is tucked near my side. If you don't keep that left arm as straight as possible, you run the risk of wrapping the club too far around your back and losing your balance.

I've kept my left arm relatively straight, my right arm has folded against my side, my chin is brushing my left shoulder, and my right knee is in the same position as it was in my setup.

See how my right elbow has folded and stays pretty close to my body? In this position, I can coil my upper body and get ready to unleash a lot of power on the downswing.

Caddie's Advice _____

Let the natural pull of the backswing determine how you coil your body. If you move your arms back from the ball properly, you'll feel your shoulders start to turn on their own, away from the ball. When your shoulders reach the end of their turn, they'll start to pull your hips. Let them. The backswing is like twisting a heavy rope. All of the tension will then release on the downswing, like the crack of a whip.

Here are three checkpoints you can think of when you work on your backswing:

1. When you get to the top, your chin should be touching, or close to touching, your left shoulder. If it isn't, you haven't rotated your shoulders enough.

2. When you get to the top, your right leg should be in the same position it was when you started the swing. Don't move your foot or change the flex in your knee. If you straighten your right knee during the backswing, you'll throw your weight onto your front foot and create a reverse pivot.

3. Imagine that the end of your club is attached to your belt buckle with a small piece of elastic cord. As you take the club back, consciously keep your hands "attached" to your belt buckle until your shoulders have fully turned away from the target. If you lift your hands before your shoulders make that turn, you'll create a loop in your swing that will almost guarantee that you hit a slice. Bad news.

The first few times you try a backswing, it will feel pretty awkward. In a mirror, try making a backswing and then stopping when you get to the top. Look at yourself in the mirror and try to copy my position in the preceding photo. Hold it for a few seconds, and then try another backswing. If you make sure to adjust into the proper position each time, you'll gradually get the feel of what a good backswing feels like.

The Downswing: Action!

The elements of the downswing are summarized in the following steps:

1. Uncoil in the reverse order that you coiled.

2. Your hips should begin the move toward the ball, followed by the shoulders, arms, and hands.

3. Pull your left hand toward the ball. Don't worry, your right will catch up.

4. Your wrists will automatically uncock at the bottom of your swing.

When you've made it to the top, what do you do now? Like any mountain climber, you come down. Luckily, there's a lot less to think about in the downswing than the backswing. It's much more of a natural move. Gravity is helping you.

One of the biggest mistakes I see beginning golfers make is their first move toward the ball after the backswing. They can be in perfect position at the top of the back-swing and then throw all that work down the drain by swinging their arms down toward the ball before they turn their hips. Remember when we took a picture of you at the top of your backswing? You had your shoulders turned from the tar-get. Your shoulder turn forced your hips to turn as well.

Caddie's Advice

If the back of your left hand is facing the target at impact, your shot will be on line.

So your hands are just above shoulder height, and you're ready to make a swing at the ball. Remember the order of the chain reaction we talked about on the backswing—arms, shoulders, hips? You need to unwind in the opposite order. Turn your hips toward the target first. You don't even need to move your hands at first. When you make that turn with your hips, your hands will automatically start to drop down. Your hips will pull your shoulders and arms through the beginning of the downswing.

When your hips have turned back toward the ball, first think about shifting your weight from your back foot to the front. Then focus on pulling the club toward the ball with your left hand. I know that sounds crazy—pulling in a golf swing? But trust me. Remember the wrist cock I talked about a little earlier? As your hips start to pull your shoulders and arms through the hitting area, keep that wrist cocked. Pulling with your left hand, swing toward the ball as hard as you can while still keeping your balance. You might think that with that wrist cocked, you'll swing right over the ball, but it won't happen. The pulling swing you're making with your left hand will force your wrist to uncock automatically.

The first few times you try this, you're bound to make some mistakes. That's okay. A lot of this is timing. The only way you can get that timing down is to hit some balls. It will feel strange at first, but if you can get yourself in the proper position at the top of the backswing, you almost can't help but make a good downswing.

At impact, I have pulled the club toward the ball with my left hand. As my hips turned back toward the ball, I shifted my weight from my back foot to my front foot. My shoulders and arms turn toward the ball, following my hips.

On a reverse pivot, your weight moves backward, away from the target, on the downswing.

The Follow-Through: Finishing What You Start

The elements of the follow-through are summarized in the following list:

1. Don't quit on it. Finish the swing high, with your hands near your head.

2. Consciously try to finish with good balance.

3. After impact, try to keep the clubhead on the target line as long as possible.

Okay, you've hit the ball. You're not quite done yet, however. You need to finish your swing. It's a very important part of the process. You can't just stop the club after you hit the ball. You'll lose clubhead speed and, therefore, distance, not to mention you could hurt yourself. The follow-through is like a natural brake for all that speed and motion you built up in the swing. Your hands and arm go past the ball and wind around your body again, until your hands end up about a foot from your left ear. If you jerked your swing to a stop right after impact, it would be like running your car into a wall to stop it. Unless you enjoy whiplash, that's not the way to go.

In keeping with our theme of balance, when you finish your swing, your belt buckle should be pointing at the target, and your weight should be directly over your left leg. Your right heel will have come off the ground during the follow-through, and your right foot will spin on its toe so you can get into that finish position facing the target. If you can't hold your finish, that's a good indication that you have a balance problem somewhere in your swing. Slow it down and take it step by step until you find where you're falling out of balance. Then work your way back up to full speed.

Many professionals visualize that imaginary line I was talking about between the ball and the target and try to make their clubhead chase the ball straight down that line for as long as they can in their follow-through. It's a practice that could help you if you have a problem jerking the club around to the left as you finish the swing.

Extra Swings

A big step in developing your golf game is trusting your swing. If you try to consciously aim the clubhead at the ball on a full-speed downswing, not only will you drive yourself crazy, you won't be able to do it. Trying to aim the clubhead while it's traveling so fast is impossible. Ben Hogan, a legendary pro, had incredible hand-eye coordination, and he said in his instruction book, *Five Lessons*, that even he couldn't aim the clubhead. To hit the ball consistently, you need to develop a system that repeats itself almost every time. Then it just becomes a question of putting the ball down in the right place on the ground so that it gets in the way of the swing. As you improve, you'll find yourself not so much swinging at the ball, but through it.

At the end of my follow-through, my weight is directly over my left foot. My belt buckle faces the target, and my right foot has rotated on its toe to allow a full follow-through.

Michelle's Swing Sequence

To give you a different, more complete view of the swing, let's take a look at my driver swing sequence. Pay particular attention to the sequence of motion—how the hands and club start, followed by the shoulders, and then the hips. The order reverses in the downswing. The hips turn back toward the target, with the shoulders and arms (and the club, of course) following.

See how my hands are hanging naturally in front of me, and not reaching for the ball?

As my swing starts, my shoulders turn back, away from the ball, while my hips stay pretty much pointed at the ball. My left knee moves slightly toward my right knee.

At the top of my backswing, my left wrist is flat, in line with the rest of my left arm. That means the club is in good position. If your wrist bends at this point, you'll have to manipulate the club on the downswing to hit it straight, and that's hard to do.

At impact, my head is still behind the ball, not moving forward toward the target. If it was forward, that would be a sign of a reverse pivot.

The momentum of my swing causes my right foot to turn, and I rotate up onto my toe. At this point, all of my weight is on my front leg.

Balance is one of the most important parts of a swing. At the finish, you should be able to hold your position without falling over.

The Least You Need to Know

◆ Balance is crucial to a good golf swing. Imagine walls sprouting from the ground at the sides of each of your shoes. Don't touch the walls with your hips or shoulders during the swing, or you'll be off-balance.

◆ Even more important than the mechanics of the swing is shifting your body weight properly during the swing.

◆ The three main parts of the swing are the backswing or takeaway, the downswing, and the follow-through.

◆ Your weight should shift to your back foot during the takeaway and then to the front foot on the downswing.

◆ Take the club back along a straight line from the ball for about a foot and a half and then coil the club around your body.

◆ At the top of the backswing, your chin should brush your left shoulder, and your hands should be just above about shoulder height.

◆ Through the swing, the right arm should fold next to your right side, while your left arm stays nearly straight.

◆ At the top of the backswing, cock your right wrist. It will naturally uncock from the force of your downswing.

◆ Uncoil your body in the opposite order you coiled it during the backswing. The hips start the move toward the ball, followed by the shoulders, and then the arms.

◆ Concentrate on pulling your left hand toward the ball as you swing through the hitting area.

Chapter

Tips to Live By, at Least for Now

In This Chapter

- Keeping your elbow tucked tight during the swing
- Cracking the whip in your swing
- Getting your weight into your swing
- Simplifying your golf life
- Taking the sting out of short chips

You've probably discovered that there aren't many quick fixes in golf. A good teacher can give you some things to think about and work on, but the only way to make long-term improvement is to practice. And when you practice, it's important to practice the right techniques the right way. If you're practicing bad habits, then that's what you'll be reinforcing. Keep hitting that slice on the driving range, and after 500 balls, you'll have a really good slice. Problems just don't magically disappear after a certain number of practice shots. You have to actively improve and change to make them go away.

This chapter is designed to give you some of the best single tips I've heard from some of the teachers I've had over the years. These tips aren't quick fixes, but keeping some of these things in mind as you practice and play will encourage you to put the pieces of your golf swing together in the right order.

The Chicken Wing

The swing should be a fluid, athletic move that you don't think much about while you're doing it. Of course, this is easy to say, but much harder to do. To get a solid, repeating swing, you have to examine the different parts and make sure that each is fundamentally sound. Among the many checkpoints in the swing, the easiest one to keep track of without an extra set of eyes is the right elbow.

In a basic, one-piece swing (the kind I've been teaching you, with the hips as the main pivot point), your left arm should stay nearly straight the entire time. Your right hand will pull the club back until your left arm is stretched back across your chest and pointed straight back from your target. When you reach the top of your backswing, your right arm should be folded against your body, with the elbow tucked next to your side. Then, on the downswing, your left hand should do most of the work, pulling the club through the ball and into the follow-through.

Take your normal backswing, but stop at the top, just before you would start to bring the club down toward the ball. Look back and down at your right arm. Is it folded tight to your body? If your elbow has separated from your body, you have what's called a *flying elbow*. This flaw isn't fatal—Jack Nicklaus has one, and he's done pretty well—but if your elbow is flying, you need to have superior hand-eye coordination to get the clubhead back down and into position through the hitting zone.

If you instead keep that right elbow tucked in during the swing, you're using your side as a brace to keep the right arm anchored in the same spot throughout the swing.

Par Primer _____

You have a **flying elbow** when your right elbow separates from your body during the back-swing. Unless you have fantastic hand-eye coordination, this flaw in your swing will lead to inconsistent ball-striking.

Imagine your right arm as the lever on a slot machine. When you reach up to pull the lever, the body of the machine isn't moving. You have no trouble grabbing it. When you pull it down, the lever snaps back into the same place every time, because the place where it's attached to the machine is stable. Your right arm and elbow are like that slot machine arm. If the elbow is floating in the air through your swing, you have to guide the club into the proper place on the downswing. If it's braced, you take one wildcard out of the equation.

Another way to determine if your elbow is staying in the right place during the swing is to take one of the soft wool covers that go over your woods and hold it in your armpit during your setup. Take your normal swing. The cover shouldn't fall out until your arms pass the ball. On a good swing, the cover will drop near where the ball was, right in front of you. If it drops during your backswing, you have a flying elbow.

Instead of folding against my side, my right elbow is sticking out—flying away from my body. It's more difficult to be consistent from this position.

Indiana Jones

One of my favorite movies is *Raiders of the Lost Ark*, which stars Harrison Ford as Indiana Jones. Jones's favorite piece of equipment is a big bullwhip. One of the most effective images you can keep in your mind during the swing is that of a whip cracking. A whip is a perfect example of using a lever and some resistance to create speed. When Indiana Jones snaps his whip, he brings the handle of it forward, and as the tip starts to move forward as well, he yanks backward with his wrist and arm to cause that lightning-fast change of direction, which makes the tip crack.

Your golf swing should be like cracking that whip. When you take your backswing and shift your weight to your rear foot (the one farthest from the target), you're setting up the whip. Then as you bring the club down toward the ball, you're forcing your weight forward and against a braced front leg, so the change of direction in your arms and hands is like the crack of the whip. If you can make the "crack" happen at the point where the ball is sitting on the ground, you'll see explosive results.

To see whether you're getting the crack in the right place, turn your club upside down and hold it with your normal grip just above the clubhead. Now swing it as you would for a normal shot. Listen for the swooshing sound. If the swoosh is happening behind you, just after you start your downswing, you're cracking the whip too early. You're losing power before you get down to the ball. Keep your wrists cocked a little bit longer on the downswing. The force of the swing will make them uncock at the right time.

Caddie's Advice

Your wrists cock automatically when you reach the top of your backswing. When you uncock them determines whether you have an early or late release. They should uncock at the moment of impact and not before.

If the swoosh happens right in front of you, where the ball sits, you've got the perfect crack. If you're swinging with a reasonable degree of power, it's almost impossible for you to have a crack that happens too late. The centrifugal force of the swing will make you release your wrists and arms before you get too far past the ball.

Weight and See

When you were a kid in science class, did you ever swing a bucket full of water around to demonstrate how centrifugal force keeps the water in place? If you did, you probably noticed that you just had to get the bucket started moving, and after that, the weight at the end of your arm carried quite a bit of momentum.

One of my best friends played college golf out in California. While he and his teammates practiced on the driving range, his coach would stroll behind them and watch. If the coach saw somebody swinging too hard, he would toss the person a clubhead he always carried in his pocket. If you've ever held in your hand a clubhead that isn't connected to a shaft, you were probably impressed with just how heavy it is. That's what the coach was trying to remind his players about. The clubhead is quite heavy. After you start it in motion, you don't have to exert all your force trying to bully it through the hitting zone to hit the ball a long way. Your biggest concern should be getting it started on the correct line.

Double Bogey

When transferring your weight forward as you swing through the ball, don't shift too early! Your hips will fly through, and you'll block the ball far to the right.

Some of the smallest players on the professional tour can hit the ball the longest distance because they understand that the crack of the whip is what creates distance, not how hard you can swing your arms. Charles Howell, III, is one of the smallest players on the PGA Tour at 5-feet-10 and 150 pounds. But he can easily hit the ball 300 yards on the fly. Annika Sorenstam is even shorter and lighter, and she can consistently hit it 285. Those two players obviously aren't as strong as someone like Ernie Els, who is 6-foot-4 and 230 pounds. So how do they hit the ball so far? They use the weight of the club and snap the whip.

Shake Hands

When I was learning to play golf, I got so excited during my backswing that I would often pick the club straight up in the backswing and swing through the ball as quickly as I could. The result was a whole lot of shanked and topped shots. The first thing my dad told me was to calm down and take a few deep breaths before I hit each shot. The next thing was to imagine that during my backswing, a friend of mine was standing 3 feet behind my ball with her hand extended for a shake. The goal was to simply turn my shoulders slowly back so that my right hand was in position to reach back and take my friend by the hand.

Practicing your swing without a club, you can actually do this drill. Set up for a normal shot, then bring your arms back in a one-piece takeaway. When you start to turn your shoulders, look behind you and reach out and shake your partner's hand. Most people don't have the body of a contortionist. When you make your turn, you won't be able to get your back to face the target like the pros, but do the best you can. Be sure to keep your hips still during this drill. Turning them backward toward your friend will defeat the purpose. You want your shoulders to turn while your belt buckle stays directly over the ball.

Finish What You Start

Whenever I give people advice about finishing their follow-through, invariably, they say, "But the ball is already gone, what difference does it make?" It makes a big difference. As I've said over and over, the most important part of the swing is the 6 inches in front of and behind the ball. If you swing through the hitting area and stop your follow-through, you're going to be slowing your club down before you get to the ball. Hitting the ball with a decelerating swing is a quick way to miss-hit a lot of shots, or at least to hit a lot of shots weak and to the right.

A full follow-through is also one of the best indicators of a solid swing. It's almost impossible to make a bad, poorly balanced swing and then wind up in a classic, well-balanced position in the follow-through. So if you make it one of your goals to get to that optimum position, you'll have some better clues about what's keeping you from getting there.

Take a normal practice swing with a full follow-through. Hold the follow-through at the end. If you can't because you would fall over, then you have a problem with balance. But after you're in the follow-through position, adjust your hips so that your belt buckle points at the target, if it isn't already there. Your weight should be over your left foot, and your right toe should be pointed at the target, with the right heel up in the air. Your hands should still be locked together as a unit and hovering near your left ear. The shaft of the club should be running nearly straight across your shoulder blades. If you aren't at that position in your follow-through, adjust yourself until you are. Then freeze for 20 or 30 seconds. Let your muscles get used to the feeling of a proper follow-through.

Take some practice swings. Each time, if you don't wind up in the proper position, adjust yourself until you are. As you take more and more swings, your body should adjust itself to get into the correct position, especially if you're thinking consciously about winding up there. You might be surprised by some of the side benefits this tip will bring. If you're finishing in a balanced, comfortable position, you're bound to make some of the right moves before you get there.

Playing with What You Have

This advice might sound so simple it's almost too obvious to bring up, but I'm always shocked that many amateur partners I play with have this problem. Let's say you have a pretty significant slice. Optimally, you could work on it with a teacher and get rid of it, but for today, you're stuck with it. If you know your ball is going to curve significantly to the right when you hit it, what do you think you have to do with your aim? Compensate for the curve and aim further left, of course. Surprisingly, many amateurs I play with don't take this simple step. They take great care in setting up so that they are aiming right down the middle, and then they are shocked when the sliced shot starts out straight and curves deep into the rough on the right.

Your slice won't magically go away if you keep aiming down the middle. Either you have to fix the slice, which is what I would concentrate my energies on, or play with the swing you have. If you're going to play with the swing you have, you need to know where to aim so that your ball will wind up in the fairway. If that means aiming 50 yards left of the fairway, then that's what you have to do.

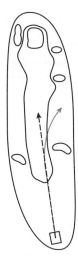 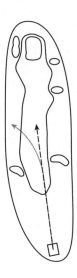

In the left figure, you can see what happens if you have a slice and aim at the middle of the fairway. Your ball will curve into the right rough. Make the left edge of the fairway your target. The opposite holds true if you hook the ball (right figure). If you aim at the fairway's center, your ball will curve to the left rough. You need to aim for the right edge of the fairway to enable your ball to curve back toward the middle.

Back to Basics

When you're struggling along, all by yourself out on the course, it's hard to remember all the things you ever heard about fixing your golf swing. In fact, even if you could remember it all, you would be so hopelessly muddled, it wouldn't help.

When I'm having a tough time, I try to keep one important thing in mind—getting back to basics. The same trick can help you. If nothing is going right, instead of over-analyzing and trying quick fixes, go the opposite way. Start from the beginning. Check your grip. Has it drifted into a too-strong or too-weak position? That alone can wreak havoc with your swing. When I'm having trouble, most often it's with my grip. Just by checking and rechecking to make sure that my hands are in the proper position, I save myself considerable swing miseries. You can, too. After you've checked your grip, slow down. Getting angry and swinging harder just compounds your struggles. Instead of using a 5-iron, relax and take a more deliberate swing with a 4-iron. Your mechanics will come back to you.

Caddie's Advice

As long as you aren't holding up your playing partners, there's no need to rush from shot to shot, especially if you're mad about the last one. When you've hit what seems to be the 100th bad shot in a row, take a few deep breaths before you move on to the next one.

Taking the Mystery Out of Short Chips Around the Green

While working with Champions Tour player and former Ryder Cup captain Dave Stockton on my short game, the best advice he ever gave me about short shots close to the green was to think of my chipping stroke as an extension of my putting stroke.

Using a 7-iron, when I hit a chip that has to travel 30 feet to the hole, I can use the same swing, with the same amount of force, as I would for a putt of that length. It greatly simplifies the decision-making process I need to go through before I take the shot. Because I can use the same swing as I would for a putt, less can go wrong.

I've played in dozens of pro-ams with hundreds of amateur playing partners. As a result, I've seen all kinds of swings, good and bad. I try to give my partners some of the tips you've been reading in this chapter to help with some of the problems in their games. But, as I'm sure you've discovered is the case in any complex undertaking, there really are no quick fixes. I can point you in the right direction here and give you the concepts that will help you make a swing change that improves your game, but your best bet for serious problems is to see a good teaching professional. He or she can help you integrate into a practice plan some of the tips I've given you here and some of the drills we'll go over in the next chapter.

The Least You Need to Know

- ◆ Set up in your normal stance and then put a head cover under your right armpit. As you swing, if the head cover falls out before your club gets to the ball, you have a flying elbow. Keep that right elbow tucked in, and the head cover won't drop out until you make contact.

- ◆ To gauge if you're getting all of your power into the swing, listen for the swoosh. Grab the club wrong-side up and give a normal swing. You should hear a swooshing noise as the grip cuts through the air. If the swoosh is behind you, then you're uncocking your wrists too soon. You should hear the noise near where your club will hit the ball.

- ◆ To get a good idea of how much weight there is working for you in the club-head, find one that's not connected with a shaft and just hold it. After you realize how heavy it is, you'll be less tempted to swing too hard.

- ◆ In the scheme of the swing, the finish is as important as the start. Follow through fully, and you'll avoid decelerating through the ball.

- ◆ If your ball flies with a curving trajectory, you need to account for the curve when you aim.

- ◆ Simplify your short game by using your putting stroke on short chips around the green.

- ◆ If you're struggling out on the course, go back to the basics. Check your grip and slow down your tempo.

Chapter 8

Drill Sergeant

In This Chapter

- ◆ Targeting: Getting everything going in the right direction
- ◆ Building balance in your swing
- ◆ Getting more turn—and more power
- ◆ Tempering that slice
- ◆ Developing the perfect release
- ◆ Hitting right down the middle—alignment tips
- ◆ Improving your putting tempo

You've heard it a million times before. Your mother probably said it to you over and over again when you were learning your multiplication tables: Practice makes perfect.

Actually, *perfect* practice makes perfect. In this chapter, I'll give you some drills to take with you to the practice range. They'll help you get the most out of your work. Nobody likes to go beat balls at the range for hours with nothing to show for it but blisters.

Looking for the Late Hit

As we talked about in Chapter 6, your arms are the last things that start down from the top of the backswing toward the ball. Your hips should unwind first, followed quickly by your shoulders, and then the arms, hands, and club. But if you've never experienced how this delayed hit is supposed to feel, it's tough to replicate. I have a simple drill that will help you get the sensation of that delayed hit.

If you can, find an old plastic rake you aren't going to use anymore and cut off half of the long wooden handle. It's important to use a plastic rake, because a metal one would be too heavy, and it would not have the broad, solid face plastic models usually have.

After you've chopped the handle down, you should be able to take your regular grip on the end of the handle, and with the broad face facing the target, the edge of the rake should hover a few inches off the ground.

Now, take the rake back slowly, as you would with your golf club. You should have enough room to take almost a full backswing. Now, on your downswing, swing with about half of your power, unwinding with your hips and shoulders first. The broad face of the rake resists the air and will force your hands to come through the hitting zone later than your hips and shoulders. The rake exaggerates the feeling you should have in your arms and shoulders during the downswing with a regular club.

Take about 10 practice swings with the rake and then switch to a regular club. You should notice your hands and arms delaying before they unwind. Your hips and shoulders will uncoil, and your arms and hands will follow, cracking the whip.

Targeting

When you're aiming for a target more than 100 yards away, it's often very difficult for your brain to translate its information on that small target into movements and changes in your stance that will help you hit the ball in the right direction.

Before you hit any shot, and before you take any practice swings, you should always stand directly behind your ball, facing your target, and visualize a path between the ball and the place you want it to go. Then pick some landmarks along that path. If there's a yardage marker on the ground 50 yards ahead and on your line to the target, picture your ball flying right over it. Extend this visualization to a point that is 5 or 10 yards in front of your ball.

Extra Swings

Have you ever been bowling? If so, you've probably noticed the little row of diamonds a few feet down the lane. These diamonds are aiming marks. It's easier to get your bowling ball to start over a certain diamond than it is to keep the pins in focus and try to fling the ball down the lane to a certain spot 20 yards away. The same principle applies in golf. If you try to adjust your aim while visualizing a target 150 yards away, the adjustments will be very vague, because the target isn't close enough to focus on. But if you pick an intermediate target, you can focus on sending your ball over that mark, just like a bowling ball rolling over the third diamond on the lane.

Pick a discolored patch of grass or an old divot hole that is on the line to your target. Then forget about the target itself and concentrate on just two things: Fly your ball over that intermediate point and pick enough club to get the ball where it needs to go. By a large margin, rookie players leave more shots short of the green than long. For a round, take one more club than you think you need until you hit a shot over the green.

Turn, Don't Sway

An easy trap to fall into when you shift your weight to your back foot during the backswing is to sway instead of turn. Your shoulders should pivot as though there is a metal bar running right down your spine and into the ground. When you sway, your shoulders drift backward, off that imaginary bar, almost as if you were tipping over.

Swaying is very common, and sometimes you can be so focused on all the other things you're doing with the golf swing that you don't realize you're doing it. Here's a good drill to practice that will let you know immediately if you're swaying off the ball.

Take your normal stance, with a 5-iron in your hand. Instead of keeping your feet shoulder-width apart, bring them together so they are almost touching. With your base narrowed like this, take a few practice swings. If you're swaying instead of turning, you'll stagger backward when you take your backswing. With your feet so close together, you can't sway without losing your balance.

Hit a few balls, until you can feel your shoulders turn instead of sway. Then go back to your regular, shoulder-width stance. The sway should have gone away!

Instead of the standard shoulder-width distance, bring your feet together, so they're almost touching (left photo), and then take a normal swing. If you sway, you'll fall over. Make a turn, as shown in the second photograph, and you'll keep your balance. It's important to keep your balance at the finish (right photo) as well.

Balance Drill

A common problem for beginning golfers is making the weight transfer from the back foot to the front foot during the downswing. Many rookies are still a little tentative with their swings, so they hang back a little bit. The result is often scooped shots that drift weakly to the right. A simple drill will help you feel the necessary weight shift over to your front foot.

Set up in your normal stance. Before you take your backswing, move your back foot (the one farthest from the ball) behind your front one and leave only the toe on the ground for support. As you can see when you take your backswing, it will be difficult to keep your balance.

When you've reached the top of the backswing, swing through to the ball like you would on a normal shot. If you don't make the proper weight transfer to your front side, you won't be able to finish the swing, because you'll fall on your butt. Your weight has to move forward, because the momentum of your arms and shoulders turning through toward the ball would make you tip if you tried to stay back.

Making the Turn

Training your shoulders to make a complete turn back from the ball and then through it to the follow-through takes some work. I've found that two drills really help me when I'm having some problems with my mechanics. They're similar, but they help in different areas.

The first drill is very simple. Take your normal stance, but instead of bending at the waist to put the club on the ground, stand upright and hold a golf ball in your right hand. Keeping your right hand at shoulder height, turn your shoulders as far back as you can without moving your knees or feet. Then unwinding from the hips first, throw the ball as you would a softball. Try to keep your weight balanced over your left foot at release. When you finish, your belt buckle should be pointing where you threw the ball.

Tossing a ball down the fairway forces you to make the same shoulder turn you need to hit a golf ball well.

The second drill is a variation of the first. Not only will this drill help you with turning your shoulders properly through the downswing, it will force you to shift your legs the right way. Take your regular stance, keeping your left hand on the club and the club on the ground where it would be at address, and bring your right hand, which is holding a golf ball, back and to the position where it would be during your normal backswing (near your right ear). Then swing your right arm through the hitting area and under the shaft of the club you're holding in your left hand. Try to throw the ball as high and far as you can toward your target. The higher and farther the ball goes, the more the sensation should feel like a full shoulder turn and follow-through. If you don't shift your weight properly in this drill, you won't be able to throw the ball very far. This drill will help you learn to use your legs.

Cutting Out Slicing

As I've talked about in earlier chapters, a slice comes from hitting the ball on an outside-in swing path. The main way this happens is that the hands get too high in the back-swing, and the subsequent loop forces your swing to come outside. You can correct a slice in several ways, depending on your specific problem, but this drill is a good general-purpose one.

First, set up with your normal stance and a mid-length iron. A 5 or 6 is fine. Take your normal grip and then slide your right hand down the shaft toward the clubhead until your right and left hands are about 3 inches apart. When you have this new grip, hit 10 or 15 balls, swinging as regularly as possible.

The split hand grip makes it easier for your right arm to fold properly against your side, which it must do instead of float in the air. After you're at the top of your swing with your hands separated and the right elbow tucked, you won't have any choice but to swing the club on an inside-out path through the ball. As you make the downswing, try not to turn the club with your right hand. Let the left hand lead the swing. If you do, you'll feel your left hand rotate, creating the perfect angle for the clubhead.

Releasing the Club

As the club swings through impact, the clubhead should be turning from open to the target (pointing to the right), to square at impact, and then closed (pointing to the left) after impact. Some players hold on through impact and keep the clubhead open, which creates short, weak shots to the right. One way to beat this problem is to make practice swings and hit short shots while holding the club in just your right hand. The club will naturally release and turn over when held in only your left hand. You'll also develop some more coordination—and strength.

Start out with your regular left hand grip on the club (first photograph) and let your right hand rest at your side. Make some slow, smooth swings with your left hand and feel the club release through impact (second photograph). Finish high and in control (third photograph).

Taking the Train

Sometimes, you need to check your alignment to make sure that you've got everything pointed in the right direction. This drill will not only improve your alignment but will help you bring the club through the ball squarely and eliminate slices or hooks.

After taking your normal stance, lay irons on the ground on each side of the ball, pointing at the target. Leave about an inch and a half of room for the club in your hand to fit into the slot created by the two guide clubs. When the guides are in place, align your feet properly, perpendicular to the target, using the two clubs on the ground as reference points. When you're aligned properly, try to hit the ball. The guide clubs force you to bring your club through the hitting area squarely, which makes for a straight shot, or else you'll hit the clubs on the ground.

Caddie's Advice

Some clubs use foot-long, rectangular slabs of wood to mark the different tee-boxes. Should the course you're playing have those kinds of markers, use them to your aiming advantage. Align your feet using the markers as a guide.

By laying irons down on each side of the ball, pointed at my target, I can use the shafts to align my feet properly. The guide clubs will also prevent me from swinging my club on an inside-out or outside-in path. I'll have to bring the club through to the ball squarely, or my club will hit one of the guide clubs.

Don't Slow Down

My biggest problem on the putting green is decelerating the club through impact, which gives me irregular distance control. I have a short-game summit meeting with Dave Stockton two or three times a year, and every time I see him and tell him about my putting woes, he takes one look at my stroke and says I'm decelerating.

Basically, you only need to take the putter far enough back in the backswing to make a fluid stroke and get the ball to the hole. The longer the putt, the more of a backswing you need. My problem is that I sometimes take the putter back too far for shorter putts and then have to slow the putter down on the swing so I don't blast the ball past the hole.

When I get afflicted with this tendency, Dave has me do a simple drill. It helps me, and I think it can help you if you're taking too much of a backswing on your putts.

Caddie's Advice

Don't place the tee too close to your ball. If your backswing is too short, you'll be popping your putts instead of stroking them.

After I set up about 5 feet from the hole, Dave sticks a tee in the ground about 10 inches behind my ball. With the tee protruding from the ground, I can't take my putter back any farther than 10 inches. The shorter backswing ensures that I won't decelerate the club through the hitting area but will make an aggressive, fluid move toward the ball.

Slow It Down

Luckily enough for me, my swing is pretty simple. Just about the only consistent problem I have with it is in the first few milliseconds of my backswing. I sometimes have a tendency to open my clubface right from the start instead of taking it back straight.

My teacher, Mike Adams, devised a simple yet effective drill for me when I struggle with my takeaway. It can help you build a more consistent, measured backswing as well.

Five inches behind my ball, Mike places another ball, directly on line with my backswing. If I make the proper backswing, my club will bump the extra ball out of the way, and I'll be able to hit my target ball without any trouble. But if I open up my clubface too soon, my club will move inside the proper line and miss the extra ball.

Takeaway drills help you keep from pulling the club back inside (left) and too close to your body. You have to flip it out away from you on the downswing, which leads to inconsistent shots. On a good takeaway (right) the club is pointing right along the target line when it is parallel to the ground.

Having that second ball really makes me concentrate on taking the club back low and slow. That deliberate, measured move helps me keep control of the club in my back-swing and bring it through the hitting area in the perfect position. It will help you, too.

The Least You Need to Know

- ◆ Use the wind resistance of a rake to feel a delayed hit on your downswing.

- ◆ Pick an intermediate target that is 5 or 10 yards between your ball and your ulti-mate target. It will be easier for you to focus on something closer.

- ◆ To work on balance, try making a swing with your back foot moved directly behind your front foot. You'll be forced to shift your weight properly, or else you'll fall over.

- ◆ To work on the shoulder turn, practice turning away from the target and then fully releasing the shoulders as you throw a golf ball.

- ◆ To beat a slice, slide your right hand 3 inches down the grip. The split will make it easier for you to fold your right arm next to your side in the backswing.

- ◆ Stop from swaying by practicing shots with your feet close together. If you sway, you'll fall over.

- ◆ Stick a tee in the ground 10 inches behind your ball on a 5-foot practice putt. The tee will keep you from taking too large a backswing.

- ◆ Place a ball 5 inches behind your target ball on a regular swing and then try to nudge the extra ball out of the way on your backswing. This will help you learn to take the club back low and slow.

Chapter 9

Troubleshooting

In This Chapter

- ◆ Topping the ball and what to do about it
- ◆ Fixing your slice
- ◆ Dealing with a hook
- ◆ Placing your swing on a diet if you're hitting it fat
- ◆ Reducing miss-hits

Hitting the ball poorly is extremely frustrating, no matter what level you're playing at. My bad shots might not look like yours, but I don't like mine any more than you like yours. After you've hit some balls, you'll get an idea of what kind of bad shots you hit more than others. Maybe you have a tendency to top the ball. Or you're having no trouble getting it into the air, but you have a bad slice. Having those kinds of struggles is nothing to get bent out of shape about. You're at the point in your game where you're going to see the most improvement in the shortest amount of time. If you start to play frequently, you'll be amazed at how quickly you'll improve. You'll still have some rough spots. Everyone does. But if you follow some of the fundamental lessons in this book and work with a good teacher, it will be easier to correct some of your mistakes.

Remember, it's more important to know *why* you're hitting a ball the way you are than exactly how to fix it. If you understand the physics and mechanics of the golf swing, you'll be halfway to fixing the problem yourself. All you'll need is another pair of objective eyes to see the parts of the swing you can't.

Couldya Take a Little Off the Top?

As a beginner, I'll bet your most common problem is getting the ball up in the air. Many rookies feel like they need to scoop the ball into the air with the club. They don't trust the loft of the club to do it on its own. But all of your clubs, even the lower-lofted ones like the 3-iron and driver, are designed with enough loft to get the ball into the air without any upward scoop move from the golfer.

If you subconsciously try to scoop the ball with your club, you'll probably succeed only in topping it. At best, you'll hit a weak shot to the right. Instead of transferring your weight from your back foot to your front as you swing toward the ball, trying to scoop the ball will make you either shift your weight backward or avoid shifting at all. That backward shift is the reverse pivot I talked about in Chapter 6. When your weight shifts backward (away from the target) suddenly in the swing, it causes your left shoulder to pitch upward. When that happens, the path of your swing changes from a circle with the ground as its lowest point to an oval with a spot 2 or 3 inches in the air as its lowest point. Because the ball isn't very tall, you can see why any shot you attempt while reverse pivoting is likely to skitter along the ground. You're only hitting the top half of it.

Believe it or not, to get the ball up in the air with your irons, you need to hit it with a descending blow to get the best use of the club's loft (the driver is a different story—for that club, because you can tee the ball in the air, you should hit it with a slight upward blow). By hitting the ground and the ball at the same time, with a powerful, downward blow, the ball doesn't have any place to go but up in the air. When you hit a shot with the right kind of swing, you'll probably see a divot (a piece of grass or dirt) come flying out of the ground after the swing. This is a good sign. If you're hitting with that downward blow, you'll hit the ball and the ground at the same time and there will be a dollar-bill–sized, shallow scraping of grass ripped out of the ground by your swing.

Caddie's Advice

Imagine hitting the spot of grass directly beneath the golf ball with your club during the swing. It will help you avoid topping a shot.

Concentrate on making this kind of divot after every full swing, and you'll find it almost impossible to top the ball. The important thing to remember, however, is that the divot is supposed to begin right at the spot where the ball was resting and continue for 3 or 4 inches forward, toward the target. If you take a big divot before you hit the ball, the clubhead will slow down from the impact and bounce off the dirt into the air, and you'll wind up topping the ball anyway!

Caddie's Advice

Topping the ball is also sometimes related to swaying during the swing instead of turning. Remember, your weight shift is just that, a shift, and not a sway. Your shoulders should stay centered over your hips.

If you're hitting it fat, that means you're making a divot before you get to the ball, like the divot on the left. On a good shot, you hit the ball and then make a divot (at right).

If you aren't making a reverse pivot, but are still topping the ball, your problem might be related to head movement. Sometimes, you're so anxious to see where your shot went, you look up before your swing is finished. Jerking your head up just before contact will cause your shoulders to lift just slightly. If you're just like every other human being, your arms are connected to your shoulders. So when your shoulders rise, your arms will, too. That means the bottom of your swing path is now an inch or two above the ground. The sole of your club will come crashing through and hit the ball squarely in its center. And you'll get the worm-burner to end all worm-burners.

Check out any action photo of a pro golfer in a golf magazine or newspaper. If you can see the ball in the photo and the golfer has already hit it, chances are you'll see him or her making a follow-through, but still looking down at the spot where the ball was a millisecond ago. If you're having trouble keeping your head down during the swing, one of the best ways to solve that problem is to go to the practice range when the sun is setting on the horizon and aim your shots toward the sun. If you don't keep your head down on the shot, you'll look up into the sun. If the sun doesn't shine where you live (don't laugh, I've been to Seattle), try this technique. Place a small coin 2 inches behind your ball. Now try to hit the ball and make a divot without disturbing the coin, and as you follow through, keep looking at the coin. Don't worry about where the ball goes. Keep your focus on the coin. Pretty soon, your topped iron shots will be a thing of the past.

If you're topping shots off the tee with your driver, you can try one of two different solutions. First, try moving the ball back a few inches in your stance. You could be topping the ball because you're reaching the lowest point of your swing path before your club actually gets to the ball. Then, your clubhead has gone too far on its way back around to your follow-through, and you're only catching the top part of the ball. Think of your swing path as a circle drawn in the air by the clubhead. If that imaginary circle stayed in the air like the smoke from one of those skywriting planes, you would see just where the clubhead got to the bottom of its path and started back up and on its way through. Your goal is to hit the ball off the tee just as the club starts this upward movement. It's easier to change the position of the ball in your stance than to change your swing, so try moving the ball back a little bit. You might be surprised by the result.

Double Bogey

On the other hand, if you tee the ball too high, you run the risk of swinging the club under it. The ball will hit off the top of the club and pop into the air. You should never tee the ball so that more than half of it sits above the top edge of the club.

If that doesn't work for you, try teeing the ball a little bit higher. When you top it, you're hitting the top half of the ball. If the ball is sitting in the air a little bit higher, you have a better chance of catching it square. Just remember that with all of these modifications, you still need to make the weight shift from your back leg to your front leg as you swing through the ball. This one movement alone, if properly timed, will eliminate most of your problems with topping shots.

Slicing: The Dreaded Banana Ball

If you are getting the ball up in the air regularly, that's great! You've met one big challenge, and that means you've discovered the concept of making the all-important downward blow. But if the ball is getting up in the air and curving in strange directions, you still have some work to do.

For beginners, the most common ball flight is a left-to-right slice. As I said in Chapter 3, a slight left-to-right flight, or a fade, isn't a bad thing. But anything severe, more than 20 yards in curve from a target straight down the middle, is something that needs to be addressed.

Slices happen for two reasons: Either you're sweeping the club across the ball from *outside in* at impact, or the clubface is open (pointing right of the target) at impact (or both, which is really bad!). Set up in your regular stance. When you look down at the ball, imagine a line running straight through the center of it to the target. Now, the longer you can keep your clubhead flying straight down this line, the more likely you are to hit the ball with a straight-on blow. If, during your backswing, you take the clubhead inside this line (toward your body), the most comfortable and convenient way for you to bring it back during the downswing is from outside of the line back in (toward your body). When the clubhead cuts back across the line this way, it hits the ball with a glancing, right-to-left blow. This blow makes the ball spin in the opposite direction, left to right. How severely your clubhead comes from the outside in determines how much sidespin the ball is hit with.

Par Primer

In an **outside-in** swing, the club comes from outside (away from the body) the imaginary line drawn through the axis of the ball to the target and cuts across to the inside at impact, imparting left-to-right spin. This is also called coming *over the top*.

If you're taking the club back and through on the imaginary line and not coming from the outside in, the only way you could be hitting a slice is by having an open clubface at impact. Remember our discussion about open and closed stances? Those same principles apply to your clubhead. Use the grooves as a guide. If the grooves come in at an angle that isn't perpendicular to that imaginary line running through the ball and to the target, your shot will shoot off in the corresponding direction. For example, if you have an open clubface at impact, that means the grooves are pointed to the right of the target. Again, you'll get a glancing blow that puts left-to-right spin on the ball.

Fixing these problems is simple in theory, but it takes a lot of practice. Changing your swing path will feel strange at first. If you're coming from the outside in, try this drill on the practice range to get an idea of how the proper contact feels. Take your normal stance. Place a ball on the ground, and an inch in front of it (toward the target) and to the top (away from your body), put a quarter down on the ground. Take some half-swings and try to hit the golf ball and then the quarter. In order to hit the coin, you'll be forced to swing from the inside (closer to your body) out (away from your body).

If you're hitting the ball with an open clubface, set up in your normal stance with a 5-iron and then bring your feet together, so the sides are touching. Take half-swings, and at the moment of impact, roll your right thumb toward the target. You should immediately start hooking the ball. Adjust the amount of roll in your right wrist, and you'll be able to temper the amount of hook you put on the ball. Spread your feet back into a normal stance and then work your way into a full swing.

Try to hit the ball and then the coin. It will help promote an inside-out swing path.

Hooks

Hooks happen for the opposite reasons I talked about for slices. Either you're coming from too far inside the imaginary line drawn through the ball, or the clubface is closed, or pointed left of the target, at impact. It's almost impossible to come from too far inside, because your body gets in the way of that kind of swing, so let's concentrate on what to do if your clubface is closed at impact.

Remember that drill I just talked about for people who were having trouble with an open clubface? To work out an open clubface at impact, you practice with half-shots and roll your thumb toward the target just before impact. To work on a closed face, you have to do the opposite. Set up as you would normally and then take a complete backswing. Stop when you get to the top. Turn your head and look at the position of the club at the top. Is the toe of the clubhead pointing at the sky? If it is, that means you're *hooding* the clubface, or causing it to come through the swing closed. The only way to hood the clubface is to have an arch in your right wrist.

Flatten out your wrist slightly, and the clubhead will come through the hitting area more squarely. You can also alter your grip slightly to correct the problem. Slide your right hand nearer the top of the grip instead of the side. The farther you move your hand, the weaker the grip, and the tougher it is to bring the clubhead through closed. Experiment until you get the results you're looking for. You can use any firm, 3-inch–long object tucked into your golf glove, near the Velcro closure, to help you feel a flat left wrist. I like to use a playing card. If I swing properly, the playing card won't have a bend in it when I'm finished.

Par Primer

A **hooded clubface** is another name for a clubface that is closed, or aimed left of the target. It's also called a *shut* clubface.

Fat, Chunky, or Thick Shots

Fat shots occur when you hit the ground too far in front of the ball. The ground makes the club slow down before it gets to the ball, and you hit a weak pop-up. The most embarrassing aspect of this kind of shot is the huge chunk of sod you usually rip up when making it. It sometimes looks like you're laying indoor carpeting when you take a really big one! Solving this problem is a lot like fixing a topping ailment. If, instead of reverse pivoting, which is a main cause of topping, you're just leaving your weight on your back foot throughout the entire swing, you could be susceptible to topping some shots. Or, if the path of your swing with an iron reaches its lowest point too far behind the ball (away from the target), you'll hit lots of dirt and not much ball. Again, changing the position of the ball in your stance might be the easiest way to fix the problem. Move the ball as near as you can to the point where your swing plane bottoms out.

Caddie's Advice

If you're having trouble with fat shots, try this trick at the practice green: Find a broken tee and stick it in the ground until a ball you put on it sits just barely over the level of the ground. Using a 5- or 6-iron, hit some shots off this mini-tee. You'll subconsciously adjust to the ball sitting up a little bit, and you'll take less of a divot.

Another visualization trick to use when you're hitting shots fat is to imagine hitting the patch of grass directly beneath the ball. That patch of grass is your target for your swing. The ball is just getting in the way.

Shanks

A shanked shot can be the most harrowing in golf. A shanked shot comes when you miss the ball completely with the clubface and hit it far down on the club, near the heel, on the hosel. The hosel is the place where the clubhead connects to the shaft, and believe me, it wasn't designed to hit a ball. Because the shanked shot is flying off the hosel, which is round, you never know where it will fly. A shank can actually be physically dangerous, because someone who is standing next to you might not expect to have to get out of the way of a shot coming from such a sharp angle.

A shank results when you swing through the hitting area while pushing the clubhead out and away from your body at an extreme angle. You're really almost whacking the ball off the side of the club. To correct this problem, lay one of your other clubs in a straight line toward the target on the other side of your ball, 2 inches from it. Then, using your trusty 5-iron, take half-swings. If you hit the other club, you're swinging on the wrong path. Concentrate on bringing the club straight down the imaginary line that runs through the ball to the target. Visualize the path of the club running through the spot where the ball is and then circling to the left for the follow-through. Slowly build up to a full swing, emphasizing the follow-through. That will help you bring the club through on the right path.

Extra Swings

Like footprints at a crime scene, the divot you take can give you clues about what you're doing incorrectly in a swing. The perfect divot is about the size of a dollar bill, starts just where the ball was resting, and points straight at the target. It should be no more than a quarter of an inch deep at its deepest point. If you're hitting the ball with a glancing blow, it will be easy to see in the divot. A person who slices will leave a divot that starts where the ball was and veers to the left of the target. A person who hooks the ball will leave a divot that veers to the right of the target. If the toe of your club is hitting the ground before the heel, which will cause the club to twist in your hand and make you hit a slice, the divot will be deep on the right side and shallow on the left. If the heel is hitting first, which causes a snap hook, you'll see the opposite characteristics. Hit a shot thin, and you won't see much of a divot at all. So remember to always fill your divots when you're through with a shot, but not until you've done a little detective work.

The Least You Need to Know

◆ The primary cause of a topped shot is a reverse pivot—moving your weight from front foot to back during the swing. Concentrate on transferring your weight from back to front during the swing, and you'll solve most topping problems.

◆ A slice is caused by either an outside-in swing or a clubface that is open (pointing to the right of the target) at impact. Roll your right thumb toward the target just before impact to perpetuate a right-to-left flight.

◆ A hook is caused by a clubface that is closed (pointing to the left of the target) at impact, or, more rarely, by a swing that is inside-out. Weaken the grip of your right hand by rotating it toward the top of the club, and it will be harder for you to hit a hook.

◆ A delayed weight shift or improper ball location in the stance causes a fat shot. Concentrate on making a good weight shift and play the ball farther back in your stance.

◆ Examine your divots to get feedback about how you're hitting each shot.

◆ A shank occurs when the clubhead is thrust outside the line at impact and the ball hits off the hosel.

Part  3

The Next Step: Some More Advanced Techniques

The quickest way to take strokes off your score is to improve your efficiency with the short clubs—the wedges and the putter. Not only are the short game and putting game the easiest parts of your arsenal to practice, that practice will pay the most dividends. In Chapter 10, I'll go over the nuances of the short game and get you burning the edges of the hole in no time. The remaining chapters in this part teach you how to get out of jams on the course and how to get the most from a lesson with a professional when you want to polish your game.

10

Little Shots: Chipping and Putting

In This Chapter

◆ Shaving shots from your score

◆ The short game: Chipping and pitching

◆ Putting techniques

◆ Reading greens

I'm sure you've had some frustrating times with your long clubs by now. Sometimes, you just can't hit straight with your driver. It happens to me, and I practice three hours a day! In this chapter, we're going to go over the parts of your game that you can make the quickest and most noticeable improvement upon—your short game.

Many amateurs I play with spend hours hitting 4-irons and 5-irons on the range, but don't practice their chipping and putting. As you'll soon discover, that's like getting ready for a test but only reading half the textbook. Follow some of the lessons and drills in this chapter, and you'll see a big improvement in your scores.

Saving Your Score

The average amateur will take more than half of his or her shots on or around the green. Driving the ball is important, and so is hitting good shots from the fairway and rough, but the quickest way to shoot better scores is to improve in the area that makes the most difference on the scorecard. For example, if you usually shoot 100 when you play 18 holes, that means about 60 of your shots come on or around the green!

Improve your short game by just 10 percent, and you can improve your score by six shots. In the same round, you might only hit your driver 14 times! So why spend three hours practicing with the driver and only 10 or 15 minutes hitting chips and putts? That just doesn't make sense.

Improving your short shots around the green leads to a chain reaction of improvement. Just think of it. If you can hit your ball closer to the hole from around the green, you'll be attempting much shorter putts. Shorter putts have more of a chance of going in.

Chipping: The Place to Improve Your Short Game

As I touched on in Chapter 2, chip shots and pitch shots are two entirely different things. Chip shots are, along with putting, part of your short game, and pitch shots set up your short game.

Caddie's Advice

Always try to keep the ball on the ground if you have the opportunity. Flop shots (those that go higher in the air) are tougher to hit and are much more vulnerable to wind.

Pitches are normally hit with the pitching wedge or sand wedge from 40 to 90 yards away. I won't talk much about pitch shots in this chapter, because they are pretty similar to a regular iron shot.

Chip shots come in different varieties and happen close to the green, usually within 30 yards. You can play a chip shot with any club from a 5-iron to a sand wedge, depending on conditions. Here are the two types of chip shots you'll learn how to use in this section:

◆ If you have open, flat grass between you and the green, the best kind of chip to play is usually a *bump and run shot*. Bump and run is one of those great golf terms that mean exactly what it sounds like—a low shot that hops off the club and then stays along the ground and rolls to its destination.

- A *flop shot* (or lob shot) is necessary if something, like sand or water, prevents you from rolling the ball to the hole. A flop shot flies very high, comes nearly straight down, and doesn't roll very far once it lands. Bump and run shots are easier to execute because the stroke is almost like that of a putt, so you're likely to make fewer errors. Flop shots are tougher to hit because you have to open the clubface and slice under the ball, making it easier to top or hit fat.

What Club Should You Use?

Professional golfers have two schools of thought when it comes to choosing a club to hit a chip shot around the green. Some, like Jack Nicklaus (who, as I'm sure you know, has had quite a bit of success), say you should use one club as much as possible around the green, because if you practice a lot of different kinds of shots with one club, you have a better chance of becoming an expert with one club than just adequate with four or five. Jack has a good point, but he also has world-class hand-eye coordination, which makes it easier for him to use his sand wedge from just about any kind of ground condition.

The other school of thought says that you should be flexible in the clubs you use around the green so you can adapt to conditions and requirements for the shot. For a beginner, I think this is the best course of action to take, because you can use each club's natural advantages to help you make a better shot, instead of trying to force something from a club not suited for the job.

For example, the sole of an 8-iron is much broader and thicker than the sole of a sand wedge. If you want to bump a ball a short distance, say 20 feet, out of thick grass, you can use the 8-iron's heavy sole to blast through the grass. You could use your sand wedge in the same situation, but trying to chop a ball out and up from heavy grass for such a short shot is much tougher. You would need to take a bigger swing, which means less control. Hit too far in front of the ball and you would move the ball only a few feet. Top it and you would knock it over the green. Play the percentages by sticking with the 8-iron.

As you play a few rounds, you'll probably find that you have one club that you like to use more than others around the green. My 8-iron is my favorite club around the green. It feels good in my hands when I'm chipping, and because I've had a lot of success with it, it gives me confidence. It's perfectly fine to have a favorite club, but be sure to practice with a few different ones so you have that flexibility around the green.

The general rule to remember when chipping is that the more lofted club you use to chip, the more height and less roll you'll get on your shot. A chip with a sand wedge generally rolls a third as far as it flew in the air. A chip with a 7-iron rolls three times as far as it flew. Now let's take a look at how to execute these two kinds of shots.

I'll use any club from a 7-iron to a sand wedge to hit chip shots. It all depends on how far I want the ball to fly before it starts rolling on the green. A 7-iron chip flies a short way and then rolls a lot. A sand wedge chip does just the opposite. Here, I have a pitching wedge, a 60-degree wedge, a 56-degree sand wedge, and an 8-iron.

Keep It Simple

When it comes to the actual technique of chipping, it's always best to keep it simple. A simple routine and a simple swing are easier to repeat consistently. In your home, I'm sure you've found that small appliances and gadgets with fewer moving parts break down less often than more complex machines. The same is true when you chip. Let's go over some basic principles for hitting chip shots.

Par Primer

An **open stance** means that your leading hip, the one closest to the target, is to the left of the target when you set up.

For a bump and run chip shot, you'll be using a lower-lofted club like an 8-, 7-, or 6-iron. Remember in Chapter 5 when we talked about stance? For a regular iron shot, you want to have your feet shoulder-width apart. But for a chip shot around the green, you need to have an *open stance* with your feet very close together. I'm in my bump and run stance in the following photo.

To hit a bump-and-run shot, I move the ball much farther back (away from the target) in my stance than I would if I were going to play a regular iron shot. By opening my stance and playing the ball back, I have the clubface hooded, which means the club plays with less loft than normal. That helps me keep the ball low to the ground. Opening your stance on this shot takes your legs out of the swing. Because the shot will be very short, you don't need your legs to generate power. Leg movement on this precise shot would cost you accuracy, so the open stance helps you keep your lower body still. Most of your weight should be on your front (left) foot, and your hands should be about 3 inches ahead of the ball at setup. Keeping your hands ahead helps you make the crisp, downward blow you need to hit this shot.

Here's the stance for the bump and run chip shot. The ball is back in my stance. My knees are flexed, and my hands are forward.

I'm playing the ball back in my stance, with most of my weight on my front foot.

I take just long enough of a backswing to give my shot power. Anything bigger might make me have to decelerate through the hitting zone, which would cause a fat shot.

I strike a crisp, downward blow, hitting the ground and ball at the same time. I'm keeping my wrists firm throughout the shot, like a putt. I finish the shot, sweeping through the hitting area and following through. Notice how firm my wrists have stayed.

Par Primer

A **divot** is the chunk of grass and dirt you chop out of the ground during a swing. It's good golf etiquette to replace any divots you've made.

On this kind of shot, you don't want much of a *divot*. Digging into the ground slows the clubhead down, and if you hit the ball while the club is slowing down instead of accelerating, you'll hit a fat, short shot.

Think about hitting the ground and the ball at the same time and sweeping the club through the hitting zone. Keep your wrists firm, like a putter swing. Remember those simple appliances in the house—fewer parts to break down!

On a flop shot, my stance is almost identical to the one I use for a bump-and-run shot. My feet are close together, and my stance is a little more open than for the bump and run. But I play the ball more forward (toward the target) in my stance—even more forward than I would on a regular iron shot. By opening my stance a little more and playing the ball so far in front, I'm doing the opposite of the hooding we talked about in the last section. Opening my stance and clubface makes the sand wedge I have in my hands play with more loft than it usually would, which means I'll be able to hit it higher and make it land without rolling very much. The swing is similar, with a little cock of the wrists. It's okay to take a little more of a divot, because you need to swing a little bit harder on this kind of shot.

To hit the flop shot, the ball must be resting on a cushion of grass. This shot is much easier to hit from the rough than from a very closely cut fairway. You need to be able to get the club under the ball to pop it up. On short grass, it's easy to accidentally hit the ground before the ball, which leads to one of those chili-dips we talked about in Chapter 2—a chunky shot that flies only a few feet. This is a difficult shot, so don't worry too much if you can't hit it too well right away.

Extra Swings

PGA Tour player Phil Mickelson is famous for a shot he calls Phil's Phlop. He developed it as a teenager in his backyard, where his dad built him a putting green and sand trap for practice. Fooling around one day, he discovered that from a downhill lie, he could face the wrong way, with his back to the hole, and hit the ball backward over his head. After he mastered it, he told his father what he could do. His dad didn't believe him and bet that it couldn't be done. Phil won the bet and took his dad's money.

Here are a few things to remember to improve your chipping:

♦ Chipping with a higher-lofted club like the pitching wedge or sand wedge will make the ball fly higher and roll less. Chipping with a lower-lofted club like a 7-iron or 8-iron will make the ball fly less and roll more.

♦ Always play a bump-and-run shot if you have a clear path in front of you to the hole. It's an easier shot to execute than a lob shot.

♦ The lower you want to play a shot, the farther back (away from the target) you should play the ball in your stance.

Of course, the best antidote for chipping troubles is practice. My favorite drill is to count out 50 balls and pace off 20 steps from a practice green. Then I chip all 50 balls onto the green, trying the get them within 5 feet of the hole. I round up all the ones that I missed on the first try and try again. I do this over and over again until all the balls are in that 5-foot circle around the hole. You can modify this drill and hit fewer balls or hit toward a larger target, but having a definite target is the most important part of the drill. It helps you visualize the shot the same way you would out on the course. Just chipping balls into an empty field won't give you as much feedback about how your chip shots wind up. Plus, there's no better encouragement than knocking a chip into the hole in practice. It makes you feel like you're making progress!

Putting

We've done so much work getting you on the green, you've got to know what to do when you get there! I just want to warn you, putting could be the most frustrating part of the game. Many times, I've hit two or three great shots to set up a short putt and then missed it and gotten pretty mad at myself. As a beginner, you're going to miss plenty of putts, but you have to remember that even the pros miss about half of the 5-footers they try. That's a putt about as long as the tub in your bathroom.

My goal is to get you to make a good swing at every putt. You have plenty of other factors to worry about, like the speed of the green, which I'll explain later in this chapter, under the section "Speed, Speed, Speed," how the putt will curve, and what bumps in the green it will bounce over on the way to the hole, but making a good swing is half the battle. The rest—except getting good bounces from the bumps in the road—comes only with experience.

Getting comfortable over the ball is the most important part of putting. I'll give you some tips about the standard stance and grip to use, but feel free to make some adjustments. The only hard and fast rule for setting up over a putt is to make sure that you are looking down directly over the ball. If your eyes are in front or behind the ball, your depth perception will be warped, and you'll struggle with both your aim and distance control.

Your Putting Grip

Most players grip the putter in one of two ways—a modified overlapping grip, or a left-hand low grip (cross-handed). The modified overlapping grip is similar to the standard overlapping grip we talked about in Chapter 4, but with a few notable exceptions. The modified overlapping grip—or some version of it—is the one used by most professionals. Instead of placing the pinkie of your right hand in the groove between the index and middle fingers of your left hand like you would in the overlapping grip used for regular iron shots, place your left index finger over the pinkie of your right hand. Your hands should feel like one unit.

Some players have trouble keeping their left wrist steady through the putting stroke. If your left, or lead, hand isn't still at impact, the putterhead will strike the ball at an angle, sending it off target. If your lead wrist bends as you hit the ball, you should consider trying to putt cross-handed. The cross-handed grip appears in the next photo. To putt cross-handed, place your right hand on the putter grip near the butt end. Then slide your left hand onto the grip until the heel rests against the side of your right index finger.

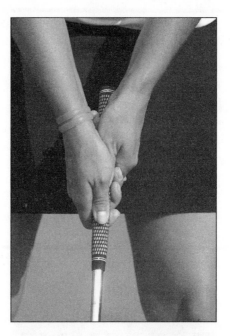

Many players putt with a version of the grip they use on full shots—and they either link the index finger of their left hand to the pinkie of their right hand, or overlap the left index finger over the right pinkie.

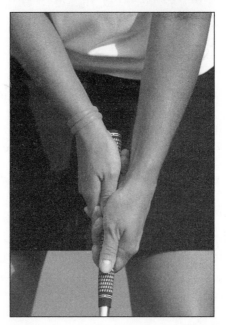

I use a left-hand low grip (cross-handed) for my putts. It's the opposite of a regular grip you would use for a shot with an iron. My left hand is low on the grip, and my right hand is high. The pinkie finger on my left hand is interlocked with the index finger on my right.

Your Putting Stance

After you've decided on a grip, just keep in mind what I said about keeping your eyes directly over the ball. You should set up with the ball in line with your belt buckle and nose, as I have in the following photo. Some people like to get into a little bit of a crouch, and others putt from a more upright stance. Decide what's comfortable for you, but remember that you need to be able to move your arms freely.

In the putting stance, make sure that you're looking directly down at the ball. My feet are shoulder-width apart.

When you're getting ready to stroke your putt, think about a pendulum on a grandfather clock. The closer you can come to taking your putter straight back from the ball and swinging it straight through on a line, the better chance your putt will go where you direct it. To test whether you're swinging the putter on a straight line, you can anchor a piece of string in the ground between two tees and set up over it. Line up your putter with the string and take a few practice strokes. Your putter should glide straight along the string. If it doesn't, you're hitting your putts with a glancing blow, which imparts sidespin on the ball. Putts with sidespin will curve on their own, usually away from where you are aiming.

Caddie's Advice

A long-shafted putter, which you can brace against your chest as you swing, is a good choice if you have trouble keeping your hands and wrists still through a putting stroke.

My shoulders rock slightly to bring the putter back. I'm not just using my arms. It's a more consistent way to make a stroke.

My shoulders rock through the stroke, and the putter follows on a line toward the target. Notice how my hands haven't twisted or flipped.

This photograph shows how nice and firm my left wrist is. My head stays in the same position through-out the stroke.

You've Got to Have a Point

The mechanics of the putting stroke are rather simple. It's deciding what direction and how hard to hit the ball that make it difficult. Let's stick with a long, flat putt for now. In the next section, we'll talk about hitting putts that curve.

When sizing up a long putt, it's tough to focus on a hole that's so far away. Your brain has trouble processing the information you need to make a good swing. It's much easier to pick out a point closer to you. Have you ever been to a bowling alley and seen the small row of diamonds just a few feet down the lane? Good bowlers don't aim their ball at the pins down the alley. They aim for a certain diamond just a few feet away. Pick a spot on the green a few feet from you that you think the ball will cross on a direct path to the hole. Then try to knock your putt right over that spot.

Speed, Speed, Speed

Even if you don't hit your putt right over the intermediate spot you were aiming for, don't worry. Judging the proper speed is a more important factor in how close your putt winds up to the hole. Most putting studies have shown that amateur golfers have much more trouble judging speed than aiming. How fast a green is depends on several factors. The shorter the grass on the green, the faster the surface will be. Imagine putting on a shag rug in your living room. You would really have to give the ball a whack to get it to move. Now imagine that same putt on some short Astroturf, like you see at some baseball stadiums. Much quicker! Also, the hardness of the surface affects the speed of a putt. The firmer a green is, the faster its speed will be. Wet greens are slower than dry ones.

The best way to judge speed on a green is to spend extra time on the practice green before going out on the course. Even pros have trouble gauging speed on greens they've never putted on. It takes time to adjust. Hit 15 or 20 10-foot putts on the practice green with the goal of leaving your misses no further than 2 feet *past* the hole. Remember, if you leave a putt short, it doesn't have a chance to go in. After the 10-footers, move 20 feet away and try the same drill. Try to roll the ball so that if it misses the hole, it goes no farther than 2 feet past the hole. At this speed, you're getting the ball to the hole, and you also have a good chance of getting a good break on putts that miss the center of the hole. They might slide in the side door!

For a final drill, take four or five balls from your bag and drop them 15 feet from the hole (about five big steps). Putt each ball to the hole and then go finish up with second putts on all the ones that didn't go in. Your goal should be to make each ball in one or two putts. If you three-putt, start the drill over again. Repeat until you putt all of the balls in two strokes or less. You're duplicating some of the pressure you'll feel later on the course by giving yourself a challenge. Vicki Goetze, an LPGA player, finishes her putting practice by taking 50 straight-in, 4-foot putts. A lot of the time, she makes them all.

A Quick Course in Reading Greens

After you have some speed control with your putter, the next challenge is learning to read the break on the green. *Break* is the amount your putt will curve left or right because of slopes on the green, how hard you hit the putt, the grain of the grass, and (believe it or not) wind.

Caddie's Advice

In general, Bermuda greens will be a little slower than bent-grass greens. Bentgrass can be cut much lower, which makes for faster speeds.

How hard you hit the putt and the slope of the green are the biggest factors that determine how much your putt will break. If you have a 5-foot putt on a slight right-to-left slope, the softer you hit the putt, the more it will curve. Play the shot aggressively enough, and it won't break at all. Of course, if you miss the hole, then you have a testy putt coming back.

If you're playing in the South, the greens you putt on might be made of Bermuda grass. We'll talk more about some of the characteristics of Bermuda in the next chapter, but on the greens, you just need to know which way the grain is running. On a Bermuda green, all the grain will run the same direction. Take a close look and you should be able to tell the direction of the grain. All of the blades will be pushed in one direction. If your putt is going with the grain, it will roll faster. If your putt is going against the grain, it will slow down. If you're putting across the grain, the ball will move slightly with the direction of the grass. Bentgrass greens, which are more common in the North, don't have grain, so you don't need to take grain into consideration on bentgrass greens.

If the wind is really blowing, it can actually have a subtle effect on your putts. Most people discount wind, but a 20-mile-per-hour gust can have a 1-foot effect on a 30-foot putt. So if the wind is blowing in your face, that putt that would have just dropped in the hole will be a foot short.

Lessons in Lagging

I told you to be aggressive enough to get the ball to the hole. This is true on most of the putts you'll take, but sometimes, as strange as it may sound, your goal should be NOT making the putt. The key to being a good putter is occasionally *lagging* the ball—leaving yourself in a good position if you miss.

For example, on a long, sloping putt, your goal should be to get the ball close to the hole but below it, which means leaving yourself an uphill putt. Short uphill putts are much easier than short downhill putts, because on short downhill putts your tendency is to be a little more tentative. A tentative, lightly struck putt is more likely to wobble off-line.

> **Par Primer**
>
> A **lag putt** is one where you are more concerned with leaving the ball in a good position for the next putt than with making the putt drop in the hole.

The same is true for a long, steep uphill putt. If you try to be aggressive and hit this kind of putt hard enough to get it to the hole, you run the risk of knocking it 2 or 3 feet past. That would leave you with a tricky little downhill putt. Go for the hole if you have a reasonable chance to make the putt. Otherwise, know your limitations and try to leave yourself in a good position to make an easy second putt.

The Least You Need to Know

- ◆ Improving your short game is the quickest way to improve your score.

- ◆ When chipping, keep the ball close to the ground if possible. Use the flop shot only if necessary.

- ◆ Practice chipping with several different clubs so you have some flexibility around the green.

- ◆ The key to putting consistently is bringing your putter straight back and straight through the shot on a straight line.

- ◆ The main factors that determine how much your putt will break are the slope of the green, the speed you hit the putt, the direction of the grain, and wind.

- ◆ Sometimes, lagging the ball to a good position near the hole is better than trying to make the putt.

Chapter 11

Specialty Shots: Getting Out of Trouble

In This Chapter

- ◆ Best techniques for getting out of the rough
- ◆ Playing from the sand when you're stranded
- ◆ Using your putter from off the green
- ◆ Dealing with bad lies
- ◆ Playing some advanced shots

Golf is a fun game, but it isn't all fun and games. When you go out and play 18 holes, you'll certainly find yourself in some sticky situations. Recognizing them and knowing that there is a way out will save you some nail-biting and aggravation. Hitting the ball in the rough or sand certainly isn't the end of the world, especially if you know a few creative ways to minimize the damage. This chapter helps you add a few new shots to your bag of tricks.

Playing Out of the Rough

The most common problem you'll find yourself presented with is playing out of the tall grass in the rough at either side of the fairway. The rough should be more difficult to play from because it's designed as a penalty for missing the fairway. In Chapter 2, we talked about the two different kinds of rough, primary and secondary. Most public courses only have primary rough, which is a few inches longer than the grass in the fairway. On a course that has only primary rough, you'll never really be faced with grass tall enough to prevent you from getting a club on the ball. We'll start with that and work our way to the tougher stuff.

The first thing you need to do when you get to your ball and it's in the rough is figure out what kind of lie you have.

The options depend on what kind of golf course you're playing on. In the North, Midwest, and Northwest, almost all courses are covered with bentgrass. *Bentgrass* has straight, thin, flowing blades that grow straight up in the air. In the warmer parts of the United States, some courses are covered with *Bermuda grass*. Bermuda has gnarly, thick blades that grow in different directions. There isn't much difference between the two grasses when they are cut closely in the fairway, but when they grow up in the rough, the difference is dramatic.

Bentgrass grows straight and in one direction. If your ball is sitting up on the top of the blades, it's a pretty simple shot getting it out. You can use your normal swing. Your club will slow down when it hits the heavier grass, so if you would normally use a 7-iron, you should probably use a 6- or a 5-iron to account for the heavier grass.

If your ball is sitting down near the roots of the bentgrass, however, you need to play it a different way. Try to determine whether the grass is growing toward the green or away from the green by checking which way the blades are leaning. If it's growing toward the green, the rough might actually help you. Your club will slide with the direction of the grass and not hit any ground, so you may hit what's called a *flier*. That's a shot that flies much farther than it would under normal conditions. If the grass is growing against you, you need to use a lofted club like a 9-iron or pitching wedge to hack it out and get back to the fairway. If you try to use a low-lofted club against the grain of the rough, it's pretty risky. The broad sole of a 3- or 4-iron can get snarled in the grass and get pulled off-target.

Par Primer

Bermuda grass is more common on courses in warm-weather climates. It has thick, gnarly blades that grow in all directions. **Bentgrass** is more common in the North and usually grows straight up in the air.

If you're playing on a Bermuda-grass course, you have a whole different set of concerns when it comes to rough. Thick Bermuda is almost impossible to play from. Your only play is to use a sand wedge and try to get back to the fairway. Trying to advance the ball with a longer club will most likely just keep you in the deep stuff. Shorter Bermuda is also pretty tricky to play from. The Bermuda blades tend to grab the clubhead as it passes through. Most commonly, the heel of the club catches in the grass and causes the clubhead to twist on impact. Your ball goes flying off to the left. Your best bet is to gauge the lie and use as much loft as you think is prudent. If two thirds of the ball is showing above the grass, you can try playing a 6- or 7-iron. Anything less than half the ball showing above the grass, and you should play safely to the fairway with a sand wedge and cut your losses.

Caddie's Advice

How much of your ball is visible in the grass should be your primary method of determining how to hit the ball. In thick grass that nearly covers your ball, you need to be more conservative and use a club with more loft.

To Chip or Not To Chip

If you're playing on a course that is well maintained, you'll probably be presented with a greenside dilemma. Your ball is 20 yards short of the green, but the path to the hole is clear and paved with short fairway grass. Should you chip the ball or take your putter and hit a long, low shot?

We've already talked about using the least amount of loft possible when hitting chip shots. More bad things can happen to a ball in the air than on the ground. The same is true when it comes to deciding whether or not to use your putter from off the green. You need to consider three things: the quality of the grass between you and the hole, your comfort level with the other possible shots, and the location of the hole on the green. Here's how to evaluate each of these factors:

◆ **Quality of grass.** If you have any kind of rough, water, or hazard between you and the green, obviously you have to chip the ball to avoid that trouble. If the path is clear, but the ground is bumpy and unpredictable, or some of the grass is patchy and thick, putting might not be the best choice under those circumstances. The ball could jump off target or get caught up before it gets to the green.

◆ **Comfort level with the choice of shots.** If you feel more comfortable with a putter than a sand wedge or pitching wedge, use the club with which you are more confident. If you're worried about the lie, go with a chip shot.

◆ **Location of the hole.** If the hole is located very close to the edge of the green that is right in front of you, hitting a good shot close to the hole with a putter will probably be more difficult than chipping with a wedge. You can hit a sand wedge high and make the shot die near the hole. It's tougher to hit a putt hard enough to get through the thicker grass and then slow down in time to stay near the hole. If the hole is located near the middle of the green, using the putter is a higher-percentage play.

Leaving the Beach: Sand Shots

Pros and beginners often feel differently about the sand. When I play in pro-ams, I often hear my amateur partners give groans of dismay when they see their ball land in the *bunker*. Believe it or not, professionals would *rather* play from the sand than from the rough! You're more likely to get a good lie in the sand, and it's much easier to put backspin on the shot.

Why do so many beginners get so worried about the sand? I think it's mostly because they aren't used to it, and they get very tentative and try to scoop the ball out. If you have the chance to get a good stance in the sand, it isn't much harder to hit a sand shot than a regular shot.

When you hit a ball into a bunker, you first need to consider your lie situation. If your ball has *rolled* into the bunker, you're probably going to have a good lie. The ball is probably sitting on top of an area of relatively flat sand. If the ball *dropped* in on the fly, you run the risk of the ball remaining in the explosion it made when it landed. That's called a *fried-egg lie*, because the ball looks like the yolk of a fried egg, and the explosion looks like the cooked egg white (see the following photo). This kind of lie is a little more problematic. It's harder to get the club to slide under the ball cleanly with this kind of lie.

Par Primer

Bunkers are sand-filled pits designed to catch wayward shots. They're often called *sand traps*, or just *traps*.

The worst-case scenario is a buried lie, in which the ball is buried in the sand. All you can do is chop at it and hope it flies out of the bunker.

My ball has wound up in a fried-egg lie. It is sitting in the crater it made when it landed in the bunker.

How you decide to play your sand shot depends on how far away you are from the hole, and how high you have to hit the shot to get it over the edge of the bunker, or lip. We'll start with greenside bunkers. These sand shots range from 15 feet to 30 yards from the hole and are generally the simplest shots to hit. Let's go over the greenside bunker sand shot procedure:

1. Go into the bunker and analyze what kind of lie and stance you have. As you would expect, a good lie and a flat stance are the ideal. I'll talk about worst-case scenarios later.

2. Open your stance very wide and dig your feet into the sand. Your left hip should point 10 yards left of your target. By digging your feet into the sand, you provide a more steady base. You're less likely to lose your balance during the shot.

Notice how my stance is open. If you drew a line in front of my feet, it would point to the left of the target. I also have the clubface open, or pointing at the sky.

3. Open the clubface of your sand wedge so that the back of the club is almost resting on the ground. (Be aware that you can't touch the sand with your club until you hit the ball. It's a stroke penalty!) You want the club to slide under the ball and blast it out of the sand. Opening the club this much should allow you to get the ball up and over all but the steepest bunker faces. If you're worried about hitting it high enough, you should probably turn around and hit the ball out to the side.

CAUTION

Double Bogey

Whatever you do, don't touch the sand with your club when you're getting ready to hit your shot from the bunker. It's called *grounding your club in a hazard*, and it's a one-stroke penalty.

4. Focus on a spot 2 inches behind the ball. Don't think "dig." Think "slide." Imagine sliding your club the length of a dollar bill, with the ball resting just on the end.

5. Make a complete follow-through. Some sand should fly out of the bunker with the ball.

Take a controlled, shorter backswing for your bunker shot. You're trying to hit a spot 2 inches behind the ball and throw the sand and the ball out of the bunker.

It should feel like the club is sliding through the sand and under the ball. Don't jam the club into the sand. Make a full follow-through, and you'll be sure to get the ball out.

Extra Swings

Sand wedges have different features that make them work better under different conditions. The amount of bounce a sand wedge has determines for what conditions it should be used. The club's bounce is the bump of metal just behind the leading edge, where the clubface turns into the sole. The more bounce a sand wedge has, the more the club bounces off the surface of the sand instead of digging in. If you're playing on firm sand, you want less bounce. Too much bounce and your club will ricochet off the sand and crash into the ball near its top, sending it screaming over the green. If the sand is fluffy, you want as much bounce as possible to keep the club from digging in and slowing down. Should it dig in too much, you'll lose clubhead speed, and your shot won't make it out of the bunker.

If you're in a greenside bunker and the lie or stance isn't so good, don't panic. You have quite a few choices. Let's run down a little checklist:

- **Fried-egg lie.** Open your stance like a regular sand shot but *close* the face of your sand wedge instead of opening it. Rotate the grip until the face is pointing less at the sky and more at the ball. This is the same as hooding the face. Play this shot like the bump and run you learned in Chapter 10, but with a more aggressive swing. Try to hit the ball and the sand at the same time.

- **Buried lie.** Play this shot almost identically to the fried-egg lie, but instead of a sand wedge, try a pitching wedge. It doesn't have very much bounce, so it will cut into the sand. Swing hard at a spot about an inch behind the ball. Remember, you've got to blast it out. This shot will roll a lot when it comes out of the sand.

- **Downhill lie.** This is the toughest shot out of a greenside bunker, because it's almost impossible to slide a sand wedge under the ball. If the lip, or edge, of the bunker isn't steep, you can try to hit a 5- or 6-iron and run the ball onto the green.

- **Awkward stance.** Having to stand with one foot outside the bunker or on a steep slope makes the shot tougher, but not impossible. Bend your knees to try to get as level a foundation as possible. Use your sand wedge and swing a little harder than normal to compensate for an off-center hit.

Of course, not all bunkers are around the green. A fairway bunker that is a long way from the green presents a much thornier problem. The clubs you will be hitting from a fairway bunker weren't designed to play out of the sand (they have less bounce and are designed to cut through the grass), so you have to take some precautions.

You won't be able to swing as hard on a fairway bunker shot as you would on a normal fairway shot because your balance and traction won't be as good. That means you're going to have to use more club than you normally would. If you're 150 yards from the hole and would normally play a 6-iron from the fairway, you probably need a 5- or even a 4-iron from the sand.

After you've selected your club, you have to set up with a wider stance than normal to keep your balance. Make your stance about 6 inches wider—your feet should be just outside your shoulders. Remember, don't touch the sand with your club! It's a one-stroke penalty. As with the greenside bunker shot, the sand will slow down your club during the swing. The key to this shot is *picking* the ball from the sand—hitting the ball and sand at the same time with almost no divot. If you hit the sand too soon, the club will slow down and dribble the ball only a few yards. Miss the sand, and you'll top the ball. Lower your expectations and be satisfied with hitting the ball in the general direction you were aiming. It's okay to hit this shot a little bit thin. You'll still get a decent result—a low, running shot.

Making the Best of a Bad Lie

Actually, the rough and sand are comparatively good places to wind up if you miss the fairway. Some places are quite a bit worse, and it takes a little more creativity to escape them. Here's how to handle the worst of the worst:

- **Landing in a divot.** Probably the most frustrating is landing in someone else's divot: You hit a good drive down the middle of the fairway, but your ball rolls into the crater caused by someone else's swing. The biggest problem with playing a shot out of a divot is that the results are unpredictable. Your club could get caught up in the grass and slow down through the hitting area, or you could catch it clean and hit a regular shot.

  The best way to deal with a shot from a divot is to adjust your stance so the ball is farther back (toward your right foot) when you set up and use a club with more loft. Setting up so the ball is farther back will force you to make a steeper swing and come down quickly on the ball, and the additional loft will propel the ball out of the divot. The shot won't have any backspin on it, so it will roll more than a normal shot.

- **Side-hill lies.** These are perhaps the most common. When you need to play a shot on a hillside with the ball below your feet, remember that the natural flight of this kind of shot is from left to right, so compensate when you aim. Bend your knees a little more than you would for a normal swing so you can bring yourself a little bit closer to the ball. If the ball is above your feet, the natural tendency for this shot is to fly from right to left. As with the previous shot, be sure to compensate when aiming. Choke up on the club to keep the ball far enough away. Remember that the ball will fly in the same direction as the hill slopes.

- **Uphill or downhill lies.** An uphill lie adds loft and reduces the distance of your shots, so use more club. Play the ball closer toward your front foot, because the club reaches the ground a little bit later in the swing. Downhill lies cause you to hit lower shots that roll farther, so use less club. Play the ball closer toward your front foot.

- **Under a tree.** If your shot rolls under a tree, you'll have a chance to test your improvisational skills. Your best bet is to take a low-lofted club like a 3- or 4-iron, choke up on the grip, and restrict your backswing. Think of hitting this shot like a really hard putt. The goal is to get the ball rolling along the ground and out of trouble.

- **Hardpan.** Baked, rock-solid ground with no grass on it, hardpan gives you some additional distance through roll but is tricky to play a shot from. It's really like hitting from the cart path, except the ground is easier on your club. You have to be careful, because when you swing at a shot on hardpan, your club has a tendency to bounce off the hard surface. That makes it easy to top the ball. Your best bet is to play a 9-iron or a pitching wedge, a club that doesn't have a lot of bounce, and use the same technique I covered for a fried-egg lie in a bunker. *Pick* the ball—hit the ball and the ground at the same time.

◆ **Pine needles or leaves.** Play these shots like you would a fairway bunker shot. The needles act similarly to sand. Pick the ball and avoid taking a big divot.

The last condition you'll really have to worry about is wind. It's tough enough to figure out exactly how far you hit each of your clubs. Add some wind to the equation, and you have a real dilemma! In general, it's best to keep the ball low when playing into the wind and high when you have the wind at your back. You'll have to judge for yourself how much a breeze is helping or hurting you, but making your shots fly higher or lower is relatively simple.

To hit a higher shot, address the ball with your hands directly above the clubhead and play the ball off your left (front) heel. This setup maximizes the loft of the club you're using. To play a lower shot, you've probably guessed that you need to move the ball back in your stance until it's about 3 inches in front of your right toe. Playing the ball back in your stance takes some of the loft off the club. Make a conscious effort to make your normal swing for both of these shots.

The Least You Need to Know

◆ When playing out of the rough, the first goal is to advance the ball to safety. Use enough loft to get the ball out.

◆ Putting from off the green is smart if you have a clear path to the hole, the hole isn't located close to the edge of the green that is closest to you, or if you have confidence in playing that kind of shot.

◆ Think about sliding the sand wedge under the ball when playing a shot from a greenside bunker. Don't *dig*.

◆ Balance and control are the most important factors when playing shots from bad lies. Widen your stance and use a more-lofted club. You'll have less margin for error.

◆ From a side-hill lie, your shot curves in the direction the hill is sloping.

Chapter 12

One Good Lesson

In This Chapter

◆ Going back to school: What a lesson can do for you

◆ Finding the right instructor

◆ Choosing between group and solo lessons

◆ Helping it all sink in

◆ Finding other kinds of instruction

We've made a good start on your golf swing in Chapters 4 through 9, but everybody has special concerns or needs, and there aren't enough chapters in any book to address them all. You can troubleshoot some of your more glaring problems with this book, but nothing beats personalized attention from an experienced teacher. This chapter covers the improvements that might be on your horizon if you decide to work with a golf instructor.

Do You Need Professional Instruction?

A teacher is more than just an extra set of eyes. As I'm sure you've discovered, some of the positions you need to get into during the golf swing are not so easy to check out for yourself, even with a mirror, so a teacher can see what you can't. A teacher should know the parts of a good golf swing and be able to demonstrate and explain them to you in a way you can easily understand. I have shown you the basic principles in this book, and you can get started on your swing, but an instructor will be able to tell you whether you've been doing things correctly. He or she can give you those fine adjustments and fixes that will connect everything we've been talking about.

A good teacher can take your club and put it in the proper position and show you how a certain part of the swing is supposed to feel. He or she can analyze the flight of your shots and diagnose your problems. An investment in one or two lessons early on is worth more than spending the same amount of cash on a new driver or other quick-fix club. When I work with an instructor on my own game, he or she isn't interested in rebuilding my swing. At this stage, it's more about watching me closely as I hit balls on the driving range and helping me make small adjustments that make the difference between playing pretty well and playing well enough to contend every weekend.

Once or twice a year, I meet with Senior Tour player Dave Stockton for a brush-up session on my chipping and putting. He's one of the best there ever was in both of those disciplines, and with his practiced eye, he usually can see very quickly where my putting or chipping stroke has broken down.

For a beginning golfer, a good teaching professional in a lesson can …

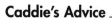

Caddie's Advice

Legendary golfer Ben Hogan said in his classic book *Five Lessons* that the key to becoming a good golfer is developing a swing that you can repeat under any circumstance.

- Get you started with good habits before bad ones become ingrained.
- Teach you efficient and fun practice techniques.
- Build your confidence.
- Answer even the most basic questions.
- Help you find success—getting the ball airborne— quickly.

Which Teacher Is Right for You?

That's a tough one to answer. It depends on what you're expecting and how much you're willing to spend. If you want someone to stand behind you at the driving range and give a few useful tips and some encouraging words, you can find a teacher who charges less than $50 an hour. If you're looking for someone to break down your swing, analyze it on video, and then help you put it back together again, we're talking about a premium investment of nearly $1,000 total, sometimes more.

Just like players, teachers have different styles and personalities. Some are all business. Others have a more relaxed, personable approach. It's up to you to find a style that works best for you.

Teachers also have different philosophies. David Leadbetter, who works with Ernie Els, Charles Howell III, and Nick Price, is well known for the technical work he does with top-level professionals and world-class amateurs. He helped Nick Faldo completely rebuild his swing, and his work with Els has been a big reason for the Big Easy's terrific record in major championships.

Butch Harmon gets credit for being almost as much of a psychologist for the players he has taught—including Greg Norman, Tiger Woods, and Justin Leonard—as swing coach. Hank Haney, who has taught Mark O'Meara for more than 20 years, centers his instruction on perfecting his students' ball flight.

You don't need to find a world-famous instructor to get a great lesson (although if one of the famous teachers is available, you should certainly take that opportunity). If a teacher has been certified by the Professional Golfers' Association of America (PGA), that means he or she should be able to give you a good lesson. In Appendix B, I've listed the contact information for the PGA of America and all the state golf associations. If you're having trouble finding a teacher, those places can help you.

Extra Swings

A PGA professional is different than a PGA Tour player or an LPGA Tour player. The PGA of America certifies men and women as teaching pros, but the PGA Tour and LPGA Tour are corporations that run the leagues and tournaments pro players compete in. To become a teaching pro, a person has to play 36 holes in no more than five strokes over the course rating. But that's the easy part. Then comes six months of apprenticeship under a PGA professional and then up to three years of special business, teaching, and management classes. So if your teacher is a certified PGA teaching pro, you know he or she has had to earn it.

I Need a Lesson. How Do I Get One?

If a public course has a golf shop where you can buy equipment or clothing, it probably has a golf professional running that shop. (You'll learn more about the different types of courses in Chapter 14.) If a golf pro is running the shop and is certified by the PGA of America, he or she can probably give you a lesson. Most private courses also have teaching professionals. Bigger ones have assistant pros who can also give lessons. And you don't usually have to be a member to get a lesson from a pro at a private club. Call in advance, and you can probably set up a lesson on the club's driving range, but you might have to pay a little bit more than the club's members do for the same service.

You don't even need to have a golf course near you to be able to find someone to give a lesson. Many driving ranges are run by certified pros who give lessons on the side.

A range in New York City at the Chelsea Piers athletic complex has four levels of hitting areas and six teaching professionals who are affiliated with instructor Jim McLean's golf academy at Doral in Miami. This range was built with instruction as one of its primary functions. As you can imagine, prices vary for each kind of facility. A lesson can cost $100 an hour at a large, modern teaching facility that has videotaping, or it can cost $15 for a half-hour on the range with the driving range pro. You need to find the right balance between quality and price. Shop around.

> **Par Primer**
>
> The head professional is the person who is ultimately in charge of giving lessons and running the golf shop. At larger clubs and facilities, the head pro has several assistant professionals, who are also qualified to teach golf, but generally have less experience than the head pro.

At some of the larger golf resorts, like Doral or Pebble Beach, well-known instructors run teaching academies. You can book a lesson at an academy and get instruction from one of half a dozen assistants who work under the head professional. The advantage to this system is that a large academy can invest in high-tech teaching aids like slow-motion videotaping systems and offer them to you for a cheaper price, because so many students come through the program. Of course, getting a complete video diagnosis might be cheaper at a resort than it would be to rent or buy the equipment yourself, but it still isn't cheap. If you're a guest of the resort, you often can get a price break on the lessons, but if you just drop by, it can be very expensive.

> **Caddie's Advice**
>
> Just because someone is certified by the PGA of America doesn't mean he or she will be a great teacher. And just because someone isn't PGA of America–certified doesn't mean he or she won't give you a good lesson. If you have friends who have received good lessons from a particular pro, get a referral, just as you would for an eye doctor.

Some of these academies take instruction one step farther. For a package price, you spend three or four days at the academy doing nothing but practicing and playing. Just like summer camp, you even sleep over. In a typical program, you spend a lot of time working on swing basics in small groups with a teacher and then test what you've learned on the driving range and the golf course. Because you're immersed in golf for the short time you stay, some of these programs can help you make vast improvements in your game, but be ready to spend several hundred dollars.

Double Bogey

If you decide to enroll in a three- or four-day golf school, make sure that the intensity of the program matches your own. If having fun and learning in a friendly atmosphere is important, a serious, highly organized program is not for you. Ask for an itinerary before you commit.

Learn Your Lesson

When you've decided on what kind of lesson to take, be sure you go into it with the right attitude. You're spending good money for the pro's time—and your own. It doesn't make any sense to waste it. Here are some basics to think about before you go and while you're there:

- **Be realistic.** Don't go into a lesson expecting miracle improvements. You'll get better with good guidance, but it also takes practice. Also, it won't do you any good to fudge about your level of expertise to the pro. He or she will know where you stand when you hit balls. Don't worry if you can't hit the ball very well. That's what the teacher is there for—to help you get better.

- **Be specific.** The more information you can give your teacher about your game before your lesson, the less time you waste when the lesson starts—which gives you more time actually hitting balls.

- **Listen.** It may sound like simple advice, but it's the most important part of taking a lesson. For a lot of the time, you'll be standing over the ball with the pro behind you or to the side, giving you feedback about a swing or helping you get into the proper position. You should be concentrating on what you're doing, but also listening to the points the pro is making.

- **Speak up.** Asking questions goes hand in hand with listening. One of my priorities in writing this book is to help you understand the language of golf from the beginning. We've gone over the basic vocabulary you'll need to play and watch, but your pro may have ways of describing certain parts of the swing with which you might not be familiar. Don't worry about looking stupid. If you don't understand or you want something repeated, ask. You won't look dumb. The pro will be glad you're paying attention and are interested in keeping up. Besides, just like this book, your teacher will start working with you on some simpler principles and then move on to more complex ones. You wouldn't learn long division before you mastered addition and subtraction, would you?

◆ **One thing at a time.** If you feel like your teacher is giving you too much to digest at one time, say so. Suggest that instead of trying to learn a whole list of things in one or two lessons, you focus on one thing, learn it, and then move on to the next. If the pro isn't willing to be flexible on this point, find a new teacher. There's no sense in paying money to stand on the practice tee getting overwhelmed by instruction. You'll just tie yourself in knots.

◆ **Enjoy yourself.** Learning to golf can be very frustrating. It might seem like you'll never be able to hit the ball where you're aiming. Some of the techniques a teacher shows you might feel funny or uncomfortable. Relax. Remember that this is a game, and one you're choosing to play. The pro and the other people around you know what it's like to be a beginner. Everybody starts out that way. If you're a good sport and keep trying, nobody will care how you hit the ball.

◆ **Do your homework.** If you sign up for a series of lessons, the teacher will probably give you some things to practice on your own between sessions. Follow his or her directions and try to do the outside work required. Not only will each subsequent lesson be more productive, your teacher will see that you are committed to learning and will be more willing to take you seriously as a student. If you don't show any willingness to practice what the pro is teaching, why should he or she make an effort? Sure, you're paying for the lesson, but most teachers get into the business because they like to help people learn. Seeing you get better is motivation—for them and you.

Extra Swings

Here are four things I've found that make golf lessons more fun. If your lessons are lacking, try making a change to incorporate one or more of the following elements:

◆ Taking lessons with a friend who is at the same level
◆ A teacher with a sense of humor
◆ Good weather (keep that in mind if you're traveling to a seasonal destination)
◆ Lots of variations in drills

Other Sources of Information

Golf lessons are the best way to improve your swing the fastest, but other resources are available to help. You've got one of them in your hand, an instruction book, but there are also magazines, videos, and computer programs. Let's take a look at some of them.

◆ **Magazines.** Several major ones, like *Golf Digest* and *Golf* magazine, devote most of their space to teaching. The instructional articles are written by top teachers and players and are illustrated with terrific photographs. The magazines do such a good job offering tips and fixes for all different kinds of problems, it makes your job harder as a beginner: You have to sift through all those words and pictures and use the ones that will help your game. A tip from Annika Sorenstam about putting a lot of backspin on the ball from a greenside bunker might be great for me or for a top amateur, but it will only hurt you if you're not ready to try such a technique. You step in that sand trap and try to do what Annika's tip suggests, and you might kill somebody on the other side of the green with a screamer! Remember to read with a critical eye. Try only the pointers that apply to your game. If you tried everything you read in three or four different magazines, you would screw yourself into the turf.

◆ **Golf videos.** The main benefit of an instructional video is that you get to see great players demonstrate different shots from a lot of different angles. You can see Grace Park or Tiger Woods hit a 9-iron at a televised tournament, but you don't usually get an extended, close-up view of the setup and the individual parts of each swing. In a video, you see each shot from several different angles and at a slower pace. And there's always your rewind button. Videos attempt to duplicate the kind of instruction you would get in a lesson, but with one major drawback: Videos aren't personalized, and they can't adapt to what you need to work on. Like anything else, with videos, you get what you pay for. Tapes cost from $10 to $40, but spending a little more pays off in better footage and more elaborate instruction.

◆ **Computer programs.** Much, much more information can be crammed onto a CD or DVD than a video tape, and you can easily access specific information through a directory. If the program is well-produced, it can offer you a video library of different golf tips and information, all sorted by subject. All you have to do is click on what you want to see. The downside? It's tough to practice a swing in your computer room, within view of the screen.

The Least You Need to Know

- You can find golf teachers at most places you can play golf—a driving range, public course, country club, or resort.

- Golf academies provide intensive instruction over three or four days, but at a significant cost.

- To get the most from your lesson, be realistic, specific about what you need, listen to what the teacher has to say, speak up when you don't understand something, follow through on between-lesson practices, and most importantly, enjoy yourself.

- Magazines, videos, and computer programs are good secondary sources of instruction. Make sure you look for tips that suit your level of ability.

Part 4

Hitting the Links, or at Least the Driving Range

In these chapters, I'll talk about the whats, wheres, and whens of practicing at the driving range and the difference between productive and pointless practicing. After that, it's time to hit the course. I'll give you the grand tour of the different kinds of courses that will be available to you. Then I'll talk about the logistics of making your tee time happen.

After that, I'll go over the rules and courtesies you should follow while you're there. Finally, we'll talk about two things that will make your golf experience more pleasant—avoiding muscle strains and pulls and golf's dress code. Not only is it important to dress appropriately for the kind of course you'll be playing, but having the right kind of shoes will help your score. You'll see how in the last chapter in this part.

Chapter **13**

Practice Before You Play

In This Chapter

- ◆ Finding your way around the driving range
- ◆ Putting drills to help you put it in the hole
- ◆ Turning your house into a practice range
- ◆ Practicing on par-three courses
- ◆ Using high-tech practice tools

Lessons, as well as all the books, magazines, and videos I talked about in the previous chapter, are great for getting started, but now it's time to go outside and give a golf round a try. But before you make that big step onto the first tee for a full 18-hole round, you should prepare yourself with some practice at the driving range and around the yard. In this chapter, I'll give you the ins and outs of practicing.

Driving Ranges: Pleasure and Pain

The best place to get ready to play golf is at a driving range. These ranges come in all shapes and sizes. Deluxe ranges have nice, new balls, natural grass, and big, inviting targets. A basic range might have fake grass mats that you hit from and a big net 150 yards away. As long as you can take a free swing and you aren't crowded in next to someone, the details shouldn't really matter.

Most communities have at least one range. If there aren't any listed in your local phone book, call some of the local public golf courses. Many of them have ranges next to the course, and you don't have to be scheduled to play the course to use the range. It usually isn't necessary to make a *tee time* to hit balls at the range. Just show up, pay, and fire away.

Par Primer

A **tee time** is the appointment you make to play a round of golf. It is made at the golf shop, usually several days in advance.

The greatest advantage the range has over a regular round of golf is that you can easily fit a practice session at the range into your schedule. You can hit practice balls for as long or short a time as you like. If you're out on the golf course, you're at the mercy of the groups ahead of you.

Extra Swings

Indoor driving ranges are becoming more and more popular, especially in northern climates. These ranges have big "bubble" inflatable roofs high enough to let you hit full shots inside, even when it's snowing outside. The only drawback is that they're usually only 150 yards long or so, which means your shots will hit into a net at the end of the range. Still, it's great to be able to hit balls in short sleeves and shorts in the middle of winter.

The disadvantage is that you're missing out on the thrill of competing and moving toward an ultimate goal. Out on the golf course, you're aiming toward a flag and hole with hopes of eventually knocking the ball in. There are consequences to each shot you hit. At the range, you're hitting out into a mostly empty space. A shot can look good in the air, but you don't have very much positive feedback about where the shot lands in relation to your target. If you hit a horrible shot, it's easy just to tee up another practice ball and fire again. In fact, the biggest mistake I see amateurs make is when they go to the practice range and hit a whole bunch of practice balls as fast as they can—hit one, watch for a second, line up another, wham! Rushing through shots like that really defeats the purpose of practicing at the range. Instead, take your time and think about every swing. After you hit the ball, watch what happens to it. How the ball flies and how far it goes will tell you a lot about the swing.

The Way Things Work

At most ranges, you either give money to the range attendant in exchange for a bucket of balls, or you buy tokens from the attendant or a token machine. Those tokens go into a ball dispensing machine. The machine has a hook that you hang your empty bucket on. After you put in the token, the machine counts out the correct number of balls and shoots them down into the bucket.

You usually can choose to buy either a large or small bucket of balls. It takes about an hour to hit a large bucket of balls, and if you haven't swung a golf club very often, that's a good way to get blisters. As a beginner, your best bet is to get the small bucket and take your time. A small bucket usually costs around $3 or $4. A larger one is usually the equivalent of two small buckets, but with a little price break from what two small buckets would cost. Of course, if you live in a big city, where there aren't as many ranges, or at a high-end resort, you'll pay a lot more.

> **Caddie's Advice** _____
>
> If you get balls from a machine, you're probably going to have to do a little housework—the machine almost always spits some balls out over the edge of the bucket. Pick them up. After all, you paid for them!

After you buy a bucket, take the balls and your clubs to one of the stalls that stretch out across the front of the range. At a range with fake grass, wood partitions usually separate the stalls. If the range is natural grass, slots are separated by a metal rack to hold your clubs or small wooden slats placed on the ground. If there's room, try to leave an empty stall between you and the next person down the line. That way, you won't be distracted by other swings. On a natural grass range, you can dump the balls into a little pile on the grass next to you and pull one from the pile with your club. If you dump the balls out on an artificial turf range, they'll roll away, so keep them in the bucket and reach down and pull one out each time you need it.

Give yourself plenty of room if you're hitting from a natural grass range, because when you take a few divots from an area, you'll have to move over a few inches to find some fresh grass. On artificial grass, I recommend hitting only from the rubber tees that stick out from the surface. Not only are your shots distorted if you hit directly from the mat, but the soles of your clubs get covered in green residue that's tough to get off.

> **CAUTION**
>
> **Double Bogey** _____
>
> Keep in mind that hitting directly off artificial turf (instead of from a tee) will distort the flight of your shots. Your club won't dig in to the artificial grass, so you won't know whether you hit a shot fat.

Caddie's Advice

Resist the temptation to swing as hard as you can—both on the range and on the course. It's very hard to control the club when you swing that hard. Swing with as much speed as you can while still feeling in control.

Some people take their whole bag to the driving range and hit a few shots with one club, then another, and so on. If you're just picking up the game, it's a good idea to hit all your clubs to get an idea of their characteristics and how they are different. But after a few introductory trips to the range, take just two or three clubs each time and concentrate on them. Pick a wood and an iron and hit a lot of balls with each club. You'll more quickly get the feel of how the swings are slightly different.

When I go to the practice range before playing a round, I start out by doing some stretches to get loose. Then I start with my sand wedge, hitting little 40- or 50-yard shots to the closest target out on the range. I work my way through the bag, from the shortest irons to the longest ones. The only wood I carry in my bag is the driver, so I end my practice by hitting 15 or 20 balls with that club. I swing at about 85-percent speed, which helps me relax and stay in control. After I hit balls on the range, I go to the practice green and hit putts.

Puttering Around

At most golf courses, a large practice green sits next to the first hole. This green usually has between 5 and 18 holes, all of them filled with little flags. Here you can work on short putts, long putts, and little bump-and-run shots from the fringe.

At a professional tournament, you'll see as many as a dozen players on the practice green at the same time, hitting putts. Watching the pros, the first thing you'll notice is that we practice far more shorter putts—from 5 to 15 feet—than long putts. On the practice green, you should practice the putts you're going to see the most when you play. During a round of golf, you'll certainly see your share of 30- or 40-foot putts, but you won't make very many of those—you're just trying to get them close to the hole. The putts in the 5-, 10-, and 15-foot range are definitely more frequent and easier to make, and by practicing at those distances, you'll give yourself a chance to make more of them. Improving your play around and on the greens—chipping and putting—is the fastest way to improve your score.

You need to remember a few rules of etiquette on the practice green:

◆ Putt at one hole at a time.

◆ Don't stand near one hole while putting at another. That way, you're only taking up one hole, and other players can use the other holes. That's just common courtesy.

◆ Don't stop another person's ball that is still rolling. You might think you're doing somebody a favor, but he or she might have wanted to see where that ball ended up.

When I go to the practice green before a round, I spend most of my time practicing 10-footers. Those putts give me a good idea of how fast the greens are playing and whether my aim is good that day. At the end of my session, I move back and try to lag five 40-footers within 3 feet of the hole. If I can accomplish that with three putts out of the five, then I'm ready to head to the first tee and play.

One of my favorite games to play on the practice green is also a great game to play with one or two of your playing partners. We call it simply "the putting contest." One person puts his or her ball down and chooses one of the holes on the practice green as the target and then hits a putt at the hole. He or she putts until the ball is holed. The number of putts it takes is his or her score for that hole. Then, each of the other competitors play the hole. Alternate who decides the next target and keep track of the total score. After 9 (or 18) holes, the person with the fewest putts wins. Not only do you practice leaving long putts closer to the hole, you re-create the pressure you'll feel on the course when you stand over those important little 3- and 4-footers.

Backyard Chipping and Other No-Cost Alternatives

Driving ranges are nice because you don't have to pick up the balls when you're done hitting them. But if you have a bag of your own practice balls, you can practice just as effectively in your own yard or any empty field. You'll save money, and you'll get a lot more exercise picking the balls up again.

If you decide to hit your own balls, you can buy a box of *range balls* from any wholesale golf distributor. The major golf magazines list these distributors in the back, near the classifieds. Or you can use a collection of any old, beat-up regular balls. Divers patrol the ponds of many courses and retrieve sunken balls and resell them. You often can buy some of the older ones cheaply—four or five for a dollar.

Par Primer

A **range ball** is a one-piece practice ball used at a driving range. Most mail-order companies, such as Edwin Watts (www.edwinwatts.com) carry them, and they don't cost more than 50 cents a ball if you order 50 or more.

When you've accumulated about 50 balls, it's time to invest in a shag bag. It looks a little like a vacuum cleaner without wheels, and a basic, good-quality bag costs no more than $30. The balls sit in the upright bag, and you hold it by a handle on the top. After you dump the balls out and hit them, you grab the shag bag and place its extended tube over a ball on the ground. The ball squeezes into the tube and gets pushed up into the bag by the next ball you pick up. It saves you from bending over and picking up each ball by hand.

A shag bag is a convenient place to store your practice balls. It's also designed to help you pick them up quickly and without any stress on your back.

Most empty spaces suitable for practicing won't be big enough to hit full shots with your driver or long irons. Plus, even if you could hit these shots, the balls would be so spread out, you would spend all day picking them up. The best clubs to practice with in an open field are your 9-iron, pitching wedge, and sand wedge. You can hit bunches of shots with these clubs into a relatively small area, which makes it easier to retrieve the balls.

If you live in a suburban area, the grounds of your local public high school are a great place to hit practice shots during the summer. Most good-sized high schools have large, open fields with grass that is reasonably well maintained. It won't be like hitting from a perfectly manicured fairway, but that might be even better, because you'll be practicing lots of shots from not-so-perfect lies. Also, unless you're using the football field for your practice area, nobody will notice—or care about—the divots.

Of course, if you aren't interested in chasing down stray golf balls in an open field, your backyard makes a perfect practice area for shorter shots. Any yard that is at least 20 yards wide will work just fine. Place a Frisbee or a plastic dinner plate at one end of the yard, pace off 15 yards, and then hit chip shots at the target (remember that one full step is about a yard). You should be able to pick up your misses in 5 minutes. If you have a large wash-tub or plastic trash can, you can also use your wedge and try to chip shots up and in. If you get really good, you don't need to go very far to pick up the balls!

I have a friend who does most of her practicing in the yard behind her condominium. Her favorite game is to put a ball down and pick targets around her yard to chip to. She'll start near the back door and chip toward a large tree halfway across the yard. She plays toward the tree until she hits it and then picks another target and plays toward that one. She has a regular circuit of targets, and each time she practices, she keeps track of how many chips it takes to get around the loop. A drill like that adds an element of competition to practicing that makes it much more fun. You aren't just hitting balls, but trying to beat your own score. You can also challenge a friend to a chipping duel. Loser buys the soda and hot dogs!

Another friend filled a child's sandbox in his backyard with the same kind of sand used in the bunkers at his local public course. His five-year-old son made sand castles as impressively as before, but my friend could drop balls in the sandbox when his son wasn't using it and practice hitting short sand shots!

> **CAUTION**
>
> **Double Bogey**
>
> If you decide to practice chipping in your backyard, make sure that anyone else who lives with you doesn't mind the inevitable turf damage that comes with practicing. Practice in the backyard, where fewer people will see the marks!

Unless you have some expensive greens-keeping equipment and quite a bit of patience, you won't be able to create a putting green in your backyard. That means you'll probably have to practice your putting inside, on the carpet. As you can imagine, a favorite shag rug in the middle of a cramped, small room wouldn't be the best choice for a practice putting green. Your best bet would be a long hallway covered with short, firm carpeting—think of a hallway in a hotel.

Extra Swings

Professional golfers sometimes take indoor practice to the extreme. At the lodge that sits near Pebble Beach Golf Links in California, the curtains in the rooms are so thick, players from the PGA Tour who were staying there for the Pebble Beach National Pro-Am hit full 9-iron shots with real golf balls into them. The thick material deadened the shot and made the ball just drop harmlessly to the floor. No windows were broken, but rumor has it the hotel staff wasn't too happy about the worn spots in the carpeting from the "divots."

The hall should be wide enough for you to take a comfortable putting stance with 2 or 3 feet to spare on either side. Your hole can be a large drinking glass lying on its side, or you can purchase a regulation-sized practice hole made from metal or plastic (your local sporting-goods store or golf shop should have one). This hole sits about a quarter of an inch above the ground and has metal or plastic tabs that look like little ramps surrounding it. If a ball rolls onto the ramps, it is collected in the center of the hole. The whole contraption looks like a flattened, circular ashtray. It really doesn't matter if your floor isn't level. If it has a rise, you can play the break just as you would on a green.

If you don't have any carpeting suitable for putting, you can buy a cheap piece of artificial turf from a lumberyard and lay it down in the basement. Otherwise, most golf shops and sporting-goods stores sell small, self-contained strips of fake grass that have a hole already attached at one end. You can roll these strips on the floor.

The basic thing to remember when you practice your putting indoors is speed control. It doesn't really matter how fast or slow the carpeting is. Trying to make each ball stop in the same area helps you learn to judge distance and speed, and that skill stays with you no matter how fast or slow real-grass greens are. It cuts down on the time it takes to adjust.

Par-Three Courses: A Rookie's Best Friend

After you graduate from the practice range, if you don't feel like you're quite ready to test your skills on a full-sized, 18-hole course, you've got an alternative. *Par-three courses* (also called *executive courses*) are just what they sound like—courses that have nothing but short holes. Playing a round at a par-three course is cheaper than a regular round of golf and takes a lot less time. You can practice shots from the 7-iron down to pitches and chips, as well as your putting stroke. You can also carry a smaller bag, because you need fewer clubs.

Most par-three courses are set up just like a regular golf course. They have a club-house where you pay for the round and pick up any equipment you need. The layouts have either 9 or 18 holes, and each hole has a distance of between 90 and 180 yards. The shortness of the holes helps players of all levels compete on a relatively level playing field. It's easier to hit a 9-iron or wedges than a driver or a 3-iron, so as a beginner you spend less time looking for your lost ball and more time hitting shots.

A round at a par-three course costs between $8 and $20, and tee times aren't usually required. In the summer, you can fit in 18 holes on an executive course after finishing work.

Most par-three courses are listed in the phone book. You can also usually get a list of them from your local golf association.

Par Primer

Executive course is another term for a **par-three course**—one that has all par-three holes and no par-fours or par-fives.

High-Tech Practice Tools

A popular new way to practice—and even take lessons—is on a golf simulator. A simulator is basically a combination of an indoor hitting stall, with a fake grass mat and nets to catch the balls, and a computer system that measures each shot and translates it into a video game–style result on a television screen. The systems are popular in bars and video arcades, where people can pay a fee to "play" famous courses like Pebble Beach, which are reproduced on the big video screen in front of you. You hit a shot into the net, and the computer draws your shot on the video screen as if you were really playing the famous 18th hole, right along the ocean.

These systems are also great for practice, because they can give you detailed information about your swing. The computer can tell you just how much slice or hook spin you're putting on your shots and how far your shots are going. You can get some very specific information about your game and get good ideas about what you need to practice. Some teachers are even using these systems to teach lessons. It's a lot more exciting than hitting balls in a plain indoor studio. You will have to pay a little bit more for hitting balls on a golf simulator—usually about $30 for an hour of practice, or a round on a famous course.

The Least You Need to Know

◆ At a driving range, balls are usually sold in two different bucket sizes—small and large. Start small; thinking about each shot is better than the machine-gun approach.

◆ After you've made a few trips to the range, focus on using just one or two different clubs on each later visit.

◆ Change your backyard into a chipping range by using a plastic plate or Frisbee for a target.

◆ Par-three (or executive) courses are a good middle step between the practice range and a regular course.

◆ Check your local phone book for range and par-three course listings.

◆ Golf simulators are a high-tech way to practice your swing or play famous courses around the world without leaving your home town.

Chapter **14**

Getting Out on the Golf Course

In This Chapter

- ◆ Distinguishing between public and private courses
- ◆ Getting a tee time
- ◆ Picking a good course for the money
- ◆ Playing a course that fits your skill level
- ◆ Finding a partner

You've hit range balls until your hands bled, chipped in the backyard until there was no grass left to mow, and worn holes in your carpeting from indoor putting. Now it's time to put all the clubs in the bag and venture out on a real, full-sized course.

There's no reason to be nervous, because this chapter will help you through the ritual. Your mortgage payment isn't resting on how many strokes you take. This is supposed to be fun! I know it won't seem like it when you're taking your tenth shot from a deep fairway bunker 200 yards from the green. But trust me, when you finish your first 18-hole round, all the worm-burners, shanks, and chili-dips will disappear from your memory.

That one high-flying, soft-landing 9-iron to the green surrounded by water or that miraculous tee shot that split the fairway will make you forget! Let's get ready for the next three-and-a-half to four hours you'll spend playing your first round of golf.

Kinds of Courses: Welcome! and No Trespassing!

Golf courses are roughly divided into two different kinds—those anyone can play for a fee, and those you can only play by belonging to the club or going with someone who belongs. Let's go over the differences between each kind.

Public Courses

Just like it sounds, a public course is open to anyone who is willing to pay for a round. Public courses are the most common type, and they also tend to be the cheapest, with *green fees* ranging from $10 to $75 for 18 holes. Some courses have a 9-hole rate, but others charge you the same amount whether you play 9 or 18.

The best-maintained and most enjoyable public courses see the most business and are tough to get on during the summer or on any weekend or holiday. In urban areas, where there is a relatively small number of courses for a large golf population, reservations are almost a necessity. Van Cortlandt Park in New York City, the oldest public course in America, had more than 100,000 rounds played on it last year. It's tough to keep a course that sees so many rounds in good shape, but it doesn't seem to matter to New York golfers. There aren't many other places to play.

Par Primer

The **green fee** is the price you pay to play at a golf course.

Caddie's Advice

Pebble Beach in California is one of the most famous courses in the world, and technically, it is public. Theoretically, anybody can play a round of golf there, but you'll have to spend about $350 for the privilege.

That problem is pretty much limited to crowded urban areas. At the average public course in a suburban area, you should have no trouble making it onto the course on a weekday. If you call a few days in advance, playing on a summer weekend shouldn't be any more difficult. Be aware that public courses are in the business of getting as many golfers on the course and through as quickly as possible. You'll be expected to play fast and keep up with the group in front of you. If you want a more leisurely pace, try to pick a time that isn't so busy. If nobody is behind you on the course, it doesn't matter how long you take to play.

Municipal Courses

Municipal courses are slightly different from public courses. Most of them are actually owned by the community and are open to anyone who is a resident of the city or town the course is located in. If you don't live there, you can't get on. Others allow nonresidents to play, but for a much higher price. A municipal course, if your hometown has one, is the best value in golf. Some of these courses have prices as low as $8 for 18 holes.

Daily-Fee Courses

Sometimes called semi-private courses, daily-fee courses are essentially higher-priced public courses that have some restrictions on when you can play. Some of these courses even have members, like a private club, but also allow anyone who is willing to pay to play on certain days. Typically, a round at a daily-fee course costs between $30 and $150. Because of the price, a daily-fee course is often less crowded than its public cousin. Also, the higher price and, in some cases, membership base helps the club maintain much better conditions.

Resort Courses

High-end hotels and resorts often have their own world-class golf course (or courses) on the grounds. If you're a guest at the resort, you can play on the course for a decent price, usually between $50 and $100. If you aren't a guest, it's still possible to get a tee time, but at double the price. And a cart costs extra. As you can see, the resorts don't encourage nonguests to play.

Private Courses

You can play a private course (otherwise known as a country club) only if you're with a member. Memberships to most country clubs cost $5,000 per year, but they can cost up to $100,000 in initiation fees and $20,000 a year. The biggest difference between private clubs and public courses is usually the conditions. Many private clubs are impeccably groomed. You get what you pay for!

Extra Swings

If you're invited to play at a private club with friends or business associates, don't panic. Generally, if you act as you would in any other casual business situation, you won't go wrong. (For more about playing golf with business associates, see Chapter 24.) Just remember that private clubs run on a completely different economy than the rest of the world. First of all, most clubs don't run on cash—members sign for anything they need, like equipment, food, drinks, or the green fee, and then get billed at the end of the month. So when you get to the course, keep your money in your pocket, unless you're tipping.

Which brings us to the second part of country club life. These places are designed so that members have to do as little dirty work as possible. Someone will take your clubs from your trunk for you, clean your golf shoes, clean your clubs when you finish playing, and shine your street shoes while you're away. Of course, nothing in life is free. Staff expect you to tip them a couple of bucks for each of these services. Don't make a big deal about it. Just be grateful and hand the attendant the tip. Before doing so, however, be sure to ask your host whether tipping in cash is allowed. If your host has to sign for it instead, just give him or her the cash to cover it.

Making Tee Times and Other Mist-Shrouded Rites

If you decide to play this game with any regularity, you'll quickly learn that making a *tee time*, or an appointment to play on a certain day and time, is a necessity. If there were no such thing as tee times, we would all have to show up at the crack of dawn and wait in a long line to get on the course. Your round is already going to take at least three-and-a-half hours. Adding four or five hours of waiting makes things quite a bit more inconvenient. A tee time saves you the trouble (most of the time) of having to wait in a long line. In a perfect world, you can schedule a 10:42 tee time for Saturday morning, show up at the course about 30 minutes beforehand, hit some practice balls, stroll up to the first tee at 10:40, shake hands with your partners, and fire away. Of course, there is no such thing as a perfect world, so most tee-time lists get a little backed up, but don't count on that margin for error. If your time comes and you aren't there, you go to the back of the line.

Par Primer

A **tee time** is an appointment to play on a course at a certain time. They're scheduled at regular intervals—usually 9 or 10 minutes apart—throughout the day.

To make a tee time, you first have to find out what kind of policy the course has. Some allow you to make a reservation only one or two days in advance.

Others let you call weeks in advance. If you ever decide to play in Scotland, you can send a letter to a public course over there and arrange a tee time six months in advance. After you find out how far in advance you can make the reservation, try to reserve your tee time as early as possible. You'll get a better selection of times. As we talked about earlier, at some courses, if you don't beat the crowd when making a tee time for a summer weekend, you won't get one.

When you ask for a tee time, the person scheduling your time will ask you how many players will be in your group. You can play with up to three other people. A group of five is an evil number in golf, because most courses only allow up to four in one group. If you want to play with five, you'll have to split up into a threesome and twosome and make two different tee times.

Shoot for getting to the course at least a half hour before you are scheduled to start. That way, you can take your time changing your shoes and warming up on the driving range and putting green. It also gives you a cushion in case one of the members of your group is running a little late. When everyone in your group shows up, go into the clubhouse and pay your green fee. The attendant will give you a receipt. It's very important that you don't lose this slip of paper—you'll need it to prove you paid. Then take the receipts of all the people in your group down to the starter. He or she usually will be situated right next to the first tee, holding a clipboard with the day's tee times. Hand the receipts to the starter, and he or she will check you off on the list. If you're early, you might be able to get onto the course before your tee time if the group scheduled before you isn't ready to go.

Caddie's Advice

After I've made a tee time, I always call the morning of my round to make sure everything is in order. If the starter (the person who is in charge of sending people out onto the course to play) is running way behind, he or she can give you that information. If you're supposed to play early, you get a chance to sleep a little more!

Double Bogey

If you know you're going to be late for your tee time, call the course and let them know. Most of the time, they can bump you back without any trouble. It's also common courtesy.

Extra Swings

Be sure to ask whether your green fee includes the use of a riding cart or not. Some courses require players to use them (because the distance between holes is substantial … and it means extra revenue for the course!) and include their cost as part of the green fee, and others will charge you extra if you want to use one. Carts don't require any special skill to drive—they have a pedal to accelerate and a pedal to stop, just like a car. Be sure to ask the starter what the cart rules for the day are. Sometimes, when it's wet out, you'll be required to keep carts on the cement paths that line most holes. Regardless of the cart rules for the day, never drive your cart on the grass near (or on) the green or tee area. Nothing will get you in trouble with the greens keeper faster.

Riding carts are a good choice for rainy days or when it's too hot to carry a bag for 18 holes.

Believe it or not, some public courses don't take tee times. For these places, you *do* have to show up at the crack of dawn and wait in line. Showing up at four in the morning to put your name on a waiting list to play golf is something you should do once, just to have the experience, and then never experience it again. I've done it a few times, and I found that after waiting all that time to play, I didn't have very much patience on the course. As a beginner, patience is an important requirement. A lot of courses that don't have tee times are wonderful and historic, but until you become a regular player, a course where you can make an appointment to play and finish in less than five hours will suit you just fine.

Bang for Your Buck

In a 50-mile radius from your home, you might have 20 or 30 different golf courses from which to choose. Some might be really inexpensive, ragged-around-the-edges public courses. Others might be high-priced, well-maintained daily-fee courses. One might be two blocks from your home. When you decide where to play, you need to take all these factors—cost, condition, location, and pace of play—into consideration. The goal is to find a course that is a good combination of them all.

You need to decide what the most important factors are to you and then try a lot of different courses that fit your criteria. Playing one course over and over will help your scores improve on that course, because you'll learn the best way to play each hole. But if you play many different courses, your game will get better overall because you'll always be challenged with new shots. Plus, one of the most exciting aspects of the game is seeing new and interesting courses.

Extra Swings

Golf Digest publishes its *Places To Play* guide every year, and its main feature is the collection of golf course reviews written by regular golfers. The guide's rating system works just like the ones hotels use. A five-star rating is the best. No stars is the worst. You can get a rough idea about the quality of a course from these ratings, and the profiles also include information on price. Just keep in mind that regular golfers are making these recommendations. Just because a few people don't like a course doesn't mean you won't.

Choose a Course That's Right for You

The other major factor to consider when choosing a course to play is difficulty. Remember Chapter 3, when we talked about course slope and rating? Here's where those factors come into play. Remember, the lower the course rating or slope, the easier a course is to play. You can pick a place to play using the criteria we went over in the previous section—cost, condition, location, and pace of play—and find one that meets those needs. But if the course you picked is too hard for the level of your game, you won't enjoy yourself. For example, the Blue Monster at Doral Resort and Spa has more than 120 sand traps, and 16 of its holes have water hazards. The Monster might be the most beautiful course in the world to you, and your uncle might own the resort and get you on for free as often as you like, but as a beginner, you won't have any fun. You'll get your brains beat in, lose 30 balls, and quit after 14 holes. Equally intimidating for beginners, the 18th hole at Doral has a fairway that is only 15 yards wide where your drive is supposed to land—it is one of the toughest holes I've ever played.

If you don't know what to expect from a course, don't hesitate to call and ask. Ask whether the course is "tight," with trees and other kinds of trouble very close to the edges of the fairway, or whether it has lots of water. Or check any one of the reference guides I mention. Most point out the defining characteristics of each course.

If a course is too easy (and that shouldn't be a problem this early in the game), you'll get bored. Start with courses that challenge you, but allow you to make mistakes without losing a bagful of balls. That means avoiding the resort courses that require long shots over water from the tee and have features that are designed to be more memorable than playable. It also means avoiding courses with an extreme number of water hazards or sand traps. If you take a look at the scorecard and it only lists one set of tees, be careful. If you can play the course only at a PGA Tour–length of 7,200 yards, that's too much golf course for you. I don't care how beautiful the scenery is, if you're paying $150 to play golf, you won't enjoy yourself if you're spending all afternoon in bunker after bunker after lake after creek after swamp.

Other courses have very narrow fairways lined with thick stands of trees on both sides. These kinds of courses are also tough on beginners who have trouble hitting accurate shots off the tee. A more forgiving course lets you get away with some wild tee shots. You might have to go to the next fairway to hit your second shot, but at least you won't be buried in the woods. It's no fun not to be able to see the hole for the trees!

How to Find Courses Near You

To get a comprehensive list of courses—both par-three and normal—in your area, call your state golf association. The numbers are listed in Appendix B. The state association can provide you with a list of its member courses and clubs. *Golf Digest*'s *Places To Play* guide, available at your local bookstore, is also helpful, but it lists more normal-length courses.

If you have access to a computer and the Internet, the World Wide Web is a great place to find where to play. Here are some of the better sites:

◆ **PGATOUR.com.** Run by the men's professional tour, this site also has a comprehensive course search feature that breaks down courses by type, cost, location, and customer rating.

- ◆ **GOLFDIGEST.com.** The *Golf Digest* magazine site is home to the Internet version of the *Places to Play* list. Courses are organized by star rating and location.

- ◆ **ZAGAT.com.** The popular restaurant review company has started a course rating system in tandem with sports network ESPN.

The Case for the Nine-Hole Round

We've been talking a lot about playing full, 18-hole rounds. Optimally, it would be great to be able to play 18 holes every time out, but most people have jobs and other responsibilities that make it tough to commit to the four- or five-hour chunk of time a full round of golf requires.

Many public courses offer a special rate for a nine-hole round. It's an ideal choice for busy people who want to get in some golf after work or for someone who doesn't want to spend all day at the course. Most youth, senior, and after-work golf leagues play nine-hole rounds. It enables more golfers to get on the course, because groups can tee off from both the first and tenth holes.

As a beginner, nine holes might offer you just the right amount of golf. Most people get a little tired near the end of an 18-hole round and lose some patience. Over nine holes, you can play for two hours and finish without getting frustrated.

Finding a Partner

I enjoy myself the most on the golf course when I'm playing with my close friends or family. This is one of the few games in which you can spend a lot of time talking and laughing right in the middle of playing. Most of the time spent on the course isn't hitting shots, but moving from shot to shot and waiting. If you aren't playing with people you like, it can make for a long afternoon. So in a best-case scenario, try to play with people you're comfortable with, at least in the beginning. If you're still learning the rules and the basics of the swing, it helps to play with someone who has a lot of experience with the game and, above all, is patient. It wouldn't be fair to expect your partner to make your round a walking lesson, but a friendly face who is familiar with the game can help you with any rule questions or swing frustrations. In the beginning, these friends are your security blanket.

If you don't have a partner to play with, you can always go to the course alone and have the starter set up a threesome or foursome for you. This is a little riskier, especially as a beginner, because you might be paired with someone who isn't interested in watching you work on your swing. If you're paired with three strangers, be sure to let them know up front that you're just learning the game and assure them you won't slow the group down. Most people you meet on the course will be nothing but polite, understanding, and pleasant, especially if you're a good sport and don't pout after every bad shot. After all, everyone started as a beginner.

During the round, be sure to keep up with the group. Don't spend too much time looking for lost balls, and be ready to play when it's your turn. If you find yourself falling behind, pick up your ball and take it to the green. Drop it there and take a few putts. The most important thing is to get some experience on the course, not what score you make. Learn when to say when.

After you've gained a little experience on the course, joining a league is a great idea. When you've figured out your handicap, you can join a league full of golfers at the same skill level. The people in your league signed up for the competition and companionship, so your partners in the threesome or foursome should be very open and receptive. It's a great place to build friendships and find regular golfing partners for years to come.

The Least You Need to Know

- The main kinds of courses are public (anyone can play), municipal (anyone in the city the course is located in can play), daily-fee (anyone can play, but with some restrictions), resort (mostly limited to resort guests), and private (you can play only with a member).

- If you're planning to play on a weekend or holiday, you'll probably need to make a reservation, called a tee time.

- If you have a tee time, try to get to the course at least half an hour early.

- As a beginner, start out on courses that fit your skill level.

- A nine-hole round is a less time-consuming, less expensive alternative to the 18-hole round.

- Try to play with friends your first few times out. If you can't, be sure to let your playing partners know that you're a beginner, but that you won't slow the group down.

15

The Eleven Golf Commandments

In This Chapter

◆ Following golf etiquette

◆ Keeping the course in good condition

◆ Taking care of your equipment

Golf is a very social game. After all, you will only rarely play all by yourself. Because most of the time you'll be playing with a group of three other people, one of the most important aspects of playing golf isn't how well you actually play the game. It's how you behave on the course.

The etiquette of the game is a collection not just of rules, but of courtesies that help everyone in the group enjoy the outing. If you can master the 11 commandments in this chapter, your skill level won't matter to your partners. They'll enjoy your company.

I. Keep up the Pace at All Costs

Whether you're a professional or a complete beginner, nothing exposes you to more scorn than playing too slowly. It's pretty simple—if everyone in your group is waiting for you at each hole to look for a lost ball, ponder over club selection, take three or four practice swings, change clubs one last time, take two or three more practice swings, and then hit your shot, they are being prevented from playing their shots at a comfortable pace. Don't be selfish. That doesn't mean you have to run to your ball, throw your bag down, and swing before you're prepared, but you can do some things to keep up with the group.

There are two schools of thought about the order of play once everyone has teed off. Many people observe the same protocol that is in effect on the green: Whoever is farthest from the hole plays his or her shot first. If you play this way, only walk ahead of someone who is hitting if you're off to the side and not in their line of fire or peripheral vision. In *ready golf*, when you get to your ball, take your practice swings and hit. It doesn't matter who is farthest from the hole. Ask your partners on the first tee whether they play "ready golf."

If you're playing with a cart, drop your partner off at his or her ball, make sure that he or she has the right clubs, and then drive over to your own ball. While your partner sets up and hits (assuming your ball is out of the line of fire), you can decide what club you need and get ready to hit your own shot. Then your partner can walk over to the cart while you're hitting. By the time you hit, he or she will be back to the cart. Then you drive to whatever ball is closest and start the procedure over again.

Caddie's Advice

Before you play a shot from the tee, remember the brand and number of ball you're playing. That way, you'll know it when you find it, and you won't play someone else's ball by mistake. You can also mark your ball with a dot of ink or nail polish to make it distinctive.

If you're carrying your own clubs, walk to your ball and check your distance from the green. If you're playing ready golf, check to make sure that nobody is in the way up ahead. If not, fire away. In ready golf, be sure to keep track of where your partners are playing from. You don't want to wander in front of a stray shot.

When you hit a shot, watch it until it stops rolling. Don't turn around and sulk—you won't be able to find your ball. If your shot goes into the trees, keep your eyes on the point where you think it went in and then make a beeline for that spot. It will narrow your search. If you can see your shot land, again pick a landmark on the ground near where the ball hit. Go to that spot and then look back to the tee-box. You should be able to roughly calculate the angle at which the ball was traveling. Walk along that line, and you should be able to find it. According to the rules of golf, you only have five minutes to look. Then you have to declare the ball lost, go back to where you hit it, and take a one-stroke penalty.

When one of your partners is searching for a ball, hit your shot first and then go over to help look. That way, when the ball is found or your partner plays another one, the group will be ready to move up the fairway.

Finally, when you're on the green, leave your cart or bag at the side of the green closest to the next hole. That way, when you're done putting, you can go to your bag or cart and on to the next hole without having to come back across the front of the green and disrupt the next group. Wait until you get to the next tee to mark your scorecard.

> **Double Bogey**
>
> If your group is waiting for you to hit a shot, don't take any more than a single practice swing—two at the absolute most. Nothing exposes a person as being unfamiliar with golf etiquette more quickly than taking three or four lazy practice swings and fooling around over a shot longer than 60 seconds.

II. Know When to Say When

When you're playing with a group of players who are significantly better than you, know when it's time to cut your losses and try again on the next hole. If you're lagging behind the rest of the group and struggling to move the ball forward, pick it up and drop it on the green. Hit two or three putts, then concentrate on the next hole. Don't be a masochist. Your first few times out, a score doesn't mean anything. After you can consistently make solid contact with the ball, you can start worrying about your score.

III. Take Care of the Course

Nothing is more frustrating than hitting a great shot right down the middle of the fairway and discovering when you get to your ball that it has landed in a *divot* that someone ahead of you didn't fix. When you play golf, you want to leave the course as close to how you found it as possible. When you take a chunk of grass out of the ground with a swing, fix the mark. If you're playing on bentgrass (mostly in the Midwest and North), find the piece of sod, pick it up, and place it back in the divot. Step firmly on the replaced divot to push it back into place. A replaced divot heals in two days. If you don't put the grass back into place, the scar won't heal for three weeks.

> **Par Primer**
>
> A **divot** is the piece of turf that gets gouged from the ground when you swing. It's also another name for the mark your ball leaves on the green when it lands after a high-flying shot.

On the Bermuda fairways of the South, don't bother replacing the divot—Bermuda that's been ripped from the ground won't grow back. If you're riding in a cart, it will probably have a little bucket or bottle of seed attached just over the rear wheel. Scoop out a little bit of the seed and spread it into the scrape mark.

When you hit a high-flying shot onto the green, check the spot where the ball landed. You'll probably see a little dent where the ball pushed the grass in. Many courses will give you a divot-repair tool—a little two-pronged piece of metal or plastic—for free if you ask. Use it to repair the dent. Stick the prongs into the ground at the back of the hole so the prongs go underneath the grass in the divot, and pull up the smashed grass. The motion is like the one you would use with a screwdriver to pry off the top of a paint can. Then tap the top flat with the bottom of your putter to level it off.

Caddie's Advice

If you aren't sure whether the course you're playing is bent-grass or Bermuda, check the scorecard. It usually will tell you whether to replace your divots or fill them with seed.

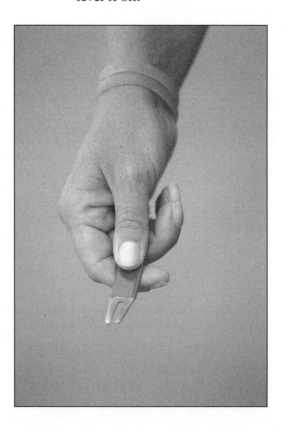

A divot repair tool has two metal prongs that go into the grass and pull it up.

From the left, first stick the prongs of the divot-repair tool into the back of the ball mark, where the grass has been pushed in. Then pull the grass gently up, first on one side and then the other.

IV. Rake Bunkers When You're Done

As a beginner, you'll probably think that a sand shot is tough enough without having to deal with hitting the ball out of somebody's footprint.

When you hit from the bunker, always use the rakes that are usually spread around the edges of the trap to smooth out the footprints and other marks you made. That way, the next person to hit it there will have a chance to hit from a reasonably good lie. Golf's hard enough without someone else making things more difficult.

To rake a bunker properly, walk out of the sand over the tracks you made when you went in, grab the rake, and go back to where you hit the ball. Rake the area where you were standing to hit the shot first, and then slowly back your way to the edge, raking your footprints away as you go. Don't dig the rake into the sand. You aren't trying to pick up leaves. Use just enough pressure to smooth the sand. If there are no rakes around, do the best you can with a club or your feet.

To rake a bunker, first go to the spot where you hit your shot. Rake that spot and then back slowly toward the edge of the trap, sweeping away footprints. Then step out and finish up the last spots.

V. Don't Throw Clubs

Keeping control of yourself on the course is more common courtesy and maturity than golf etiquette. It's perfectly okay to get mad and swear after a bad shot, but let it go after that. You're going to hit bad shots every round you play in your life. I'm a pro, and I hit plenty every time out. Curse your luck, but don't sulk. It makes you a less pleasant partner. And never, ever throw clubs or other equipment. I've seen people dump entire bags into a lake after a bad shot. It isn't worth it. Besides, you'll either have to get wet saving your stuff or buy some more.

VI. Be Quiet and Still When Someone Else Is Playing

Having said golf is a social game, I can't stress enough that you should be silent when one of your partners is hitting a shot. Making noise while another person is swinging is considered the ultimate in rude behavior on the course.

From the time a person gets in his or her stance and is addressing a shot, don't jingle change or dig through your bag. Try not to cough or sneeze. Don't choose the moment your friend is in the middle of his backswing to ask your other friend what club she's thinking about using. Even if that kind of noise or chatter wouldn't bother you at all, many people are very sensitive to noise during the swing. Nothing quite matches the dirty look you'll get when you drop your golf bag in the middle of a friend's swing, and she sends a shot slicing two fairways over into a swamp. Try not to let that happen.

Caddie's Advice

Most public courses don't have rules against cell phone use like private ones do, but if you do bring a phone, use common courtesy. At the minimum, turn the ringer off and leave the phone on vibrate—and in your pocket, not in the cup holder on the cart. Better yet, turn it off and leave it in your bag. You can quietly check messages every few holes.

The same holds true for your arms, legs, clothes, and shadow. None of them should be moving if you're in your friend's peripheral vision during a swing. Be especially careful about casting a shadow over the ball. That's one of my pet peeves. Fold your arms to keep your shirt from flapping, and don't turn around and walk away during the swing. It will divert your friend's attention just long enough for her to send a ball screaming over the interstate that runs down the left side of the hole! There's no way to control a gust of wind that makes your pants start flapping, but I'm sure you can appreciate how vulnerable your partners are to distraction during a golf swing, which takes a lot of concentration.

VII. Don't Step on Someone Else's Line on the Green

When you're on the putting surface, think of the patch of grass between your partner's ball and the hole (called the *line* on the green) as sacred ground. You don't want to touch it, go near it, or step on it. It would be extremely impolite. If you're wearing golf shoes, stepping on your playing partner's line would create little dents in the grass from the spikes. Those little dents can make a putt jump off line. You might be trying to beat your partner, but do it with your play, not by sabotage.

No matter where a player's putting line is, avoid stepping too close to the hole at any time. When you go to get your ball out of the hole, stand a few feet from the hole and reach over to get the ball out. Stepping next to the hole turns the grass there into a lumpy mess, creating big problems for the players coming behind.

VIII. Don't Kid Yourself: Play from the Proper Tees

If you had plenty of free time to kill, you could sit on a little folding chair next to the first tee of your local public course on any given day and count dozens of beginning and intermediate golfers who play from sets of tees too difficult for them. As we went over in Chapter 3, most courses have championship tees, which are blue or black; regular tees, which are white; and women's tees, which are red. Some courses also have a gold set between the championship and regular tees. Invariably, some groups are determined to play their round from the back tees, even if they're not quite good enough. All they succeed in doing is making the round too difficult to enjoy, not to mention slower.

Don't be proud. If you're a beginner, play from the white or red tees. In fact, you should play from the white or red tees in almost any circumstance until your handicap improves to at least 11 or 12. That's why different tees exist—to differentiate between skill levels.

IX. Be Courteous to the Starter

For no other reason than that he or she controls when you'll get on the course, you must be courteous to the starter. You're also a nice person. That should be a good enough reason. Even if the starter is short with you or downright impolite, keep in mind that shooting back with a snide comment might get you bumped two hours down the list of tee times. You'll spend the morning cooling your heels on the practice putting green.

X. Take Care of Your Equipment

A golf bag filled with dirt-encrusted clubs tells a lot about its owner. Taking some pride in your equipment and keeping it in good shape will make you look better, and more importantly, the equipment will last longer.

Caddie's Advice

Don't use anything metal to scrape dirt from the grooves of your clubs. You could scratch the finish and make it easier for the clubs to rust.

It's most important to maintain your clubs' faces. After you hit a shot, you'll notice that the grooves on the face of your iron will be filled with dirt or mud. Wipe the club-head with a towel to get rid of the big chunks and then use the sharp point of a wood tee to scrape the dirt out of the grooves. This isn't just for cosmetic purposes. You'll lose distance and control of your shots if you hit with grooves that are filled with gunk.

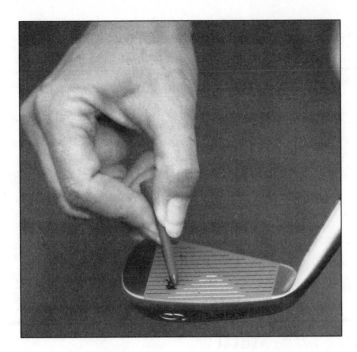

Use a wooden tee to scrape dirt and mud from a club's grooves. Don't use anything metal to do this—you'll ruin your club's finish.

At each tee-box, you'll notice a small contraption on a pole. Some have a round handle on the top, and others have a crank on one side. Both serve the same purpose—to clean your golf balls. If the ball washer has a knob on top, pull up on it. A plastic holder will slide out, revealing a hole in which to place the ball. After you've put the ball in, lower the holder. When the ball is in the washer, jerk the handle up and down quickly until the ball is clean. Pull the handle all the way out again, and the ball will roll out on its own. Washing your ball in one of these things is just about the noisiest thing you can do on a golf course aside from running over someone's foot with a cart, so don't do it when your partner is about to swing. If the washer has a crank on the side, open the little hatch on top and drop your ball in. Then turn the crank quickly until the ball is clean. Open the hatch and rotate the crank until your ball pops out. Set it on the tee and fire away.

After you finish a round, take all your clubs from the bag and wash the clubheads with a wet cloth. Dry them as best you can with a clean towel and then wipe off the grips with a damp cloth. Spread them out and let them dry.

Always scrape the excess grass and dirt from your spikes before you take them off at the end of the day. Not only will you keep the grass from getting in your trunk or your golf bag (or wherever else you keep your golf shoes), but you'll be able to tell whether you need new spikes put in.

A package of new spikes comes with a little wrench with two claws. Insert the claws into the small holes at the base of the cleat and twist off the spikes. Screw the new ones in firmly but don't tighten them with all your strength. When spikes wear down, the claw holes also get worn out, which makes it tougher to get them out.

First, put the ball into the plastic holder (left). After a few rapid jerks of the handle (center), pull the holder all the way up and the ball will pop out on its own (right).

XI. Relax and Have Fun

It's a game, not a job, and you're out there with friends. Relax, take the bad shots with the good, and enjoy yourself!

The Least You Need to Know

- Most important, keep up with your golf partners and be quiet when another person is swinging.

- Leave the course in the condition you found it: Repair your divots, rake bunkers, and don't abuse the course by smashing clubs down in anger.

- Take care of your equipment. Clean the grooves on your clubface after a shot, wipe down your clubs after each round, and don't throw your clubs.

- Be courteous at all times. Keep your group moving on the course, don't shoot from tees that are too challenging for you, and be nice to the starter.

- Relax and enjoy yourself.

Chapter 16

Rules of the Game

In This Chapter

- ◆ Hitting from a tee
- ◆ Hitting into a hazard: What happens now?
- ◆ Moving the ball without penalty
- ◆ Taking greenside responsibility
- ◆ Allowing replays and do-overs

You won't get any penalty strokes if you break one of the commandments of golf etiquette we talked about in Chapter 15. You'll just aggravate the people you're playing with. In this chapter, I'll talk about the situations that *will* cost you penalty strokes—golf rules. And if you don't get enough here, Chapter 22 will give you more examples of the application of rules, as well as rules for dealing with some strange situations.

I think it's more important to be a courteous and pleasant partner than to know all of golf's rules down to the letter. So as long as you follow the commandments in the last chapter and remember the basic golf rules I'll go over in this chapter, you'll know what to do in 99 percent of the situations you find yourself in.

Get a Rule Book and Read It

Before you play for the first time, you might want to invest a few dollars in a copy of the USGA's *Rules of Golf*. It's a little paperback book with about 100 pages, and you get it free if you join the USGA (for $35 per year), or you can buy one at any pro shop or book store. Some of the stuff in the rule book won't mean much to you, like the section on rules for a match-play tournament. Just browse through the main body of the book, which contains all the basic rules of golf. You aren't going to be tested, so don't read it like you would a textbook. Just familiarize yourself with the main points and learn how the book is organized so you can go back and look something up quickly.

Caddie's Advice

A rule book is small enough to slide right into the front pocket of your golf bag. Keep a copy in there, and you'll be able to quickly look up a rule if you run into a problem.

An important thing to remember about this game is that you are your own rules police. No referees wander around the course watching you to see whether you bend the rules. It isn't your partners' job to blow the whistle on you if you do something illegal. One of the basic themes of golf is being honorable enough to call penalties on yourself. When you play, your partners won't force you to follow the rules, but they'll appreciate it when they see that you do.

To Tee or Not To Tee

The tee-box is the only place on the golf course you can put a wooden peg called a tee in the ground to help improve your lie. After you hit the ball from the tee, you have to leave the ball on the ground and hit it as you find it until you get to the green. On the green, you can put a small marker (usually a coin or a small, flat, circular piece of plastic) in the spot where your ball was, clean the ball, and then place it back on the spot. I'll talk about that technique later in this chapter. When you hit from the tee-box, you must play from between the corresponding tee markers (the blue, white, or red tees) or no more than two clublengths behind them. If you hit from in front of the markers, it's a two-stroke *penalty*.

Par Primer

Remember, a **penalty stroke** is an extra shot added to your score for some rules violation.

When you tee the ball up for your driver, you want about half of the ball to sit above the face of the club.

When teeing a ball up for a shot with an iron, the tee should be pushed much further into the ground, so the ball sits up just above the level of the grass.

Hitting from a tee helps you hit the ball higher in the air when you use one with your irons, and it helps you hit using your driver without the club skidding against the ground. To tee the ball for a shot with an iron, stick the tee head up between the middle and third fingers of your left hand. You should be able to make a fist and see the pointed end of the tee sticking out from between those fingers. Then take your ball in the palm of the same hand so that it rests on the top of the flat part of the tee. Bend over and punch the pointed end of the tee into the ground by putting pressure on the top of the ball, which should still be resting on the flat top of the tee. Move your fingers out of the way and then slide the tee almost all the way into the ground. Only the top quarter of an inch should show under the ball. Now, when you take a regular swing with an iron, it will be easier for the clubhead to swing through without hitting the ground very much so that you can knock the ball higher in the air. Also, you don't have to worry about the quality of the grass underneath, because you'll barely be hitting it.

When you're teeing the ball up to hit a driver, follow the same procedure but keep your fingers locked around the tee. Push the pointed end into the ground until your knuckles hit the grass. This is the approximate height the ball should be teed up for a driver—about an inch and a half—so that half of the ball is above the face of your driver (that means you have to tee it higher if you have a driver with a really big head). With the ball sitting a little bit higher, you can make a swing without bumping the clubhead against the ground before you hit the ball. Hitting the ground before the ball would slow the clubhead and take distance away from your shot.

Caddie's Advice

If you find yourself popping a lot of shots too high into the air with the driver, try teeing the ball a little lower. If you're having trouble getting those shots in the air, tee it a little higher.

Hazards: As Bad as They Sound

Hazards are the danger zones of the golf course. If you knock your ball into one, you usually have to add extra strokes to your score just for the privilege of hitting another shot.

As I discussed in Chapter 3, there are several different kinds of hazards. A water hazard is simply a pond, lake, stream, ocean, creek, or river that's between you and the green and is marked off by yellow stakes. A lateral hazard, which is marked with red stakes, lines the perimeter of the hole and shouldn't be between you and the green if you draw a straight line from the tee to the flag. How you play from each of these hazards is slightly different:

◆ **Playing from a water hazard (yellow stakes).** If you go into one of these, determine the spot where the ball went into the water. Drop your new ball as near as you can to this spot without moving closer to the hole (that means you have to hit over the water again if your first ball didn't make it!). Or you can back up as far as you want on the line of flight the ball took into the water. Which means that if there's 50 yards of rough in front of the water you just blasted a ball into, you can back up 75 yards into the fairway and hit your next shot.

Here's an example to make things clearer: If I hit my first shot on a par-three into a water hazard in front of the green, I drop my new ball as close as I can to the spot where the ball went in, no closer to the hole. I take one penalty shot for going into the hazard, so I'm now hitting my third shot.

◆ **Playing from a lateral hazard (red stakes).** The only difference between a lateral hazard and a water hazard is that you can drop your ball two *clublengths* from the spot the ball crossed the edge of the hazard, but no closer to the hole. You can't back up as far as you want, like you could if you hit the ball into a water hazard. The penalty is still the same—one stroke. So if you hit your third shot into a lateral hazard, add one shot to your score for the penalty. Then you're hitting your fifth shot with a new ball.

Occasionally, you'll be able to see your ball resting on the edge of a lateral hazard. If the ball is inside the red stakes, you are allowed to go into the hazard and try to hit it, but the rules are the same in there as they are in a sand trap. You can't touch the ground or anything else in the hazard with your club before you hit your ball, and you can't move anything (like rocks or branches) to improve your stance or lie. I would only hit the ball out of a hazard if at least three quarters of the ball is exposed, and you don't have to take off your shoes and socks and get into the water to take your stance. Otherwise, you run the risk of blasting up a bunch of mud and water, covering yourself with gunk, and leaving the ball in the hazard, which means you'll probably have to take the penalty anyway. The only thing worse than losing a penalty shot in a hazard is getting wet and muddy *and* losing a penalty shot in a hazard.

> **Par Primer**
> A **clublength** is the length of the longest club in your bag from the tip of the shaft to the head. Lay the club down on the ground as a big measuring stick when you need to determine one or two clublengths.

Whenever you have to drop a new ball, the procedure is fairly simple. Hold the ball at shoulder height with your arm extended, palm facing the ground. Open your hand and let the ball fall. Don't try to guide it or put any spin on the ball. If the ball starts rolling back into the hazard, you can stop it, pick it up, and drop it again.

Out of Bounds: Stroke and Distance

The three worst words in a golfer's vocabulary are "stroke and distance." Not only do you have to take a penalty stroke when you hit a ball outside the white stakes that line

Caddie's Advice _____

If you think the shot you just hit may have gone out of bounds, to save time, you can immediately hit what's called a *provisional ball*. The provisional ball only counts if your first one is lost or out of bounds. If your first ball is out of bounds, pick it up, take a penalty, and go play the provisional ball.

the outer edge of the course, but you have to go back to the spot you hit the out-of-bounds shot to hit the next one instead of being able to drop near where it went out of bounds. It really is a painful penalty, because you lose both the penalty shot and the yardage you advanced on the shot.

When trying to figure out whether your ball is out of bounds, first find the ball and then make an imaginary line between the white stakes. If the line crosses between your ball and in-bounds, guess what—time to go back to the tee and hit another.

When Moving Your Ball Won't Cost You a Stroke

You can pick up your ball and drop it in a better position in two common situations: when it stops on a cart path, or on ground under repair. Ground under repair is usually circled with a dotted white line in spray paint. If a course has flood damage or is being dug up for construction, you don't have to play from those areas.

To *get relief*, pick up your ball and wipe it off. Find the nearest point (no closer to the hole, of course) that you can take a clear stance (meaning you aren't standing on the cement path, or in the ground under repair area). Move one clublength away from that spot and drop your ball. If you hit onto a cart path or ground under repair, you don't *have* to take a free drop. If the ground under repair is in better shape than any nearby area where you could drop, you might be better off leaving your ball where it is. But that won't happen very often.

Often clubs have local rules about getting relief from certain fences, bleachers, or other temporary structures. They'll be listed either on the scorecard or in the golf shop. For instance, if you're playing in the British Open and you blast a shot into the grandstands surrounding the 18th hole, you don't have to climb up into the crowd and hit your shot from there. Of course, if there were no grandstands, your ball would be sitting in the grass 20 yards from the green. So you could pick up your ball and drop it in a clear spot no closer to the hole than where you landed with no penalty.

Par Primer _____

Legally picking your ball up and moving it to a better position is called **getting relief**.

Other Nefarious Schemes That Inflate Your Score

Aside from hitting your ball into a hazard or out of bounds, the two main ways you'll accumulate penalty strokes are through lost balls or unplayable lies.

If you hit a shot into the woods next to the fairway and the area isn't designated out of bounds, you can wade in there and try to find the ball. One of three things might happen:

- You might find the ball and try to hit it out into the fairway.

- You might find the ball in an unplayable lie, which means you don't have a chance to get a club on it or advance it in any way. If this happens, you can pick up the ball, take a one-stroke penalty, and drop it two clublengths from the spot, or you can go back and hit it from where you played your last shot (which is much more painful, because you lose the yardage).

- You might look for five minutes, not be able to find the ball, and declare it lost. Then you have to go back to the location where you hit the lost ball *and* take a stroke penalty. A lost ball is the least pleasant of the three outcomes.

> **Par Primer**
>
> Stray branches, twigs, stones, leaves, or garbage are called **loose impediments.** You're allowed to move those out of your way as long as you don't move your ball.

Another way to accumulate a penalty shot is to move your ball accidentally while you brush away any *loose impediments* before you get ready to swing.

For example, you're allowed to sweep away twigs, stones, or other debris from around your ball as long as you aren't in a bunker or hazard. However, if you brush a twig away and your ball happens to be resting on it, you get a one-stroke penalty if the ball slides off the twig and rolls a few inches. So be careful.

> **Double Bogey**
>
> Remember, you can mark your ball only if you're on the green. It's illegal to mark your ball on the fringe, the short grass around the green.

Tending the Pin and Other Greenside Bromides

After you make it to the green, you have even more rules and responsibilities to take into consideration. The most important one is marking your ball properly. After all of the players in your group have hit their shots on or near the green, those who are closer to the hole should place a small coin or plastic ball marker in place of the ball. That way, whoever is farthest away can hit a shot at the hole and not worry about his or her ball crashing into somebody else's.

To mark your ball, take your coin or marker and place it on the ground 3 or 4 inches behind your ball. Slide the marker toward the ball until it's almost touching. Let go of the marker and pick up your ball. Tap down the marker with your putter. After you're on the green and you have your ball legally marked, you can pick the ball up and clean off any mud or dirt.

To mark your ball, place a coin just behind your ball (away from the hole) and then take the ball away.

According to golf etiquette, the person farthest away from the hole plays first. Wait until it's your turn to play before you replace your ball on the marker. Set the ball down on the ground just barely in front of the marker and then slide the marker away.

If you've marked your ball and someone else is farther from the hole than you, it's your job to take the flag out of the hole. When you walk toward the cup, make sure that you don't step in someone else's line. That's sacred ground! When you get to the hole, ask whether anyone wants the pin tended. If your partner has a really long putt, he or she might want the flag in the hole to help aim. If someone does want the pin tended, grab the flag near the top with your arm fully extended, keeping your feet as far from the hole as possible. After your partner hits the putt and before the ball gets near you, quickly take out the flag and move away from the hole.

> **Double Bogey**
>
> If one of your playing partners is just off the green on the fringe or in the rough, ask whether he or she wants the pin in or out before you take it from the hole. Some people prefer to leave it in for chip shots. It helps them focus more clearly on the target.

Strange Situations

There will be times when you're in such a strange situation you won't know what to do. The first thing to remember is that the point of the rules of golf is to do what is fair. If you take a moment to think about the situation, you'll probably be able to come up with a reasonable solution that's fair to you and your opponents. Chances are, what you decide will be close to what the rule is. Even if you're carrying a rule book with you, it doesn't cover every situation.

I was playing at a nice course just outside New York City a few years ago when something really bizarre happened. My partner drove his tee shot down the middle of the fairway, as did I. We were walking to our balls when a red fox ran out onto the fairway and picked up my partner's ball and took off with it. The hole was lined with woods on both sides, and the fox bolted into a little opening in the trees on the left side. We were both laughing hysterically, and I ran over to the edge of the trees to see where the fox went. It was sitting there in a clearing 20 yards from the fairway, with the ball in its mouth, looking at me. At its feet was a small pile of about ten balls. Obviously, this had happened before. I took a step toward the fox, and it dropped the ball and ran off. After we finished laughing, we wondered where my friend was supposed to hit his shot from. We decided that the fairest thing to do would be to replace the ball as close as we could figure to the place where the fox stole it from.

You won't be faced with felonious foxes too often, but in situations like that, use your best judgment. A 10-foot alligator lives in one of the ponds near the clubhouse at Grand Cypress in Orlando. If the alligator is sunning itself on the edge of the pond and your ball rolls near him, don't be a fool and go get it. Drop one without a penalty, and let sleeping gators lie!

Breakfast Balls and Mulligans

Many people you play with will have one or two "special" rules they play by that you won't find in the *Rules of Golf*. The most common is called a *mulligan* or *breakfast ball*. Both of these strange terms mean the same thing—if you hit a really bad shot off the tee, you don't have to count it, and you get another try.

If you are playing with mulligans, most groups only allow one per 9 or 18 holes. It isn't an open invitation to take another shot any time you don't like the way one turned

Par Primer

A **mulligan** is an extra shot taken from the tee when you don't like how the original one turned out. It's sometimes known as a **breakfast ball**.

out. If you do get a mulligan, remember that they're only allowed on the tee. You can't use one in the fairway or on the green. Mulligan management is crucial—if you stub one a few yards, but it's still in play, you might want to save your mulligan for a time when you hit a tee shot in the water or out of bounds. Then you can really save yourself some strokes.

The Least You Need to Know

◆ You can use a tee only when you're playing from the tee markers at the beginning of a hole. Place your ball between the markers or no more than two clublengths behind—never ahead.

◆ In general, when you hit into a water hazard, drop at the nearest point to where the ball entered the water, no closer to the hole, and take one penalty stroke.

◆ If you hit a ball out of bounds, you must take a penalty shot and hit again from the same spot.

◆ An unplayable lie costs you one penalty shot, and you can move the ball two clublengths from the spot.

◆ If you lose your ball, you must go back to the spot you played the shot and hit again with one penalty shot.

◆ If your ball stops on a cart path or in an area marked "Ground Under Repair," you can get relief without penalty.

Chapter 17

Course Management: Getting From Here to There

In This Chapter

- ◆ Strategizing for par-three holes
- ◆ Playing par-fours
- ◆ Chopping it down to size: Approaching par-fives
- ◆ Extricating yourself from sticky situations

Even if you just started playing golf last week, you can still start every round you play with a plan. That means having a plan for your round as a whole and also mini-plans for how you will play the different kinds of holes you'll face at the course. In this chapter, I'll go over the basic game plans you'll need to get the most out of your par-three, par-four, and par-five experiences.

The Goal: Play the Percentages

No matter how well you plan, you're going to face some risky shots on the golf course. There's no way around that. As a beginner, your goal should be to take as much risk as you can out of the equation. As you improve and gain confidence, you can afford to take a few more chances in your control over the ball.

The secret to avoiding big scores on a hole is thinking critically about worst-case scenarios. Every time you step onto the tee, you should look around and figure out the worst possible place your ball could go on the shot you're about to hit. After you've picked that spot, you know that's the place to avoid at all costs. Then check off the different directions. If I miss my shot way right, what happens? Will I go out of bounds? What if I go way left? Is there a clearing over there that wouldn't be so bad to play from? What if I hit this shot too far? Is there water up there?

Every time you get ready to hit a shot, you need to ask yourself those kinds of questions. For example, if you hit a slice, you know that most of your long irons and woods will curve from left to right. Survey the hole. If most of the trouble, like thick stands of trees or a pond, is down the right side, you should be aiming far into the rough on the left side of the hole. That way, if your shot flies relatively straight, you might be in the fairway, and you'll be on the safe side of the hole. If your ball slices as expected, you'll be in the middle—or at worst, on the right side—of the fairway. You're taking some of the risk out of the shot. It wouldn't make any sense to aim right down the middle on this hole. Your slice might take the ball right into the trouble.

If you do decide to take a deliberate risk on the course, do it either when the reward is great or the penalty isn't very severe. Let's say that you're playing a long par-five that is wide open. No trees or other kinds of trouble are lining the fairway, so if you hit a shot a little bit wild, you won't suffer too much. You have 180 yards to the green, and your ball is sitting on a nice patch of fairway grass. You have two choices. If you really swing hard and hit a solid 3-wood, you've got a chance to hit the ball on the green. But you really feel the most comfortable hitting an 8-iron and laying up in front of the green so you have an easier shot the next time.

What do you do? Well, there isn't very much risk in trying to hit the 3-wood. You don't have any water or out-of-bounds to worry about. If you top the ball or hit a worm-burner, the ball probably will roll 50 or 60 yards, which still leaves you with a decent shot to the green. There's really no reason not to try the 3-wood. But think of how your decision-making would change if a stream ran right in front of the green. If you miss-hit your 3-wood just a little bit, you might hit into the water. That's a penalty stroke. Now the risk outweighs the reward, and the smart play would be to *lay up* short and play your next shot onto the green.

Par Primer

If you're too far away to reach the green with one shot, try to place your shot in a position that makes your next shot, the one to the green, as easy as possible. This preliminary shot is called a **lay up**.

Par-Threes: Close to the Green Is Close Enough

Early in your golf career, you're probably going to have the most success on par-threes—holes that range from 90 to 230 yards. Playing from the white tees, you won't see too many par-threes longer than 180 yards. As a beginner, you're probably going to be more comfortable hitting shorter shots with irons than long shots with a driver.

The biggest decision when you are on the tee of a par-three hole is club selection. You need to take into consideration the distance between you and the hole, the wind, and the elevation of the green compared to the tee-box. Learning to gauge these factors will not only help you on a par-three, but on any shot to the green on any course. Let's take a quick look at these factors:

♦ **Distance.** Eighty percent of your decision on what club to play will be based on your distance to the hole. The scorecard will tell you the distance from your tees to the middle of the green. Some courses use different color flags to show that the hole is located in the front (toward the tee), middle, or back (away from the tee) of the green. Other courses give you a little map that shows where the holes are that day. Other times, you'll have to use your eyes and your judgment, and adjust your yardage accordingly.

♦ **Wind.** In most circumstances, wind will have a minimal effect on your ball. Only when you can feel the wind tugging at your clothes do you need to start worrying about *taking more* or *less* club, at least at the beginning level. If you can feel a strong breeze on your face, use more club. On a 150-yard hole, if you would normally use a 6-iron, try a 5-iron or 4-iron into a strong breeze. Of course, if a strong breeze is at your back, use less club.

♦ **Altitude.** The difference in elevation between the green and where you are standing will also have an effect on what club you choose. If you're hitting to an elevated green, you need to use more club. A green that's below the level of the tee requires less club than normal. Again, it's a judgment call just how much.

> **Par Primer**
>
> In golf lingo, to **take more club** means to use the next longest club in the set to get more distance (from a 5-iron to a 4-iron, for example). To **take less club** means to go from, a 4-iron to a 5-iron, for example.

Your strategy for a par-three hole should be to expand your aiming area to include not just the green, but a 15-yard wide area around the edge of the green. Think of the green as the bull's-eye of a target. The area just outside the bull's-eye is still worth points, just not as many as hitting the bull's-eye. If you can hit your shot consistently either on the green or no more than 15 yards off, you'll make a lot of bogies. As a beginner, a bogey is a victory. You're shooting for a four.

When you play your shot to an area just off the green, even a below-average chip shot should put you in a position to two-putt for your four. If you miss the green, your goal should be to place your chip shot no more than 20 feet from the hole. Don't obsess about sticking the chip within 2 feet of the cup. Start with 20 feet. When you can chip inside that radius consistently, change your goals.

If you do hit the green with your tee shot on a par-three, congratulations! That's a victory! You're getting better! If your ball is more than 20 feet from the hole, your goal on that first putt should not necessarily be making it. You want to lag your putt with the intent of leaving yourself the easiest possible short second putt. Visualize this shot the same way you did your tee shot. The hole is the bull's-eye, but a 4-foot area around the bull's-eye is just as good. Try to roll that putt into the 4-foot radius. On some, you'll hit your putt quite close, and you'll have a short par putt. On others, you might not be so successful. Taking three putts on a hole isn't the end of the world. It happens to the best of us.

Refer to the following par-three checklist:

1. Determine your yardage to the hole. The distance on the card is to the center of the green. Is the hole up front? In back?

2. Pick a club that will get you to the hole. Most amateurs leave the ball short because they don't use enough club.

3. Decide which side of the green is more favorable should you miss. For example, if there's a pond on the right, aim for the left side of the green to take the trouble out of play.

4. After you decide on a club, commit to it. If you're stuck between clubs, take the longer one and make a smooth swing.

Par-Fours: Do What You Can to Be Straight off the Tee

Remember what I said about bogies on a par-three? As a beginner, a bogey is also your first goal on a par-four. To meet that goal, the first and most important step is to keep your ball in play off the tee. It doesn't matter what club you use. If you can hit your ball at least 170 or 180 yards straight off the tee, you'll be in good position to make a bogey. The average par-four is about 375 yards, so that 170-yard shot will leave you about 200 yards from the hole.

One more 170-yard shot will leave you just short of the green. Then, if you can execute a decent chip and two putts, you've made your bogey and earned another little victory!

As you can see, the farther you can hit your ball with a reasonable degree of accuracy from the tee, the easier the job becomes to get your ball near the green. Beginners run into the most trouble on par-fours when they insist on using a driver off the tee, even if they only hit one good shot out of ten with it. If you're always playing your second shot on a hole from a few yards in front of the tee or the deep grass of the secondary rough, you'll give yourself more trouble than you need. Practice with your driver on the range until you have confidence with it. Until then, use your 3-wood or any other club you can hit reasonably straight off the tee. Like I said, extra distance is a bonus, not a requirement. I would rather be straight and short than crooked and long.

Refer to the following par-four checklist:

1. Hitting your tee shot in the fairway is imperative. Take whatever club you can hit straight and use it off the tee.

2. If you can't get to the green with your second shot, try to place it in the optimum position for your next try. For example, if there's trouble in front and to the left of the green, try to play your second shot down the right side of the fairway so you have a better angle at the hole on your next shot.

3. If you do have a chance to make it to the green on your second shot, lower your sights. Don't just focus on the green, but on a 20-yard area around the green, much like on a par-three.

Par Primer

On a par-four or par-five, a shot hit with intent to reach the green is called the **approach**.

4. Follow the earlier par-three checklist for your *approach* shot.

Par-Fives: Advance the Ball—You've Got Room for Error

The best part about playing par-five holes is that you can incorporate the strategies you've learned for the par-threes and par-fours. When you get within 100 yards of the green, go through the same checklist you would for hitting a tee shot from a par-three. From the tee until the approach on a par-five hole, your strategy should be similar to that of the par-four, with a few differences.

A par-five is much longer than a par-four—usually from 460 to 600 yards. As a result, it's a little more important to get distance off the tee. That doesn't mean you should sacrifice too much accuracy. If the par-five hole you're playing has a tight fairway (trees or other problem areas very close to the sides of the fairway), sacrifice distance from the tee to hit the ball relatively straight. If the hole is a little more wide open, this is your chance to experiment with your driver. On a wide-open hole, even a wild shot with the driver shouldn't hurt you too much. At worst, you'll just play your second shot from the fairway of the next hole over. There's nothing wrong with that. Just be careful and keep your eyes open for people hitting shots near you on that hole. They might not be expecting you or watching out for you.

No matter what kind of shot you decide to play on a par-five, do your best to advance the ball on each swing. Because these holes are so long, shanked or topped shots are particularly damaging to your score, because they don't give you very much distance. As I mentioned earlier, unless the hole is constricted by trees or water, you can afford to risk using a little more club to gain distance. Accuracy isn't as much of a premium until you make your approach shot.

Refer to the following par-five checklist:

1. Accuracy is less of a premium off the tee on a par-five. You need to get some distance. Go with your driver or 3-wood.

2. When off the tee, advancing the ball is your biggest priority. Even if you don't hit a shot perfectly, getting it down the fairway and toward the hole is important.

3. When you're in position to try for the green, follow the earlier par-three checklist.

Thorny Problems and How to Deal with Them

In the scenarios I presented in the previous section, I didn't touch on some of the difficulties you'll inevitably run into on a given hole. If course management were as easy as I just made it sound, golf would be a simple game. But you know as well as I do that golf isn't easy. You can have a plan, but part of that plan has to include getting yourself out of tricky situations. Here are some of the most common ones and the best ways to try and escape them:

◆ **Water in front.** When I play with beginners, I usually ask them what their biggest fear is on the golf course. Most of the time, they say that hitting over a water hazard makes them the most nervous. I can understand why. If you're still working on building a swing you can have confidence in, seeing that expanse of blue in front of you can be disconcerting, especially if you're having trouble getting the ball up in the air. I can't give you any tip that will make your ball float, but the best thing to do is to focus on a spot 15 yards past the water hazard as your real target. Judge the distance to that spot and then take the club you're most comfortable with hitting that yardage and fire away. If you can, don't think about steering the shot as you swing. Give a normal, aggressive swing. If the ball goes in the water, don't worry too much. You can buy three for a buck.

◆ **Fairway bunkers.** These shots present difficulties for even the professionals, so don't feel bad if fairway bunkers give you fits. Your first priority when hitting from a fairway bunker is getting the ball out of the sand. The only thing worse than a shot from a fairway bunker is two shots in a row from the same fairway bunker. For beginners, I recommend hitting a sand wedge or pitching wedge and not even worrying about distance. Play it just like the greenside sand shot you learned in Chapter 11. Aim for a point 20 yards outside the bunker in the fairway and make that your intermediate goal. When you're safely out of the sand, you can play for the green on your next shot. If you want to try to use a longer iron from the sand, widen your stance so you have a stable base. Choke up a little bit on the club and try to pick the ball directly off the surface of the sand. In other words, try to take as little a divot as possible.

◆ **Tight squeezes.** If you're stuck in the trees, but you have a small alley out to the fairway, your highest-percentage play is to keep the ball as close to the ground as possible. Using a 3- or 4-iron, hit this shot like an aggressive bump and run. You want your ball to take one low, quick hop and then run along the ground out of the opening and back onto the fairway. Tree branches get more and more tangled the higher you go on a tree, so the lower you keep the shot, the fewer things your ball can get tangled in.

◆ **Blind shots.** Aiming for a target you can't see can be a little disconcerting. The easiest way to take the uncertainty out of this shot is to walk or drive ahead and get a look at the target and then go back to a point where you can see both your ball and the target. Find an intermediate target on or close to the ground that your ball will fly over if it's on target and aim for that. If the target is on the other side of a hill, go to the top of the hill and look for a distinctive tree growing in the background behind that target. When you address your ball, aim for the top of that distinctive tree.

◆ **Carry to the fairway.** Much like shots over water, a shot that requires a carry over a swamp or weedy area to the fairway can give a beginner fits. If the distance to the fairway is relatively short, under 150 yards, use the same visualization technique I talked about for the shot over water. Aim for a spot 15 yards past the edge of the water and take enough club to get it to that spot. The additional loft you'll be using on a mid-iron instead of the driver will give you a greater margin for error and a better chance to get the ball up in the air and over the trouble.

My favorite trouble shot is a low, running hook out from under trees. If I get in trouble off the tee and send my drive into the forest down the left side of the fairway, I have a simple, effective plan for extricating myself. If I can't hit my shot directly toward the hole, but there's an opening to the right, I take a 4- or 5-iron and close the face (point it to the left of the target). Playing the ball back (away from the target in my stance), I use a three-quarters–strength swing and punch the ball out. If I do it properly, the ball will hook down the fairway and roll for quite a ways.

The Least You Need to Know

- ◆ Play the percentages in your golf game. Don't take unnecessary risks.

- ◆ On a par-three, think of the green as the bull's-eye and a 20-yard ring around the green as a part of your target.

- ◆ On a par-four, your primary goal is to keep your tee shot in play.

- ◆ On a par-five, advance the ball on every shot. Distance is more of a premium.

- ◆ Take the highest-percentage avenue of escape available to you when you're in trouble.

Chapter 18

Golf and Fitness

In This Chapter

- Getting your muscles in gear
- Taking care of yourself on the course
- Performing on-course triage: First aid

The golf swing is a pretty violent action. It takes sweeping moves from your arms, shoulders, hips, and legs. Whenever you use so many different muscles in such an aggressive, quick movement, you run the risk of pulling or straining something. If you use the simple warm-up drills we'll be going over in this chapter, you'll save yourself some uncomfortable mornings after playing golf when you wake up stiff and sore.

I'll also go over what safety precautions you need to observe when you're playing and what kind of first-aid supplies you should carry with you in your bag.

Five Basic Warm-Up Stretches

If you're late for your tee time and rushing to get your clubs from the trunk and to the first tee, the last thing on your mind will be stretching.

But if you want to get the most from your body and limit muscle soreness and stiffness the next day, stretching and warming up before you play is absolutely vital.

With a good set of warm-up exercises, you start moving the muscles you'll be using in your golf swing slowly, getting them gradually ready for the next four or five hours of golf. And if you follow a regular stretching routine five or six days a week, whether you play a round of golf or not, over the course of a few months, you'll notice a dramatic increase in flexibility. That increase in flexibility is what gives you extra distance from your driver—the more you can turn your shoulders in relation to your hips in the backswing, the more quickly you can swing. A quicker swing means more distance. Ever since I started working out with a trainer, I've seen a dramatic improvement in my game, just because of my fitness.

The major groups of muscles you use in the swing are the ones in the shoulders, arms, and upper and lower legs. In a best-case scenario, you should thoroughly stretch each of these muscle groups before you play a round or hit balls at the range. The five drills I'm going to describe here are basic ones to use before you play, or even during a round as you wait on the tee. They all use a golf cart as a brace, but if you're walking and carrying your own bag, you can just as easily use a tree. Let's go over the stretches:

◆ **Shoulder and chest stretches.** This stretch helps you loosen the big muscles across your chest and back, which are normally wound very tightly. By holding this stretch for about 10 seconds, you gradually loosen that tension, which makes it easier for you to bring the club back smoothly and completely in your backswing. It also feels really good!

Stand next to the front roof post of your golf cart. Take a small step forward (toward the front of the cart). The post should be about a foot behind you. Reach across your body with your left arm and grab the post with your left hand. Don't turn your shoulders toward the cart. After you've got a hold of the post, turn your shoulders away from the cart until you can feel the big muscles across your back stretch. Pain isn't the goal, just an easy stretch. Hold this for 10 seconds. Let go and then take one step away from the side of the cart, until you can reach your right arm straight from your body and grab the post. After you've grabbed the post, move forward toward the front of the cart until you can feel the muscles across your chest stretch. Hold for 10 seconds and let go. Go over to the other side of the cart and repeat these two exercises, but using the opposite arms and hands.

Standing one step away from the cart's front roof post, facing away from the cart, straight from your body and grasp the bar.

◆ **Hamstring and calf stretches.** This stretch helps you loosen the long muscles in the backs of your legs. Keeping your legs straight, hold your driver straight up and down against the ground, and lean forward and stretch against your driver. The farther you can drop your head between your arms, the more you'll stretch those hamstrings.

By bracing yourself against your driver, you can get a great hamstring stretch in.

◆ **Lower back stretches.** The number-one physical problem of all golfers over the age of 50 is low back pain. Many of those problems come from outside of golf, but why put any more stress on your body than you have to when you're out enjoying yourself? This single stretch, held for 20 seconds, helps you loosen the muscles that run vertically down your back.

Place your feet close together, near the rear wheel of the golf cart. Grab the handle next to the cart's seat. Hold it with both hands, like you would if you were doing a pull-up. Slowly slide your hips down and back, as if you were going into a skiing tuck position or a baseball catcher's squat. Pull your hips back against the resistance of your hands holding the handle, and you'll feel the muscles stretch in your lower back. Hold for 20 seconds.

◆ **Lunges.** This exercise also works your hamstrings, and it loosens the upper body and thighs. Take your driver and slide it behind your neck. Hold one end in each hand and brace the shaft across the back of your shoulders. You should feel a slight stretch across the front of your chest and in your upper arms. After you have the club in place, step with your right foot onto the floor of the cart.

◆ **Torso and back stretches.** To finish, hold a club behind your back, across your shoulders, and stand with your feet a little bit closer together than in your regular golf stance. Then slowly make a full backswing turn and then a full forward swing turn. Repeat this five or six times. Now you should be ready to play!

Holding a club behind your shoulders, take a narrow stance and make slow back-swing and forward-swing turns. Holding the club this way really loosens the back, torso, and chest.

In the Gym

As a sort of addendum, I'll give you a list of some of the other stretches I do in the gym, in case you're interested in building a flexibility program of your own in addition to the on-course drills I just talked about.

When I'm at the gym, I work on the major muscle groups I talked about earlier, but I also try to do extra work on my hip flexors and waist. I found that when I built up the muscles in my stomach and increased the flexibility in my hips, I could turn much more easily, which has helped me increase my distance. Here are a couple of the exercises I do three times a week:

◆ **Hip flexor.** With my back flat on an exercise mat, I put my left foot on a wall. Then I cross my right leg over my left and put my right foot on my left knee. With my right hand, I press gently on my right knee. The pressure causes my right hip flexor to stretch. I'll hold that for 15 seconds and then alternate legs and do the same for the left. Taking it one step further, I leave my right foot on my left knee, and with my shoulders pressed to the floor, I turn my hips to the right until my right hip is flat on the floor. Then I alternate as before. This stretches the muscles in my sides.

With your back flat on the floor and left foot against the wall, cross your right leg over your left, putting your right foot on your left knee. Push gently on your right knee until you feel the stretch in your right hip.

◆ **Hamstring.** This drill isn't very practical on the course because there isn't anywhere to lay down, but in the gym, it works great. I lay with my back flat on the ground, bring my knees as close to my chest as I can, and pull them toward me with my hands, as hard as I can. I get a good stretch in my gluteus muscles (buttocks), hamstrings, and lower back.

With your back flat on the floor, grab your knees and pull them to your chest as hard as you can.

Taking Care of Yourself on the Course

You have much less chance of getting injured out on the golf course, than say, in a basketball game, but you need to take certain health factors into consideration. If you're playing on a sunny day, you need to be very careful about your exposure to the sun. It's easy to get a bad sunburn if you aren't used to being exposed for four or five hours at a time. A good hat and some sunscreen are an essential part of your preparation.

Most courses have water coolers situated every few holes, usually at the tees. Drink plenty of water. If you aren't a big fan of tap water, bring along a sports drink like Gatorade. When you make the turn (finishing 9 holes of 18 rounds), you'll often have the opportunity to stop at a snack bar and get something to eat and drink. In addition, on many courses an attendant in a cart with a cooler on the back will drive around selling drinks and snacks. However, it's usually cheaper to bring a candy bar or sandwich with you than to buy the snack-bar food.

Double Bogey

It's perfectly acceptable to bring a sandwich and candy bar to a public course to munch on during a round, but if you're playing at an upscale club, bringing a bag lunch is considered tasteless.

On a hot day, you really can't drink enough. Golf might not seem like the most physically taxing game, but if you don't drink enough fluids, you will feel drained and tired at the end of your round. Your swing will suffer, and you'll lose concentration easily. Bad swings and lapses in concentration never help you out on the course.

If you drink alcohol while you play, you should drink in moderation, because not only are you probably driving a golf cart around the course, you'll most likely be driving a real car home afterward. If you do decide to have a few beers on the course, remember that alcohol has a dehydrating effect, so alternate between beer and big glasses of water.

Lastly, no matter what you're drinking or eating, remember to keep all your garbage in your cart or bag. Throw it all away at the end of the round in a garbage can. Don't toss it on the course. For one, it's littering, and your partners will think you don't have respect for the course. Also, more than one person has been stymied in the rough or a bunker when their ball has landed on a piece of paper or plastic somebody left lying around. If you're playing by the rules, then you have to play that ball as it lies.

Golf Bag First Aid

The most common injury that occurs on the course is a blister. You can prevent most blisters with a good golf glove (which I'll talk more about in later chapters), but if you do have a blister, it's helpful to have a bandage to cover it with. In fact, it makes sense to dedicate one of the smaller pockets of your golf bag as a first-aid kit of sorts. You don't need to put too many things in this pocket, just a few essentials to tide you over in case of a mini-emergency:

◆ **Bandages.** Four or five strips of different sizes can cover blisters or other little cuts you might get out on the course.

◆ **Bug repellent.** A small can of bug repellent is worth its weight in gold on wet mornings in the summer. I grew up in South Florida, where some of the mosquitoes grew as big as small birds. We never left home without some extra bug spray.

◆ **Adhesive tape.** A miracle product, adhesive tape works great in place of a bandage if you've got a blister on your finger. Just wrap a few layers of the tape (cloth works best) around the affected finger, and off you go. Adhesive tape can also keep a loose part of a club grip in place until you get a chance to get it fixed properly. Keep a small roll handy.

◆ **Sunscreen.** Keep a small tube of it in your bag in case you forget to put some on before you come to the course. When the hot August sun starts rising over the trees, you'll be glad it's there.

◆ **Aspirin or pain reliever.** I don't know how many times my playing partner has asked me whether I had any aspirin. I never do, and I always wish I had one or two of those little packets stuck somewhere in my bag. They don't take up much space, and you never know when you'll get a headache.

◆ **Extra socks.** The first time I developed a blister on my heel during a round, I didn't have an extra pair of socks or a bandage in my bag. By the time I hobbled into the locker room after the round, the heel of my sock was covered in blood, and my foot was raw. Ever since, I've always carried bandages and an extra pair of socks. If I do get a blister, I put a bandage on it and slip on the extra pair of socks over the ones I'm already wearing, so I have an extra layer of cushioning between the shoe and my foot.

Extra Swings

Lightning is the most serious danger you can face on the golf course. Nothing could be more serious—if you get zapped, you can be killed. People on the golf course are susceptible to lightning strikes because oftentimes they are the tallest things in the middle of a wide-open field. Plus, a golf club makes a pretty good lightning rod. Or they take cover underneath a tree, which is the absolute worst place you can go.

If the weather looks ominous, the first thing you need to do is listen. Most courses you play at will sound a warning horn if lightning has struck in the area. Don't finish out that putt. Get back to the clubhouse as fast as you can. Leave the ball there. Nobody is going to take it. If you don't hear a warning horn, but see lightning in the distance, get back to the clubhouse if you can or make for one of the weather shelters spread out around most courses. These shelters have lightning rods on top that will deflect any strikes. If no shelter is available, put down your clubs and stay in the open.

Golf and My Handicap

One of the biggest decisions I ever had to make was to turn pro right out of high school instead of playing for at least two years in college. One of the main factors in my decision was the fact that I have diabetes. We've learned a lot about this disease, but there are a lot of things we still don't know. When I was 17 and 18 years old, I wasn't sure (and neither were my doctors or parents) just how long of an active athletic career I'd be able to have. Because my health was a wild card, I decided to turn pro out of high school to be able to maximize my professional career. Luckily enough for me, my parents had the time to travel quite a bit with me those first few years, and I developed a good routine to deal with my disease.

Now, it's hardly a factor. The two most obvious things I worry about are getting enough exercise and eating reasonably well. Accomplishing these two things takes care of many of the problems most diabetics have, and I've been lucky to avoid any severe complications. I've also known my own limitations. I have to be very sensitive to what my body tells me. If I feel tired, I don't push it. I go home and get some rest. I think my career will be extended because of those precautions.

Regardless of whether your problem is diabetes or something else, the best thing for you to do is to get good, up-to-date information from your doctor about the things you can and cannot do. Golf is a wonderful game because people of all ages and condition levels can play. No matter how well or how poorly you hit the ball, it's still a nice walk in beautiful surroundings. It can be very therapeutic.

The Least You Need to Know

♦ Warm up the major muscle groups you'll be using in your swing—the shoulders, back, hamstrings, and arms—before you play or practice.

♦ On a hot day, plenty of water is available around the course. Drink it.

♦ Bandages, bug repellent, adhesive tape, sunscreen, aspirin, and an extra pair of socks are always good things to have in your golf bag.

Chapter 19

Dressing the Part

In This Chapter

- Dressing for success: What to wear on the course
- Staying cool and dry: Sun and rain gear
- Starting off on the right foot: Choosing the right golf shoes

Unless you live in a *very* liberal community, you won't be playing golf naked. That means you're going to need some clothes. Most of what you'll be wearing, you already have (but please, no jeans …), but you will need a few specialized things like golf shoes. I'll talk about those things in this chapter.

Golf Is Not a Game of Polyester

If you've ever seen footage of a pro golf tournament in the 1970s or early 1980s, then you know all about bad fashion. For a while there, it seemed like those guys were having a competition to see who could look the silliest on any given day—lime-green polyester, mismatching plaid patterns, the works. The women's tour was a little better, but not much. The mini-dresses they used to wear might still be fashionable for a night on the town, but thankfully we don't have to wear them to play golf in anymore.

Luckily enough, as younger people started to embrace golf, the clothes have improved. Now, you can buy golf clothes that are actually fashionable and wear them on or off the golf course. And a lot of sportswear not specifically designed for the golf course is acceptable as well. You've got a lot more choices.

Of course, many people still seem to take great pride in dressing loudly. At any course, you're bound to find a guy with radical plaid slacks and a lemon-colored golf shirt, or a woman sporting a matching maroon and teal sweater-and-shorts combination. In this day and age, I think it has more to do with making a statement of individuality than it does with bad taste. At least I hope so!

No Shirt, No Shoes, No Service

When you're thinking about what to wear to the course, you need to keep a few things in mind: the dress code of the club you'll be playing, comfort, and the weather.

Regardless of what course you play—public, private, or otherwise—a shirt with a collar (for men and women) is a must. I realize some courses don't mind if you play in a t-shirt, but I believe golf is a game with sophistication and class. Take pride in your appearance and wear a collar. A polo or tennis shirt is fine.

> **Double Bogey**
>
> When a club has a long-pants requirement, they usually enforce it. If you forget and wear shorts, the pro will be happy to sell you a pair of pants (of the grossly overpriced, designer variety, of course) from what's available in the pro shop. That will put an extra $85 or $100 dent in your wallet.

Some courses have more strict dress requirements. They might ask you to wear long pants or shorts that reach at least knee-length. Generally, if you're playing at a public course, knee-length shorts are acceptable. No matter how comfortable they are, keep the running shorts or cut-offs in your drawer. At a private club, men are often expected to wear long pants, but women usually can wear knee-length shorts or skirts.

At no time should you take your shirt off while out on the course (men or women). If your body isn't so great, nobody wants to see it. If it *is* great, nobody wants to be distracted! Here's a simple uniform that is acceptable for any course you play, regardless of whether it is public, private, or resort.

For men:

- Polo shirt or golf shirt, in a solid color or subtle pattern
- Solid-colored belt that matches the color of your shoes
- Khaki, navy, or black pants

- ◆ White socks
- ◆ Golf shoes (preferably polished)

For women:

- ◆ Polo shirt or golf shirt, in a solid color or subtle pattern
- ◆ Loose-fitting, knee-length shorts or skirt or pants
- ◆ Ankle-high white socks
- ◆ Golf shoes

These are basic, boring outfits that don't really show your personality, but they are safe fashion choices. When you get a feel for what the dress code of the course you're playing most frequently allows, use your imagination. Just like your regular clothes, your golf clothes should reflect your personality. For years, Gary Player wore nothing but black shirts, pants, and shoes. He had no trouble mixing and matching in the morning!

It's important to follow the dress code of the course, but it is equally important to wear clothes that are comfortable. To make a good golf swing, you need freedom of movement in your upper arms, back, and waist. Wearing clothes that are too tight might restrict your swing. You'll also be doing a lot of squatting and bending to rake sand traps, pick up balls, and check the line of a putt on the green. Few things are as embarrassing as ripping your pants during a deep-knee bend because they were too tight. If you're out in the middle of the course, you have nowhere to hide that big rip, so you'll have to live with it until you get back to the clubhouse. Spare yourself the aggravation and think of practicality before you think of seductiveness.

I also don't recommend wearing any expensive fabrics like silk on the course. If it's a hot day, you'll be sweating. If the course is a little bit wet, your pants and shirt will be covered with flecks of mud. Good-quality cotton is your best choice for shirts and pants because it's lightweight and breathable, and if it gets dirty, you can clean it without too much trouble. That beautiful silk shirt might look great on the hanger, but after you sweat through 18 holes, you'll wish you had something a little more absorbent.

When I play somewhere that's colder than my native Florida, I keep in the trunk of my car a plain black or gray sweatshirt that's one size too big for me. If it's a little chilly, I can slip the sweatshirt on over my golf shirt and I still have enough flexibility to take a normal swing. Don't wear

Caddie's Advice

Stick to 100 percent cotton clothing. It's more comfortable than other fabrics, and it breathes, keeping you cooler.

one that's too oversized, though—the sleeves will hang down over your hands, and you'll be pushing them up all day.

Keep the Sun Out

Of all the things I wear on the course, my hat is my favorite. The LPGA has its own dress code when it comes to shirts, shorts, and pants, but we can wear whatever kinds of hats we want. My hat is the way I express my individuality. I think it makes it easier for my fans to recognize me from far away.

Caddie's Advice _____

If you have thinning hair, it's crucial for you to wear a hat on sunny days. As you may have already discovered, scalp burns aren't so pleasant.

The big hat didn't start out as a fashion statement, however. I have very fair skin, and if I didn't wear a hat or put on a lot of sunscreen, I'd get sunburned pretty quickly. Baseball hats only covered the top of my face, but the larger hat with the brim all the way around kept the back of my neck out of the sun, which is intense in a Florida summer. I wore those big hats so often that they became my trademark. I've got dozens in a big closet at home.

Quite a few pro golfers who are now in their 50s and 60s have had to deal with small skin tumors on their faces because of their long-term exposure to the sun. Luckily, many of them managed to catch the skin cancer in time, but you should learn from them and avoid too much sun from the beginning. Regardless of your skin tone, always wear a hat and strong sunscreen. Fortunately, you can now purchase sunscreen that isn't greasy and that sprays on like bug spray. It's great for golfers because greasy sunscreen is a nightmare to clean off your hands, and if you don't get it all off, it can make you lose your grip. I recommend putting strong sunscreen on the tops of your arms (especially your forearms) before you tee off and then wearing a hat with a brim that at least covers the top part of your face.

GoreTex: Your Rainy-Day Friend

Some people just hate to play golf in the rain. It doesn't matter if it's just sprinkling or if the clouds are really threatening. They just won't go out unless the weather is reasonably nice. Others will play through anything—wind, rain, and sometimes even snow. You have your own tolerance level for weather that's less than perfect.

In places like Florida, weather can move in and out very quickly. The sun might be shining when you leave in the morning, but by the 10th or 11th hole, rain is pouring down. That's why you need at least a rain jacket in your bag and preferably an entire rain suit.

You can get a plastic, slicker-type pullover for about $15 and can keep it folded in your golf bag in case it rains. If you only play a few times a year, one of these is more than sufficient. If you decide to play more frequently, you should probably invest in a GoreTex (or other breathable, water-resistant material) rain shirt. A rain shirt looks just like a sweatshirt, except it's made of water-resistant material. A nice one will cost you between $45 and $100. Make sure it's big enough to fit comfortably over your golf shirt and a sweater. Use the same general rule of thumb for rain shirts as for sweatshirts—if it hangs over your hands, it's too big. A good rain shirt will keep you dry in a drizzle and enable you to make a reasonably complete swing. You'll be a little bit hindered no matter what kind you wear, just because it's another layer of clothing, but the rain shirt shouldn't bind you at all.

You can buy a complete rain suit, which includes the rain shirt and a pair of water-resistant pants, at any golf shop. The pants slide on over your regular pants or shorts and keep your legs dry. A rain suit will cost anywhere from $60 to $200.

One new piece of rain gear I like is the short-sleeved rain shirt. It covers more than a vest, but the short sleeves make it less restricting than a long-sleeved shirt. Some of them even have a zip front, making them easy to get on and off.

> **Caddie's Advice**
>
> If your ball is sitting inside a water hazard, but on the water's edge, put your rain pants on before you swing, so any water or mud you blast up won't get on your clothes.

Golf Shoes: Getting a Grip

I've saved the golf shoes for last in this chapter, but in many ways, good spikes are the most important part of the uniform. If you swing with any kind of power, you need golf shoes with cleats on the bottom to keep your feet anchored in the grass. An occasional player can get away with playing in tennis shoes, but if you expect to play the game seriously and want to be taken seriously by your playing partners, golf shoes are one of the first investments you need to make, along with golf clubs.

You can buy a good pair of golf shoes for less than $40, and one pair will last two or three seasons if you take care of them. Waterproof models are also available, but you can expect to spend at least $60 for shoes with that feature. If you can afford it, I recommend buying waterproof golf shoes, because walking 18 holes with damp feet is something you shouldn't have to experience. Wet feet blister faster, and that squishy feeling you get from wet socks just isn't very nice. Spending $20 or $30 more for those waterproof shoes will pay off after one round on a really wet course.

Let's go over the basics of buying a pair of golf shoes:

◆ **Sneakers versus spikes.** For a long time, the only advantage golf shoes had over sneakers was traction. Basketball or running shoes were much more comfortable than the stiff leather golf shoes, but serious golfers sacrificed some of that comfort for the confidence they got from the one-and-a-half-inch spikes on the bottom of golf shoes. Now, major sneaker manufacturers are making golf shoes that are designed to feel like basketball or running shoes with cleats. The comfort level has increased tremendously. As a result, the traditional golf shoe companies have been making more sneaker-type golf shoes themselves to keep up. Even the traditional, saddle-shoe types now have sneakerlike inserts that make them more comfortable.

Put all of this together, and it means the average golfer has more choices. Having that many options will help you, because some manufacturers' shoes tend to run wide, and others tend to run narrow. Some have higher arches, and others are relatively flat. The variation in the different brands makes it easier to find a pair of shoes that fits your feet properly.

◆ **What kind of spikes should you use?** Until about 10 years ago, you only had two choices. Golf shoes either had the standard, three-quarter–inch spikes, or they had small plastic nubs, like softball shoes. The plastic-nubbed shoes were significantly inferior to spikes and were really used only by people with serious knee injuries who couldn't risk having their feet planted in the turf with spikes.

> **Extra Swings**
>
> Most golf shoes have individual threaded holes for each spike. A normal shoe has four spikes on the heel, and seven or eight arranged around the ball and toe of the shoe. With a special wrench, you twist the spike into the shoe as you would a screw into a board. An average plastic spike wears down after about 10 rounds. It doesn't cost much—$10 for a new set—so don't risk losing traction by letting them go too long.

In the early 1990s, several companies started to market soft spikes, which are plastic or hard rubber nipples or swirls that screw into the same standard threads as a metal spike. Metal spikes leave little holes in the green as you walk. Soft spikes were designed to minimize this damage. Because the soft spikes are better for greens, most clubs forbid metal spikes. Most of these clubs will put the new spikes in your shoes for you if you don't have them (for a fee, of course). A side benefit of the rubberized cleats is that they are more comfortable to walk in than metal spikes. They do, however, wear out much more quickly. Pros haven't completely endorsed soft spikes yet because they don't grip as well as metal spikes in wet conditions, but they're improving every year, and the gap has almost closed.

◆ **These boots are made for walking.** No matter what kind of spikes you choose, remember that you're going to be doing a lot of walking in your new golf shoes. Try on several pairs before you decide. Walk around the store a little in each pair. Don't expect that the shoes will break in and be more comfortable later. If they pinch your feet in the store, they'll murder you on the course. If you can, wear a pair of dress shoes to the store when you're browsing for golf shoes. If you're wearing a pair of your favorite old sneakers, new golf shoes might feel unnatural when you try them on. Also, be sure to try the shoes on with the kind of socks you'll be wearing when you play. Golf shoes that fit great with your thin dress socks might not feel as great with some cotton athletic socks. You'll be walking between 8 and 10 miles during an average 18-hole round. You don't want shoes that will hurt your feet.

◆ **Get the wet out.** Waterproofing is an important feature on golf shoes. You can buy bargain-basement shoes that aren't waterproof, but the slick leather finish prevents you from using any kind of spray to make them waterproof yourself. The wide stitching along the sole also makes it tough to keep the water out. Shoes that are made to be waterproof have double rows of stitching along the sole and a chemical treatment on both sides of the leather that keeps moisture out. With the best shoes, you can stick your foot into a pond halfway up the side of the shoe and your sock will stay dry. Of course, you pay for that privilege—top-of-the-line waterproof golf shoes can cost as much as $300.

Caddie's Advice

When I find golf shoes that really feel good, I buy two pairs and alternate them. That way, both pairs last longer than if I bought one pair, wore them out, then went out and got another. It saves you money in the long run.

◆ **Women's shoes.** With the explosion in popularity of women's golf, most of the major shoe companies make several different models of women's shoes. Because this is the case, avoid buying a smaller-size man's shoe. The proportions of a man's foot are different than a woman's, and even if the shoe fits the general length and width of your foot, you won't get as good a fit as you would with a women's shoe. I've tried to

Caddie's Advice

In the last few years, golf sandals have become more popular for casual rounds. They're obviously not waterproof, but they are incredibly comfortable, and your feet stay nice and cool. They're way too casual for use at a private club, however.

stay away from specific product endorsements in this book, but FootJoy, the largest golf shoe maker in the United States, offers nearly as many women's models as they do men's shoes, and they really pay attention to the differences in men's and women's feet. All other things being equal, they give you the biggest choice of styles and colors.

The Least You Need to Know

- Check the dress code of the course you will be playing, but wherever you play, wear a shirt with a collar.

- Wear loose-fitting clothes that won't hinder your arms and shoulders and won't make it tough for you to bend over.

- Keep a waterproof jacket and pants in your bag in case it rains.

- Golf shoes will help you keep your footing during a swing.

- Most courses don't allow metal spikes because of the damage they do to greens. Soft spikes are your best option.

- You'll walk between 8 and 10 miles during an 18-hole round, so make sure that your golf shoes are comfortable.

Part 5

Beyond the Basics

It's time to concentrate on some of the more advanced themes in the game. In Chapter 20, you'll get everything you need to know about accessories—things you need in addition to your clubs, shoes, and balls. Then we'll move on to something more exciting—gambling. Of course, if you're going to gamble, you need to know the rules. We'll take a much more thorough look at them in Chapter 22. In Chapter 23, I'll teach you how to keep your eyes open for cheating.

The last two chapters of this book deal with some issues larger than the game itself. Chapter 24 will touch on golf and business—playing this game with your boss or co-workers and what's appropriate. If you like what you've read in this book, you'll find information in Chapter 25 about how to join some of the golf associations around the country.

Chapter

20

Accessories: All That Other Stuff

In This Chapter

- ◆ Choosing the right golf bag for the kind of golf you play
- ◆ Considering pull carts and other major accessories
- ◆ Finding a golf glove that fits you
- ◆ Taking care of your equipment
- ◆ Keeping tabs on tees and other small accessories

You've got a set of clubs and some golf shoes. You went out and bought a dozen golf balls. You're ready to go out and play. Wait a second! It isn't quite that simple. You still need a few detail accessories before you're ready to play.

Some golf mega-stores have aisles and aisles dedicated to accessories—ball retrievers, plastic practice balls, tube inserts for your golf bag, hand-held scoring and distance calculators. You could spend hours, and hundreds of dollars, on all these products. Some of them are worthwhile, but many are junk. In this chapter, I'm going to focus on the few major accessories you need before you go out and play your first round. After you've played a few times, you can wander all those aisles and decide for yourself whether you really need an electronic grip for your 5-iron that beeps when your backswing is too fast, or a practice green with little motors under the surface that will automatically shift to give you a different break for every putt.

A Good Bag Is a Life-Saver

If you are going to be serious about playing golf, your clubs and your bag are two areas you shouldn't skimp on. If you plan to ride in a cart most of the time, the importance of a golf bag is diminished a little bit, but if you're ever going to carry your clubs (and I highly recommend walking as much as possible when you play), you want a bag that makes this a pleasure instead of a pain.

Bags come in several different varieties. A tour bag is the giant leather model you see the professionals using on television. A tour bag is completely waterproof and has lots of big pockets to carry a full rain-suit and any other extra goodies the caddie needs during the round—it's also got lots of room for sponsors' logos. Notice that we don't have to carry our tour bags. In fact, we're paying someone specifically to lug that thing around all day. A full tour bag weighs more than 50 pounds. My caddie is invaluable to me for the advice he gives me during the round, but it's also a big help that he's carrying that big bag. I pay him 5 percent of all the money I win in tournaments, and 10 percent of any winner's check. He earns every dollar.

The next size down from a tour bag is a cart bag. Cart bags aren't quite as big as tour bags, but they are a little too bulky for the average golfer who is going to carry clubs and play at the same time. These bags are made of leather and nylon and are designed to be used on a riding cart. You don't need one of these.

If I had to play and carry my own bag at the same time, I would leave the big tour bag or cart bag sitting in my garage. Instead, I would use a travel or carry bag, which is much smaller and lighter than a full-size bag. Most are made from plastic and nylon, and they have special straps designed to be easy on your shoulder. A carry bag will fit all of your clubs, a few balls, and some other small accessories, but not much else. That's okay, however, because you can leave most of the extra stuff in the trunk of your car.

Carry bags vary in size, quality, and price. You can buy a tiny, three-quarter–size carry bag for a child, or you can get a deluxe model with plenty of pockets and a special backpack-type strap that goes over both shoulders. The backpack strap is a great feature that moves the weight from one shoulder and spreads it out over both. It makes carrying your bag much more comfortable.

Just like clubs and shoes, you generally get what you pay for. Discount golf shops sell a few bags for about $50, but these are at the extreme low end. They don't look very nice, have very basic features, have only a few pockets, and they aren't very comfortable to carry. If you're only going to play once or twice in a year, then this kind of bag is sufficient.

If you're willing to spend more than $100, you can get a high-quality, light carry bag that will stand on its own when you put it down. When you set the bag down, two plastic legs that sit tight against the side of the bag while you're carrying it will pop out. That way, the bag sits on a little tripod and doesn't get wet or dirty on the ground. A bag on a stand is also much easier to move clubs in and out of. If you're going to buy a new bag, a stand is one feature I think is really worthwhile.

Caddie's Advice _____

If you decide to travel with your clubs, you'll need to invest in a club cover. A cover, which costs anywhere from $40 to $150, slides over your entire bag and protects it and your clubs.

The bag on the left is an intermediate-size cart bag. It has more room and pockets than a carry bag but is rather bulky to carry. The tour bag on the right is made from top-grain leather, and is used mostly by professionals. It's so heavy, pros have to hire someone to carry it!

A carry bag like this one is lightweight, yet it has enough room for all of your clubs. This model has legs that extend automatically when you put it down.

Extra Swings

If you do decide to carry your bag, the process has a definite science. By carrying it the right way, you'll save your clubs—and your back—from getting beaten up in the process. To start, stand your golf bag on the ground. If you're right-handed, stand the bag next to you on the left side. If you're left-handed, stand it on the right. The strap should face to the outside. Grab the top of the strap, near where it connects to the bag, and lift the bag to shoulder height. Set the thick part of the strap on your shoulder. The bag should now be resting off the ground on your shoulder. With the hand that's closest to the bag, push down on the tops of your clubs. This will make the other end of the bag rotate up into the air. Now, keep that hand resting on the heads of your clubs to keep them from knocking together when you walk. If you like, you can use your other hand to stabilize the bottom end of the bag. The bag should be resting almost horizontally across your back.

Of course, the more you're willing to spend, the more elaborate the bags can get. When you're looking for a bag, keep in mind the features that will be most important to you and make sure that the bag you buy has them. If you have lots of little accessories that you like to carry with you on the course, you'll need a bag with lots of pockets. If you like to carry your street shoes in your bag as you play (and then put your golf shoes in the bag when you finish), you'll need a bag with at least one relatively large pocket. If you want some place to carry an umbrella, you'll need to have a bag with such a slot. Again, you can get as many features on a bag as you like, but at some point you start to sacrifice room and size for weight. A carry bag is designed to be just that, a bag that's easy to carry.

You Don't Need No Stinking Pull Cart

Many courses now require golfers to ride in a cart, but most public courses allow you to carry your own clubs or use a pull cart, or if you live in the British Isles, a trolley. A pull cart is simply a handle and set of wheels that attaches to the bottom of your bag and enables you to drag your clubs along the ground instead of carrying them on your shoulder. Pulling your clubs is only marginally easier than carrying them, especially on hilly courses.

This standard pull cart has a removable handle and a clip to hold a scorecard and bag of tees.

Every so often, I see an amateur open the trunk of his or her car and struggle to pull a bag, with pull cart attached, out of the trunk. As we walk to the tee, he or she will invariably tell me how great it is to have the pull cart and not have to rent one from the club. I have to shake my head, because a pull cart almost never costs more than two bucks to rent. Sometimes, clubs can't give them away for free, because so many people like to ride in motorized carts these days. Why would you invest $150 in a nice pull cart to drag with you from course to course when you could rent one whenever you needed it for two bucks? A pull cart is something I don't think you need to invest in. You won't play enough in two years to justify the money you spend, and carrying your clubs is the best way to experience the round, anyway. Also, it's a pain in the butt to have to detach your cart from your bag every time you want to hook your clubs to the back of a motorized cart.

Gloves That Fit, Well, Like a Glove

In Chapter 19, I talked a little bit about how to avoid blisters on your hands when you play. A good golf glove is the best way, and not only does it help you avoid blisters, but it improves your grip on the club.

There isn't any real science to buying a glove that fits. Always try it on before you buy. If the salesperson or pro won't let you, buy the glove somewhere else. Remember that your glove should always go on the top hand (farthest away from the clubhead). If you're left-handed, you need a glove on your right hand. Righties need a glove on the left hand.

When buying a glove, the most important factor to consider is fit. The glove should stretch snugly across the palm of your hand, and the fingers should not be too short or too long. If you have any extra material in the palm or where your fingers hold the club, you're risking a blister, because those folds will rub between the club and your skin. Different companies' gloves fit in different ways, so a women's large from FootJoy won't fit the same way as a Nike glove will. Try on as many as you can and pick the one that fits the best. When you find a glove that fits across your palm and your fingers, make sure that you can secure it properly across the back of your hand with the Velcro strap. If the Velcro won't reach across the back of your hand or it reaches too far across and won't stick, you need to find another glove.

Caddie's Advice

If you look at your new glove, you'll notice a pearl-colored snap just below the Velcro closure. The top of that snap comes off, and you can use it to mark your ball on the green.

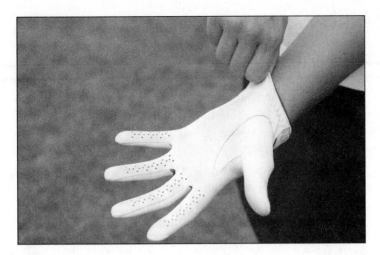

To make sure that your glove fits properly, pull it on firmly and then pull the Velcro tab firmly across the top of your hand. The glove should fit snugly across your palm, without any bunching. You should be able to wiggle your fingers without any hindrance from the glove.

Be sure to keep the cardboard and plastic sleeve the glove came in, so that when you finish your round, you can slide the glove back into the package. That way, it will stay flat and dry. If you wad it up and stuff it into one of the pockets in your bag, it will get stiff and wrinkled. You'll have trouble getting your hand into it the next time you play, and you'll wind up having to buy another one.

Golf gloves are available in several different kinds of material. Cabretta leather is the softest option, and it feels very nice on your hand. But leather that soft isn't very durable and will develop holes pretty quickly. In addition, cabretta gloves aren't waterproof, so if you get them wet, they will shrivel up and stiffen. A good-quality cabretta leather glove costs around $15. Most glove companies now make a synthetic leather glove that has the advantage of being waterproof. Synthetic leather doesn't feel as soft on your hand but will last longer and keep its shape.

Keep It Clean

Luckily, you can keep your equipment clean and in good shape without having to buy many extra accessories.

Clean Clubs Are Happy Clubs

Any golf shop will sell you a simple club-cleaning kit for less than $10. In it is a red plastic tool that you can use to scrape the dirt and mud from the clubs' grooves. You need to keep the grooves free of debris if you want the clubs to do what they're supposed to do. If you use a sharp-edged object from around the house to clean the grooves, don't use anything metal! It will scratch the finish, and that will lead to rust.

In addition to the simple club-cleaning kit, you can do most of your maintenance with a chamois, towel, and old toothbrush. After you play, dampen the chamois with warm, slightly soapy water and wipe down the grips of each club. Dry off the excess water with the towel. The grips will last longer with this little bit of extra care. Every month or so, fill your bathtub with 5 or 6 inches of warm water. You can dump a little bit of shampoo in there for soap if you like. Dunk each of your clubheads in the water. Using the old toothbrush, scrub the grooves of each club to get the dirt and debris out. Make a pass over the back of the club to clean it off, too. Most important, when you're finished, rinse the clubs off with clean water and dry them thoroughly. Again, rust is your main enemy if you don't dry the clubs. If you maintain your clubs this way after each round, they'll look nicer and last longer.

An important part of cleaning your clubs after a round is checking to see whether you need new grips. Most grips have little dimples or lines on them. Like the treads of a tire, these markers are the easiest indicators to check for grip wear. If the dimples or lines on the grip are starting to fade, you need to start thinking about new ones. After you've cleaned and dried your grips, grab a club and put your left hand on the grip where you would if you were starting your swing. Then, with your right hand, grab the shaft a few inches below the beginning of the grip. Try to pull the club out of your left hand's grasp. If the grip slips at all in your left hand, you need to get new grips.

Regripping Kits and Advice for Do-It-Yourselfers

You can either buy the pieces and replace the grips yourself, or you can take your clubs to the golf shop of almost any course or driving range, and the pro will do it for you. If you decide to take it to a pro, you'll pay between $3 and $5 a club, and that includes the cost of the new rubber grips. If you decide to get oversized or real leather grips, they will cost more.

> **Double Bogey**
>
> Not only do slick grips make your hands slide on the club, they can be dangerous. On damp days, a club with an old grip can slide right out of your hands on the backswing or follow-through. Always check for grip wear.

If you decide to do it yourself, you can buy the parts from a component company like Golfsmith. Golfsmith's regripping packages (available online at Golfsmith.com) include all of the tools necessary to regrip a club and usually come with a how-to booklet. In general, to regrip a club, you'll need the new grip, a sharp hobby knife, grip compound (which glues the new grip to the shaft), fine sandpaper, and some clean rags.

With the hobby knife, slice down the side of the old grip from the end nearest the clubhead to the butt of the club. Then, using your fingers, peel the old grip off the club. Use the sandpaper to rub off any of the old adhesive and then wipe the shaft with a damp, clean rag. Spread a thin layer of grip compound over the shaft and quickly slide the new grip on. Most grips have an alignment mark on them that you line up with the top of the shaft. Obviously, this is a very general description of how to replace a grip. Follow the specific directions that come with the regripping package for the best results.

Unless you enjoy the physical aspect of replacing grips as a hobby, I would recommend getting your grips replaced by a pro. You don't save all that much money by doing it yourself, and until you get some experience, it's tough to get it exactly right.

Shiny Shoes

Clean your golf shoes just as you would any other pair of leather shoes—with saddle soap or other shoe cleaner. Be sure to use the bristly spike cleaners most courses have near the door of the clubhouse to get the clumps of grass and dirt off the bottoms of your shoes before you take them off and put them away. That way, the trunk of your car or the bottom of the pocket of your golf bag won't be filled with dead grass and dirt.

If you play at a private club, the locker room attendant will clean and polish your golf shoes for you after your round. He gets paid by the hour, but you should tip $4 or $5 for this service.

Tees for Two

The cheapest accessory you're going to need before you play is a plastic bag of tees. If you're playing at a private course, you don't even need to buy them. You can grab a handful from the box near the starter's window. But if you aren't planning an outing at your neighborhood country club, you'll have to buy them.

Usually, a plastic bag of 20 tees costs around 50 cents if you buy them from the golf shop. You can go to a sporting-goods store or off-course golf shop and buy a bag of 1,000 tees in rainbow colors for no more than $10.

Tees come in different sizes and composition. You can buy very short tees to use on par-three holes, when you tee the ball up just barely off the ground. You can also buy 4-inch–long tees if you like to tee the ball way up off the ground. These tall tees are more popular than ever because of how big driver clubheads have gotten. Most tees are made from wood, but you can buy more expensive ones made from plastic that are virtually unbreakable. You just have to remember to pick them up after you hit! Some companies are starting to make tees from biodegradable material, so you can leave the broken tee on the ground, and in a few hours it will decompose into the grass.

To tee up your ball, hold the tee by its fat end between your index and middle fingers. Cup the ball in your hand, resting it on top of the tee. Push the tee into the ground with the ball until your knuckles hit the ground.

Other Gadgets

I could fill 10 more chapters with a description of the hundreds of gadgets and gizmos you can buy for your golf game. Instead, I'll just touch on a few of the ones you'll most likely run into:

- ◆ **Ball retriever.** This telescoping metal pole fits in your bag like a club and extends to reach 8 or 10 feet into a water hazard. The claw head at the end can snag balls. It's handy for when the water in the hazard is clear and you can see your ball, but don't wander next to the water, trolling for lost balls in the middle of the round. Your partners won't appreciate the delay.

- ◆ **Scorekeeper.** Made from metal or plastic, this device looks like an umpire's balls-and-strikes counter. You make a click on it every time you hit a shot or take a penalty, and it keeps track of both your hole and round scores.

- ◆ **Distance finder.** These are illegal in tournament play. Cheap ones are made from plastic and look like a cheap set of opera glasses. You line up a mark in the view-finder with a target, say, the flag, and a row of numbers at the bottom gives you an estimate of the distance. New, deluxe distance finders shoot a laser at your target. The laser bounces off the target, comes back to the reader, and the distance shows up digitally at the bottom of the screen. One of these machines, originally designed for hunters, will run you at least $500.

When I play a round, here's what I have in my pocket: A coin to mark my ball, long tees for my driver and shorter ones for par-threes, a divot repair tool, and an extra ball.

The Least You Need to Know

◆ A good-quality carry bag with pop-out legs is your best investment.

◆ A golf glove should fit snugly across your palm, and you shouldn't have any extra material at the tops of your fingers.

◆ If you're right-handed, you need a glove for your left hand. If you're left-handed, it's the opposite.

◆ Keep your clubs and grips clean between rounds, using soapy water, a groove cleaner, chamois, towel, and old toothbrush.

◆ Clean your spikes off with the bristly scrubber located near the door of the club-house before you store them in your bag or trunk.

◆ Tees come in small plastic bags that sell for around 50 cents. You can buy them in bulk at a sporting-goods store.

Chapter 21

Gambling (a Little) Never Hurt Anyone

In This Chapter

◆ If there's money involved, know what you're getting into

◆ Vocabulary lessons: high-stakes lingo

◆ Snake, Wolf, and Junk: playing the games

◆ Be a good winner—and loser

If you're just picking up a club for the first time, you should probably skip this chapter for now. You don't need to worry about golf and gambling until you've played enough rounds to establish a handicap—at least 20 in most cases.

But after you've taken that step from beginning golfer to high-handicap regular player, you can start to enjoy some of the little side wagers with your playing partners that make the game even more interesting. This chapter will help you get started.

Don't Play Fast and Loose

No matter what, if any, bet you make on the golf course, the cardinal rule is to always know the stakes. Learn about the different games and dollar values associated with them. Get a rough idea of the maximum amount you're willing to lose before committing. It's just like going to Las Vegas and playing in a poker game that's too big for you. You shouldn't be betting with money you can't afford to lose or in amounts that will put a strain on friendships. It's one thing to tease a friend about beating him or her for $10. It's another to make him or her take a trip to the nearest ATM to pay up.

Be especially careful if you're playing with a group of people you don't know or with whom you have never played golf. When everyone is standing on the first tee haggling over the terms of the bets, with strangers you have no idea if they're telling the truth about their skill level. Can you imagine if you and I were playing, and before I hit my tee shot, I told you I was a 15-handicap? If you were a 27-handicap, you would get to subtract one shot from your score on each of the 12 hardest holes on the course (27–15 = 12) to make the competition even. Of course, I'm really a +2 handicap, which means I should shoot around 69 or 70—from the back tees. That means you would be getting 17 fewer shots than you really should to compensate for the difference between our handicaps (27 and +2, or a gap of 29 shots). Of course, that's an extreme example, but many people fudge a few shots here and there when they bet on the golf course with people they don't know.

The first few times you decide to bet on the golf course, keep the stakes very low and only do it with people with whom you are very familiar. They will be the ones likely to be the most interested in giving you a fair competition. An evenly balanced match with a little bit of money riding on it is one of the most exciting things about playing golf! If I win a tournament on the LPGA Tour, it's worth about $200,000, but on practice days, I play with some of my friends who are also out on tour. Not much else matches the excitement of our head-to-head matches, which might only have $25 or $30 riding on them. Taking a single dollar from your brother or sister in a hard-fought, fair match is infinitely more satisfying than cheating someone out of $100 by inflating your handicap and getting more strokes than you deserve.

Talk Like a Pro, Even if You Don't Have the Game

The most important factor in making a friendly wager on the golf course is leveling the playing field as much as possible. With the use of handicaps, which I talked about earlier in this book, it's possible to create a balanced match regardless of the skill levels of the players involved. In the process of figuring out how to make a match even, the most common terms you will hear are *getting* and *giving* strokes. Let's go back to the example I gave in the last section. Let's say I'm a 15-handicap and you're a 27-handicap. If both of our handicaps are accurate, the basis for our bet should be that I *give* you 12 shots. On the 12 hardest holes, before we compare our scores, you'll be able to subtract a stroke from your tally. You're *getting* 12 strokes from me.

Par Primer

To **get** or **give** shots or strokes means to adjust your score to make a match more even. You get shots from a player with a lower handicap than you. You give them to a player with a higher handicap.

Extra Swings

Be sure to remember the difference between your handicap index and your course handicap when you make any bet. Your handicap index matches up with a course handicap number on a chart in the golf shop. That chart will tell you how many handicap strokes you get at that course. At a course with a lower course rating, which means it is easier, your 15.1 handicap index might translate to 16 handicap strokes. At a harder course, you might get 18. Three shots make a big difference in close games.

After you've figured out the lingo of negotiating strokes before the match, you need to learn about some of the on-course customs. If we were playing in an official tournament, we would have to play every hole completely, from start to finish. But when playing a friendly game with some wagers involved, you're going to be faced with the opportunity to concede short putts to your opponent. As a courtesy, a putt that is shorter than the length of your putter can be conceded. Just tell your opponent that his or her putt is "good." In theory, you can concede any length of putt, but it's usually only a good idea to do so in two situations: when your opponent is putting for such a high score that conceding the shot won't really make much difference, or if the putt is short enough that missing it would be unlikely.

For example, let's say I'm having a terrible time on the par-three you and I are playing. I hit two balls in the water and then skull my chip shot over the green. I finally hit my second chip on the green, and I have a 20-footer for a quadruple-bogey seven. If you hit your tee shot 5 feet from the hole, it's probably safe to concede my putt, because even if you take three putts to get into the hole (which is unlikely from 5 feet!), you'll still beat me by three shots on the hole. Conceding the long putt when it doesn't affect the outcome of the hole just speeds the round along. It also saves your opponent a little bit of frustration. This is a civilized game, you know!

When you're betting, one term that comes up frequently in several different games is a "press." If you've lost a certain number of holes in a bet, a press is like a double-or-nothing risk. You're making another bet with hopes that you'll win it to offset the bet you're losing.

For example, say we're playing a game where each hole won is worth a quarter. According to the rules of the bet, presses are allowed at two-down, and after I fall two holes behind you, I can offer you a press. If you accept, a new bet starts immediately, on top of the other bet. So if four holes are left, and I lose all four, I lose four more quarters in the original bet, plus four more in the press. If we split the four holes, I still lose my two quarters for being two holes behind you in the original bet, and nobody wins any money in the press. Each game has its own situations when pressing is allowed, so be sure to ask before you play. Remember, games with lots of presses are the ones that turn out to be the most expensive if you lose, because often at the end, four or five times the amount of one bet is riding on the last few holes. Be very careful when considering whether to press.

Choose Your Poison

I have a book on my nightstand that is 300 pages devoted strictly to golf betting games. There are literally hundreds of different games you can play, and I couldn't possibly do a good job of explaining them all to you, because I don't know how to play most of them. To get you started, I'll go over some of the most common games people play; that way, most of the time, if someone offers you a bet on the first tee, you'll have a general idea of what he or she is proposing. If someone offers you something a little more exotic, don't be afraid to ask for the rules to be explained before you accept. You won't look stupid. Your opponent will respect you for being cautious. Make sure your opponent explains all the rules. That way, you won't get seven holes into the game and then hear your opponent say, "Oh, I forgot to tell you …."

The following sections give you the rules for the most common types of bets.

Nassau

The most common bet in golf is the Nassau. Basically, it's a three-part wager. If somebody proposes a $1 Nassau, the person who wins the most individual holes on the front nine wins $1. The person who wins the most individual holes on the back nine also wins $1. The whole card then is tallied, and the person who won the most holes out of the 18 played wins the third $1 bet. If a hole is tied, nobody wins it, and it doesn't carry over.

For example, let's assume you and I have the same handicap, so neither of us is getting any strokes. We're playing a $1 Nassau. If we tie the first hole with a pair of pars, that hole is wiped out and doesn't count for the bet. We play the second hole, and you win it with a par. You win one hole. We keep playing, and keep track of who wins each individual hole. Let's say that after winning the second hole, you also win the third, fourth, fifth, and sixth (I'm really playing badly!). You're leading four holes to none, and we have only three holes left to play on the front nine. So, you've closed out the bet on the front nine. I can press you, which we talked about a little earlier. If I press, we start

another little side bet and keep track of who wins more holes in that one. If you keep up your hot streak and win holes seven, eight, and nine, you've won the front nine bet, you're seven holes ahead for the overall bet, and you've won the press, which ends after nine holes. Each of those bets is for $1. So for a $1 Nassau, without any presses, the most you can lose is $3. Each press is another $1 bet. Unless you and your opponents decide at the beginning that presses are *automatic* at a certain point, you don't have to press if you don't want to, and you don't have to accept a press from your opponent.

You can play a Nassau individually against one opponent, or you can team up with someone and play against two others. In the team format, both you and your partner play the hole, and then your team uses the best score of the two and compares it to the best score from your two opponents.

Par Primer

An **automatic press** is a rule in a bet that forces a person to make a second bet, or press, when he or she falls behind in the original bet. For example, two-down automatic presses are common, which means that after one person or team falls two holes behind, another bet automatically starts.

Caddie's Advice

If you feel like you've been playing poorly, but winning some holes in your bet by luck, don't feel obligated to accept your opponent's press. Sooner or later, your luck will run out, and you'll lose money.

Skins

This is the format you see the pros playing for big money on television. In a skins game, each hole is worth a certain amount of money. The player who wins the hole gets that amount of money from each opponent. Unlike a Nassau, skins do carry over from hole to hole. If two holes are tied, then the third hole is worth three skins. If you and I are playing with two other people in a quarter skins game (where the winner of each hole gets a quarter from each opponent), any time that two or more in our group tie a hole, that hole carries over. It doesn't matter if you and I make pars and the other two make 12s; if anyone ties, the hole carries over. If you have a competitive skins game going, some holes can be worth five or six skins.

When you finish the round, calculate how many skins each player won. If you won ten skins, I won four, and each of the other players won two, I subtract the four I won from your ten, and then pay you a quarter for each of the remaining six. The two other players in our group do the same, subtracting their two from your ten, and then pay you a quarter for the eight left. They then each have to subtract their two from the four I won and pay me for the two left over.

Greenies, Sandies, and Other Strange Nicknames

Greenies and sandies are extra side bets that go along with a regular Nassau or skins game. A greenie bet can be won only on a par-three hole. To win, you simply have to be the one who hits your tee shot closest to the hole. The only requirement is that the winner's ball must be on the green. If nobody in the group hits the green, the greenie carries over to the next par-three. If you hit an approach shot into a greenside bunker, then *get up and down from there*, and win the hole, you earn a sandie.

Par Primer

To get up and down from off the green means you hit your chip shot or sand shot onto the green and then sink the putt that's left over.

Extra Swings

Before the days of the PGA Tour, male touring pros were just that, people who drove around the country by car, playing in whatever tournaments would have them. The tour was a loosely affiliated group of events that offered winners as little as $1,500, and nothing at all to the people who finished outside the top 10. Unless a player was a Byron Nelson, who won 11 straight tournaments in 1945, the winnings available on tour weren't enough to support one person, much less a family. Many of the top pros added to their income by staging exhibitions and gambling. Because televised golf hadn't yet been invented, people didn't have a clear idea what the top players looked like. So someone like Sam Snead could arrive at a public course in suburban America and take on that club's top player in a high-stakes match. Snead didn't lose many matches, and often the money he won paid for the gasoline he would need to get to the next tour stop.

Both greenies and sandies are usually worth the same as one hole in a regular bet. If you're playing a $1 Nassau, each greenie or sandie is worth $1. Most courses have four par-threes, so if you're betting greenies, you could win or lose as much as $4. The number of sandies in a match depends on how many bunkers a course has and how many times you or your opponent can get up and down from off the green. Any other side bets you choose to make on a hole are called *specks* or *junk*. That way, you can tally up each bet for a given hole, and then say, simply, "I won three specks on that hole," instead of elaborating on each bet.

Snake, Wolf, and Other Wild Games

Some other fun games have different strategies. Snake is very simple. Each time a person in a foursome three-putts, he or she has "the snake," and the pot increases by a set amount. If I three-putt on the first hole, the pot might be $1, and I have the snake until the next person three-putts. Basically, you don't want to be holding the snake at the end of the round, because you then have to pay out the amount in the pot to the other people in the group.

In Wolf, the person who tees off last on a hole can choose one of the other people in the foursome to be his or her partner—for just that hole—or can decide to go "lone wolf" and try to shoot the best score alone, against the other three. Winning the hole by yourself is worth three times the normal bet amount.

Playing with a Partner

Skins and Nassaus can be contested between two players. If you're playing with a group of four, the two most common formats are a scramble and best-ball. Both are used in betting, but they're also common formats for outings and gatherings where no betting is involved. They are good ways to get groups of players unfamiliar with each other together.

Scramble

The scramble is the most fun format for beginners to play. Played with anywhere from two to four golfers on a team, in a scramble everyone on the team hits his or her tee shot. The group then decides which one was the best, and then everyone hits his or her shot from the spot of that ball. The process continues until the hole is completed. On the green, all the members of the team putt from the same mark.

This game is great for beginners because it diminishes bad shots and emphasizes good ones. For example, if you're just starting out, you won't be very consistent with your driver off the tee. That's okay in a scramble, because there should be someone on your team who is strong in that area. If you hit a good shot, then your team can use it. If you hit a bad one, pick up your ball and try again from your partner's better spot in the fairway.

Extra Swings

When you're playing in a scramble format, sometimes your team will be required to use a minimum number of tee shots from each teammate. That means that at least once or twice, your team will have to use your shot. If your team is counting on you, remember the lessons we went over in Part 4. When in doubt, play conservatively. Sacrifice distance for accuracy and hit a club you're confident you can place in the fairway. On a long par-four or a par-five, your best choice might be a three-wood.

The bad shot doesn't hurt the team, and you get another chance to hit a good shot to the green from the fairway. On the greens, you can take your best shot at a putt, and you're valuable to the team even if you miss. The other players can see how your putt broke (or didn't break) and adjust their putts accordingly. Because a scramble is truly a team game, you quickly gain a sense of camaraderie with your partners.

Best Ball

In best ball (sometimes called better-ball), each player on the team (usually two golfers) plays his or her own ball for the entire hole. The team uses whomever's score is lowest for the hole—counting any handicap strokes, too. At the end of the round, the low score from each hole is tabulated and added like a regular scorecard for an individual. In a common variation of this game, each member of the team hits a tee shot. Then, like in the scramble, you play the second shot from the better of the two drives. After each teammate hits from the spot of the better drive, each plays his or her own ball into the hole.

Alternate Shot

Alternate shot format is less common than scramble and best ball, and it's not a great game for beginners to play. In alternate shot, one member of the two-person team hits the tee shot, and then the other teammate hits the second shot. The person who hit the tee shot then hits the third shot, and so on. This continues for the whole round, even on tap-ins (inches-long putts) on the green. The weaknesses in a beginner's game are particularly exposed in alternate shot, especially if both members of the team don't have much experience. Probably the only thing worse than having to play your own bad shots is watching someone else have to play them. Of course, you'll have to play your partner's bad shots, too!

Etiquette for Winning—and Losing

In a best-case scenario, every match you play with a bet on the line will be a fair, closely contested one. If it turns out that way, you'll know that the conditions of the bet were set up just right—nobody was given too many strokes, and nobody was humiliated and left penniless.

Of course, if every match is closely contested, you're going to win some, but you're also going to lose some. Behaving gracefully in both situations will make you a great partner, and a great opponent. Nobody ever enjoys losing, but if you're a classy winner, your opponent will enjoy playing with you again.

If you are winning your bets, but the round isn't over yet, don't get cocky. Taunting your opponent or otherwise mouthing off will only make you look silly. If you do wind up winning, your opponents (who might also be your friends) will leave with a bad taste in their mouths. If you're the victim of a comeback, that makes your taunting seem even more ridiculous.

> **CAUTION**
>
> **Double Bogey**
>
> Nobody likes a bad winner. If you're up big, remember that one day you'll be the one getting creamed. You wouldn't like getting taunted, would you?

If the person you're playing against is really struggling, the worst thing you can do is offer swing advice or try to diagnose his or her problem. He or she is playing poorly and losing money to you as well. The last thing he or she wants to hear is your theory on the flying elbow. Think about how you would feel in the same situation. If you wouldn't want someone to say it to you, they certainly don't want to hear it from you. Talk about something else, like the NCAA basketball tournament or how your favorite team is doing in the baseball pennant race. Or say nothing. Let him or her work out the problems in silence.

If you are the one who is struggling, try not to be a poor sport. Nobody likes to play with a whiner, and throwing clubs is downright immature. It might be the hardest thing to do in golf (or any other sport), but try to be a graceful loser. It's certainly okay to get upset about a bad shot or an unlucky break, but get mad, blow off some steam with some curse words, and then let it go. Don't moan and groan about the shot two holes later. Not only will your partners and opponents not want to hear about it, if you're still hung up on a shot that trickled into a creek three holes ago, you aren't giving your full attention to the hole you're playing. And that could cost you even more money.

When you finish the 18th hole, it's time to settle up. The cardinal rule if you're going to gamble is that you need to be able to cover your losses. It is extremely bad form to say, "Sorry, I'll have to pay you later." Don't get in over your head. When you finish the round, walk off the 18th green to the clubhouse bar or restaurant and go over your scorecard. After you've figured out how much you owe, pay up. If you won some money, accept it with a smile, and then buy your opponent a beer or a Coke. If you play regularly with the same group of people, they'll remember you as a good sport who plays by the rules, and they will always be happy to have you in their foursome.

The Least You Need to Know

- Be careful. Know what you're getting into before you bet.

- The most common betting game is the Nassau, which is a three-part wager. One bet covers the first nine holes, the next covers the last nine, and the third covers all 18 holes. Whoever wins the most holes in each part of the bet wins that part.

- In a scramble, all of the golfers on your team hit a shot from the same spot. You pick the best one, and then everyone goes and hits from that spot.

- In best ball, each team member plays his or her own ball. The team then uses the best individual score.

- Never bet more than you can afford to lose. Settle your bets immediately after you finish the last hole.

- Win—and lose—gracefully. If you win some money, buy your opponent a beer or a soda.

More Rules to Golf By

In This Chapter

- ◆ Taking and scoring penalty strokes
- ◆ Handling lost balls and unplayable lies
- ◆ Dealing with obstructions
- ◆ Repairing marks on the green
- ◆ Knowing the other important rules

We spent some time in Chapter 16 going over the bare-bones basics of the official *Rules of Golf*, which is published by the United States Golf Association. I'm going to repeat some of that information in this chapter, but I'll elaborate on some of the individual rules a little more fully. I'll also go over several other rules we haven't talked about yet—ones you're going to need to know when you start to play regularly.

Penalty Strokes

According to the *Rules of Golf*, you get slapped with penalty strokes for two main reasons: Either you hit your ball somewhere you weren't supposed to and cannot play it legally (out of bounds or into the water), or you hit it and now you can't find it. The penalty shots are the cost for the privilege of putting a new ball into play (even if you manage to dig your first ball out from the bottom of the pond).

Common Penalty Stroke Situations

The following list goes over the most common ways in which you can be assessed a penalty stroke, as well as examples of each:

Caddie's Advice

When you drop a ball behind a water hazard, there's no limit to how far back (toward the tee) you can go to make the drop. If dropping right behind the hazard leaves you an uncomfortable distance to the green (between clubs, for instance), move back until you can take a full swing.

♦ **Water hazard.** If I'm playing a par-three hole with a pond directly in front of the green, and I hit my tee shot into the water, the first thing I have to do is check the stakes around the pond. If they are yellow, then the pond is a standard water hazard. I have to assess myself a one-stroke penalty and then determine where my ball crossed the edge of the hazard. After I figure that out, I have to drop my new ball with that spot between me and the hole. My tee shot that went into the water was my first shot. The penalty shot for putting a new ball in play was shot two. So my first shot with the new ball is number three. If I hit that shot onto the green and then take two putts, I've made a double-bogey five.

♦ **Lateral water hazard.** A lateral hazard, set off by red stakes, is different than a yellow-staked hazard in that it is to the side of the hole, and not directly in the line between the tee and green. If you hit into a lateral hazard, the procedure is a bit different than for a yellow-staked hazard. If I hit my tee shot on a par-four into a lateral hazard 160 yards from the green, first I have to determine the spot where my ball first crossed the edge of the hazard. Then I take my penalty stroke and drop my new ball two club-lengths from that spot, making sure my drop is no closer to the hole than where my shot went into the hazard. If for some reason I can't make a drop in that area (if there's a cart path or ground under repair, for example), I can move farther away from the hazard as long as I am parallel to the spot where my ball went in and no closer to the hole. Like the yellow-staked hazard, my tee shot into the lateral hazard was my first stroke, the penalty was my second, and my shot with the new ball will be my third.

♦ **Out of bounds.** White stakes mark the edge of the property the course sits on, or areas in the middle of the course that are off-limits for play. The stakes are set about 5 feet apart, and an imaginary line runs between each one. The line acts as the boundary. If I hit my tee shot on a par-five, and it hooks over the out-of-bounds line that runs down the left side of the hole, I must hit another shot from the place I hit the first, on the tee, and take one penalty stroke. Hitting out of bounds hurts you much more than hitting a shot into a water hazard, because not only do you have to take the penalty shot, but you have to hit again from the spot of your original shot. You lose all the distance you gained from where you hit to the out-of-bounds spot. So, the second shot I hit from the tee will be my third shot overall for the hole—my first drive, the penalty stroke, and then my second drive.

Many courses have wooded areas just off the fairway that make it difficult to determine whether a borderline shot has gone out of bounds or stayed in. In that situation, you should hit a second shot, called a *provisional ball*. Then go see whether your first shot did go out of bounds. If it did, you can play your provisional ball as your third shot. If the ball stayed fair, then play on with it and pick up your provisional ball.

Par Primer

Hit a **provisional ball** if you aren't sure whether your first shot stayed in-bounds. If it didn't, then instead of having to go back to the tee and delay your group, you can simply play the provisional ball. You must declare that you are playing a provisional ball to your playing partners.

Penalty Strokes for Lost Balls and Unplayable Lies

Hazards and out-of-bounds areas aren't the only dangerous places on the course. In two other circumstances, you can cost yourself penalty strokes—for a lost ball or an unplayable lie:

◆ **Lost ball.** If I hit my second shot on a long par-four into the thick stand of trees on the left side of the hole, I have to determine whether the area is set off by out-of-bounds stakes. If it isn't, I have to go into the trees to try and find my ball. After I'm in the forest, three things can happen: I find my ball and it's in a place where I can hit it; I find my ball and it's in a place where I can't hit it (like a thick bush or a rabbit hole); or I can't find my ball. If I can play the ball, I hit it toward the green, if possible. If I can't hit it, I'll talk about that option in just a minute. If I can't find it, then I have to declare the ball lost. A lost-ball penalty is very painful. I have to go back to where I hit my last shot (like for a shot out-of-bounds), but I have to take a two-shot penalty. Very painful, indeed.

♦ **Unplayable lie.** Using the same example, let's say I go into the forest and discover that my ball is halfway down a rabbit hole. I can see enough of the ball to identify it as mine, but I have no chance of getting a club on it. I can declare it unplayable, and then I can do one of three things after I add one penalty stroke to my score: I can drop the ball two clublengths from where it currently sits, as long as it's no closer to the hole; or I can go back on a straight line from the hole through where the ball is, as far back as I want, and drop the ball; in a worst-case scenario, I can go back to where I hit the shot that got me in this mess. Stuck deep in the woods, I might have to choose the third option and go back to where I hit the original shot.

Caddie's Advice

Remember, you have five minutes to look for a lost ball. When your time is up, take your medicine and go back and hit another.

The Art of the Drop

You'll expose yourself as a beginner very quickly if you nonchalantly toss a ball from your bag into a general spot near where you should be dropping. To drop your ball correctly, your hand must be at least shoulder height. You must drop the ball with your palm facing the ground, and you aren't allowed to try to direct where the drop goes by putting spin on the ball with your fingers or hand.

Caddie's Advice

If you are on a slope near a water hazard, you're allowed to stop the ball after you drop it if it's about to roll into the hazard again. If you try to drop twice, and the ball won't stop rolling toward the hazard, you can place your ball on the ground at the point where it hit the ground on the second drop.

To make a good drop, use one of these two techniques. In the first, hold your arm out straight in front of you at shoulder height, as if you were going to take something from a shelf at eye level. Hold the ball with your palm facing down, with your first two fingers and your thumb. Then simply let go of the ball. In the second method, you can reach over your right shoulder with your right hand (as if you were going to scratch your ear) and drop the ball over your right shoulder.

Other Penalty-Stroke Situations

In a collection of other isolated incidents, you can also earn penalty strokes. For example, as I discussed in Chapter 16, if you touch your club to the ground in a hazard (sand or water) before you hit your shot, you have to assess yourself one penalty stroke. If you attempt a putt while on the green and you don't take out the flagstick, you're penalized two strokes if your ball hits the pin. Teeing off in front of the tee markers at the beginning of a hole will also cost you two penalty strokes. If you accidentally play your partner's ball, you must take two penalty strokes, but finish out the hole with the wrong ball before you change back to your own. Otherwise, it's another two-stroke penalty for not playing your ball where it lay.

Extra Swings

One of the strangest penalties in the history of tournament golf came in the 1984 U.S. Open at Oakland Hills Country Club in Birmingham, Michigan. T. C. Chen, who was leading the tournament by two strokes on the seventh hole of the last round, missed the green with his approach. On his chip shot to the green, his club hit the ball twice, once on impact and then again, a half-second later as Chen made his follow-through. The double-hit cost him a two-stroke penalty, and he made a quadruple-bogey eight on the hole. He lost the lead and wound up finishing second to Andy North. Since then, because of an unfortunate coincidence in initials, Chen has been known as "Two-Chip Chen."

There are quite a few other instances in which you can get a one-stroke penalty. You don't need to memorize them, because a lot of them are so rare, you'll probably never encounter them. Did you know that if you hit your own caddie with a shot, you're penalized two strokes, but if you hit your partner's caddie, there's no penalty at all? Under the strict *Rules of Golf*, if your partner asks you what club you used for the shot that hit your caddie, you get a two-stroke penalty for hitting your own caddie, and your partner gets two extra strokes for soliciting advice from someone aside from his or her caddie. Some of the rules are mind-boggling, and nobody will expect you to be a nit-picker about them. If you keep track of the major ones and have a rule book handy for the not-so-common ones, you'll be able to take care of at least 95 percent of the rules questions you come across.

Par Primer

If you're playing in a tournament and have a rules question, you can ask an official to make a decision for you if you aren't sure what to do. That's called getting a *ruling*.

On the Green: Marking and Fixing

The biggest distinction you need to make when you get to the green is the difference between a ball mark and a spike mark. Why is it so important? According to the rules, it's legal to fix any and all ball marks (dents in the grass made by a ball hitting the green), but illegal to fix marks made by a person's cleats. It doesn't matter if you made the spike marks or a person who was there last night did. If a spike mark is smack in the middle of your putting line, you have to leave it the way it is. You can't tap it down with your putter or fix it with your divot repair tool.

Many players have questioned the logic of the rule. Why, they ask, is it legal to fix a ball mark and not a spike mark? The United States Golf Association, the organization that makes the rules for the game, says that a spike mark on the green is just like a divot on the fairway. If you encounter one, you must play the ball as it lies. A ball mark is something you create as you're playing the hole, so you are allowed to return the green to the condition you found it. The rules don't make any distinction between the ball mark you make and ones that are already there, so it's legal to fix as many as you like. The spike marks are considered "the rub of the green," which means the conditions as you find them. You cannot improve the conditions between your ball and the hole. It might not be the most logical of rules, but it's important to follow it. Your partners won't take too kindly to you if you feverishly tap down all the spike marks between your ball and the hole.

> **Caddie's Advice**
>
> It's illegal to fix spike marks between your ball and the hole, but after all of the players in your group putt out, you are allowed to tap them down. As you leave the hole, tap down a few marks and spare the next group some aggravation.

As I talked about in Chapter 16, to mark your ball legally, it must be on the putting surface. You can't mark it if it's on the fringe. To mark your ball, place a coin or other flat marker down on the green several inches behind the ball, and then slide it until it is just under the edge of the ball (but not quite touching). Let go of the marker and then pick up the ball. Clean your ball before you put it back down. To replace your ball, set it down just in front of the marker, and then slide the marker back and away.

If your marker is in another person's line to the hole, ask whether he or she would like you to move it. If he or she would like you to move it, ask which direction. Then, using your putterhead as a ruler, measure one clubhead's width from the mark (laterally, and not closer to the hole) and move your mark. When the other person finishes putting, replace your mark in its original position. If you forget to put your marker back, guess what: You get a two-stroke penalty.

Obstructions

Across the golf course, you'll find all kinds of obstructions. Some are natural, like trees or large rocks. You can't do anything about those. You have to play around them. But if an obstruction is artificial, like a tractor parked next to the fairway, or some bleachers put up next to the 18th hole for the pro tournament that comes to town next week, you do get to move your ball out of the way.

If your ball rolls behind or under an obstruction, you're allowed to pick the ball up and drop it at the nearest point of relief, no closer to the hole. This happens fairly often at professional tournaments, when television camera stands, bleachers, and temporary stands are sitting all over the course. You'll run into obstructions much less frequently at your average public or private club.

Temporary obstructions at places like that tend to be things like construction equipment, lawn mowers, or garbage bins that have been dragged to the edge of the course to collect construction debris. The same rules apply to these obstructions as the temporary ones that abound at a professional tournament.

Caddie's Advice

If you do take a free drop away from an obstruction, remember that you can leave yourself enough room to take a full, unimpeded swing.

Loose Impediments

Loose impediments are natural objects like branches, stones, or leaves that aren't imbedded in the ground and don't stick to your ball. You can brush these out of your path, but your ball can't move in the process. If it does, you get a penalty stroke. For example, if I hit my tee shot near some trees and a little branch that fell out of the tree is lying near my ball, right where I would take my stance, I can move the branch without penalty. But if moving the branch makes my ball shift, I would have to take a penalty stroke.

Anything still alive is not considered a loose impediment. If you go into some long grass or shrubs and try to hit your ball, you can't break off any living branches to clear a path for your backswing. You also can't yank out any tall weeds behind your ball, even if the ball doesn't move. If you do, it's a two-stroke penalty.

Caddie's Advice

Just as you cannot pull out or break off any live plants, you can't flatten the grass directly behind your ball to get better contact. That's considered improving your lie, and it's a two-stroke penalty.

Local Rules

Each course or club can make local rules that apply only to their courses. These rules are usually written on the back of the scorecard. Local rules address abnormal situations that the USGA's Rules Committee hasn't specifically addressed. The only require-ment for these rules is that they don't specifically waive a penalty that the *Rules of Golf* establishes. For example, a local rule can't make an out-of-bounds tee shot on a cer-tain hole cost you nothing. The *Rules of Golf* set up situations where local rules are most likely to be established, including:

◆ Clarifying which objects are and are not obstructions.

◆ Determining areas of the course that are under repair.

◆ Identifying extreme wetness, mud, or other temporary conditions that make areas of the course unplayable.

Local rules come into play when the course is so wet that balls embed in the ground when they land. Course or tournament officials then can enforce a lift, clean, and place rule for the day, allowing players to extricate their balls, clean them, and then set them on a dry piece of ground in the immediate area.

More and more courses are also starting to protect environmentally sensitive areas such as wetlands by either making them out of bounds or allowing players a free drop should their ball enter.

Strange Situations

Every year, things happen out on the golf course that don't really fit with any of the *Rules of Golf* established by the United States Golf Association. Sort of like the Supreme Court, the USGA's Rules Committee gets together and makes rulings on some of the new situations with which it is presented. The subjects of these rulings can range from the absurd to the logical. Twenty years ago, somebody got the idea that a long shaft on a putter would be an innovative idea. The USGA then got together to decide whether such a putter fit with the rules, and decided to put the long-shafted putter on its conforming clubs list. (There's been a lot of debate about that, and some people think long putters might eventually be banned.)

To take another example, the committee had to decide what is supposed to happen if a ball comes to rest underneath a dead animal. The dead animal is a moveable obstruc-tion and can be legally moved aside, as long as the ball doesn't move with it. A live animal is a temporary obstruction, and the ball can be picked up and dropped at the nearest point of relief. Of course, if your ball stops by a live, dangerous animal, your point of relief ought to be at least 50 yards away! Forget about the golf ball, too.

The *Rules of Golf* are tough to memorize, and it doesn't help that the USGA makes all these rulings every year to go along with them. If you buy the complete set of rules and rulings, you get a book the thickness of a high school civics test. You can get a small, scorecard-sized, soft-cover book of rules for free when you join the USGA (I'll go into more detail about how to do that in Chapter 25).

The Least You Need to Know

- The major areas in which penalty strokes come into play are hazards, out-of-bounds, and rules violations.

- You get a two-stroke penalty for most rules violations.

- On the green, the most important distinction to make is between spike marks and ball marks.

- It is illegal to repair spike marks during a round, but you can repair ball marks without penalties.

- Local rules are made by the club to address special situations that are unique to that club. They are usually written on the back of the scorecard.

- The USGA issues interpretations of its *Rules of Golf* every year for situations that aren't covered by specific rules.

23

Cheating

In This Chapter

- ◆ Why cheating isn't worth it
- ◆ How to spot a cheater
- ◆ Dealing with someone who bends the rules
- ◆ Cheating versus poor sportsmanship

Unlike many other sports, golf doesn't have referees or umpires. Nobody is watching your every move to make sure that you don't break any rules. The defining principle of golf is self-regulation and integrity. That is, you're supposed to be honest enough to call any penalties on yourself. Most of the time, you'll be off on your own, looking for your ball. If you find it and notice that it's stuck behind a rock or a foot out of bounds, you're the only one who will know whether you bump the ball into a little better position or play it as it lies.

Now I'm not asking you to be completely suspicious of everyone with whom you play. That would take a lot of the fun out of the game. Most people you play with will be fundamentally honest, and if they do break a rule, it will either be because they aren't aware they're doing something wrong or because the game you're playing isn't serious, so nobody is harmed. It's the rare instances when you're playing in a competition or betting on a game and your opponent tries to take advantage by cheating that I'll be talking about in this chapter. If you're playing a friendly game, any cheating that goes on won't matter very much to you. But if you're playing in a competition or betting and money is riding on the game, you have to know when and how to speak up.

Cheating: It's Not Worth It

If you're a beginner, you should be more concerned about learning to hit the ball than about rules or cheating. Your first few times out on the course, you're going to be getting used to the surroundings and worrying about getting the ball off the ground. When you become a little more experienced and start to be an active part of the foursomes you're playing in—when you've played enough rounds to get a handicap, around 20—then you can start to worry about cheating.

As you progress from a beginner to an intermediate player, you'll need to look at several different barometers to figure out how much improvement you are making. The most obvious is your score. The scores you turn in determine your handicap. If your handicap goes down, that's an indication your game is improving. But in order to get an accurate handicap, you have to submit accurate scores. If you bend the rules, you won't be submitting accurate scores. If your handicap is artificially low, it might give you an ego boost, but it will only hurt you out on the course. For one thing, you'll always be competing at a disadvantage. If the computer says you're a 10 handicap, but you're really only skilled enough to be a 14, when you play people with lower handicaps than yours, you won't be getting as many shots as you should.

The competitive disadvantage you get from fudging your score affects you in the long term. In the short term, you might end up losing some friends. When you play regularly with the same group, if you're using some creative scorekeeping or bumping your ball to get a better lie, your partners will eventually figure it out. At the minimum, they won't trust you, even when you aren't cheating. At worst, they won't want to play with you anymore. It's a pretty hollow feeling to play the best round of your life, legitimately, and have your golfing buddies discount it because they don't think you played by the rules.

The best way to put score fudging in perspective is to remember that in the long run, your score is not going to matter to anyone but you. If you're in a competition, of course it's important to be honest and record your score fairly. Other players then have a stake in the score you shoot. But if you're out playing a friendly round one Saturday morning with your family, you're only trying to kid yourself if you try to manipulate your score. Your partners won't care tomorrow if you shot 101 or 99 or if you shaved two penalty shots off your score to get there. You'll just be deluding yourself and depriving yourself of a real sense of accomplishment when you make it under 100 for the first time legitimately.

How to Spot Mr. or Ms. Fast-and-Loose

That said, there will be times when you're doing your best, but your opponent is bending the rules to gain an advantage. If you recognize cheating when it first starts, you can do something about it with the least amount of embarrassment for your opponent. When you know your opponent is cheating, you can stop worrying about it and worry about your own game. If you're playing for money, you can tell him or her to stop. If he or she doesn't, the bet is off. If he or she does stop, great. Problem solved.

As you can imagine, you can bend the rules in golf in many ways. I'm going to touch on a few of the most common. Through experience, you'll learn some of the others. Be on the lookout for these types of fudging.

> **Extra Swings**
>
> The official rules of golf (in the United States) are administered by the United States Golf Association (USGA), and they come in two parts. The first part is the actual rule book. It's pretty dense reading, but it's small enough to fit in the pocket of your golf bag. Even the best players in the world keep a copy handy, because some tricky situations can leave you wondering what to do. The second part is the decisions book. This is a fat, spiral-bound book full of descriptions of every conceivable situation on the course and what to do to follow the rules. It's a great book to leave in the bathroom for light browsing!

Ball Bumping

Far and away the most common type of fudging happens on boring shots from the fairway or rough. One of golf's fundamental rules is playing the ball as it lies. If you're playing on a course that's in poor condition, sometimes the urge to move your ball off a bare patch of dirt or a divot mark is overwhelming. If you and your partners decide before the round to play *winter rules*, which means that in the fairway you can move your ball a few feet to a better lie, then bumping isn't a problem. If you aren't playing winter rules, or if you're in the rough at any time, bumping is strictly a no-no.

Par Primer

Winter rules are unofficial rules that come into effect early or late in the golf season in cold-weather climates when conditions aren't as good. Under winter rules, if your ball is in the fairway, you can move it a few feet to a better lie.

If you aren't riding in the same cart as your opponent, catching him or her bumping the ball is very difficult. You're busy looking for your ball and worrying about what shot to hit next, while somewhere in the distance, he or she is moving the ball to a better spot. This is one of those times you're just going to have to be trusting.

The Magical Ball-Mark Improvement

When you're on the green and putting, you should be paying more attention to your own shot than your opponent's, but you need to keep two things about his or her shot in mind. First, don't step on the line between his or her ball and the hole. Not only is it a two-stroke penalty for you to do so, it is very bad manners. The other is to keep a rough idea of where your opponent marked his or her ball. A few inches' difference between where the ball was and where your opponent marked it won't make too much difference for a 20- or 30-foot putt, but if he or she is moving the mark 6 inches closer for a 6-foot putt, you can see why it starts to become a problem.

Another time that's open to a little bit of creative ball marking is when you ask your opponent to move his or her ball from your line. As I talked about in Chapters 16 and 22, it's perfectly legal to use your putterhead as a ruler to move a ball mark one way or the other to allow another player a clear path to the hole. When you move that ball mark out of the way, never move it closer to the hole, and always on a perpendicular line. Some players take advantage of this movement to mark their balls 5 or 6 inches closer to the hole. Again, this advantage doesn't mean much 30 feet from the hole, but for closer putts, that little extra can mean the difference between the ball dropping in the hole and dying just short.

> **Caddie's Advice**
>
> Make it a habit of marking your ball properly every time you play, even if it's just a friendly game. It will soon become routine, and you won't even have to worry about it in a competition or other serious event.

The Miraculous Deep-Woods Scouting Mission

When your opponent takes off into the woods to look for a wayward shot, for the most part, you're going to have to have a little trust. You can't follow your opponent into the woods and make sure he or she finds and plays the correct ball or doesn't drop another ball when the first one turns up. Golf balls turn up in strange places, so the first time your partner goes into the jungle and manages to punch out to safety, give him or her the benefit of the doubt. But if your opponent is routinely finding his or her ball in waist-high grass and thick stands of trees and playing perfect recovery shots from these tough positions, you should begin to get a little bit skeptical.

Of course, the easiest way to deal with the problem is to make sure that you know where your ball is and then go help look for your opponent's. If you're in the woods, too, that makes it more difficult for him or her to put a new one into play.

Extra Swings

One of my favorite movies of all time, *Goldfinger,* has a great golf scene starring Sean Connery as James Bond. He's undercover and playing a match against the evil Goldfinger. The match is close, and on the 17th hole, Goldfinger hooks his ball into thick rough down the left side of the hole. Goldfinger and his sinister caddie, Oddjob, trudge off to find the ball, while Bond waits at his own ball in the middle of the fairway. Almost instantly, Oddjob drops a second ball down his pant leg, then signals to his master that he found the ball. Just after Goldfinger plays his second shot safely, Bond's caddie says, "I can't believe he found that ball." With a smirk, Bond answers, "He didn't." The caddie wonders, "How do you know?" Bond moves his foot a few inches. "I'm standing on it."

Bond lets Goldfinger finish the hole with the illegal ball and then tee off with it on the 18th hole. The match is tied, and on the 18th green, Bond intentionally misses his short putt to lose the hole and the match. Bond then walks to the hole to get Goldfinger's ball for him and discovers the wrong ball. "I'm sorry, but you must have played the wrong ball back there at 17. That means I win the hole, and the match." Goldfinger storms off the course in disgust.

That Whiff Didn't Count

On occasion, if you're playing with someone who is a beginner as well, you'll see your opponent take a practice swing, then set up and take a mighty lunge at the ball, and completely miss it. A whiff might be the most embarrassing shot in golf, so it should be no surprise that sometimes, a whiffer acts like the miss was just another practice swing. This, of course, is ridiculous, because anyone could see that the whiffer was set up over the ball, not to the side as he or she would be for a practice swing. Take comfort in the fact that everyone in the group will recognize a whiff when they see one. If the poor whiffer has the audacity to try to play the miss as a practice shot, chuckle to yourself and move on.

Those White Stakes Are Out of Bounds?

We've already talked about bumping a ball that sits just out of bounds into legal territory. Unless you see it happen, there isn't much you can do about that. You can, however, make sure your opponent doesn't hit a ball from out of bounds. That's what the stakes are for. In most cases, it should be easy to see from 25 yards away whether your opponent is playing a ball from out-of-bounds territory. Most often, this kind of situation occurs when one person has a very liberal interpretation of just where the imaginary out-of-bounds line runs between the white stakes. According to the rules, the line is considered to run straight between each stake. To determine whether a ball is out of bounds, simply stand directly behind one of the stakes that brackets the ball in question and line up the stake on the other side. If the ball isn't on the fair side of the line, it's time to go back to the tee.

Creative Scorekeeping

If you're the one who is in charge of keeping score, sometimes one of the people you're playing with will give you a score that is almost too hard to believe. You saw him or her duffing it around in the rough for 15 minutes and then taking a few chops in the bunker next to the green. Now that person tells you that he or she made a bogey (instead of an even worse score).

Creative scorekeeping happens for three main reasons. Often, new players aren't quite sure how to tally penalty strokes and add them to their score, or else they just plain forget about a couple of miss-hits or other bad shots that happened early in the hole. No big deal.

The second reason is that the person made a really horrible score and doesn't want the ugly number to go on the scorecard and *ruin the round*. If that person made an eight on a par-three, he or she might claim a six, just to keep the damage under control and his or her ego intact.

The third reason, and the least common in my experience, is that the person in question is really trying to be sneaky and cheat you. If you both are beginning golfers, you'll be making double-bogeys more often than pars, so if you're playing a match, the difference between a double-bogey and a triple-bogey is fairly significant. It could be the difference between winning and losing a hole. And because both of you are still learning, you aren't apt to hit your tee shots and approach shots right down the middle. You'll be off to the sides (and often on opposite sides) of the fairway, minding your own business and hitting your own shots.

When you get to the green, it's a simple thing to keep track of how many putts a person takes, but who knows whether your opponent didn't count that little duff back there in the fairway bunker? Again, most people will be honestly mistaken, not deviously scheming. But you have to keep your eyes open.

Extra Swings

If you're on your first trip around the course, remember the advice I gave you earlier in this book—know when to say when. Taking your lumps on a hole is only necessary when you're playing in an official tournament or competition, or when there's a bet riding on the hole. We all know how frustrating it is to make a really bad score. Just ask Tom Weiskopf. At the 1977 Masters Tournament, he hit his tee shot in the water at the par-three 12th hole. Then, instead of dropping, he held out his hand and asked his caddie for another ball. Plop. He hit the next shot into the water as well. Like a machine gun, Weiskopf blasted three more balls in the water, for a total of five. Then, on his sixth shot from the tee, he finally hit the green. Two putts later, he had a 13, the highest score ever recorded on that hole. Tom's is a pretty extreme example, but that kind of hole happens to us all.

As I write this, I'm thinking back to a par-three I played a while back at an LPGA event in Arizona. I hit two balls in the water and took a quadruple-bogey seven. By the time I putted out, I was ready to pack up my things and go back to the hotel.

Fire or Brimstone: Dealing with a Cheater

As I said earlier in this chapter, if you are aware of someone bending the rules intentionally early in the round, do everything you can to resolve it as soon as possible. Give them the benefit of the doubt the first time, just to make sure that you aren't the one who is mistaken; then if you see something obvious a second time, try to take care of it with as little embarrassment as possible.

Remember, you only need to confront someone about breaking the rules if their actions are going to affect you—namely, if you're both playing in a competition or tournament or if there's betting going on. If everyone is out playing a friendly game, just ignore it. Nothing good will come from a confrontation, and embarrassing the person won't do anything for you.

> **Double Bogey**
>
> If you do decide to confront someone about cheating, keep in mind that the person might not realize that what he or she is doing is against the rules. Don't be sanctimonious.

If you are in a competitive situation, the two situations that are easiest to deal with are, thankfully, the ones that occur the most frequently—bumping the ball and giving an incorrect score. If you see your opponent move his or her ball with a foot or club to get a better lie, wait until you get to the next tee and ask whether winter rules are in effect. Your opponent can answer in one of two ways. He or she can say yes, we are playing winter rules, which means you can now move your ball in the fairway as well. Or he or she can say no, we aren't. If he or she says no, don't mention anything about the ball-moving incident you just saw—yet. Wait for it to happen again and then immediately confront the person. Say, "I thought we weren't playing winter rules." Don't yell or curse. Just say it in a matter-of-fact way. That should do the trick.

If your opponent does it again, on the next tee, tell him or her that all bets are off (if you're betting). If you're playing in a competition, tell your opponent that you won't sign his or her scorecard. That's your way of saying you won't vouch for that score. Then forget about it and concentrate on your own game.

The best way to deal with scoring discrepancies is, again, to give the person the benefit of the doubt the first time. Then keep track of the person's score more carefully on subsequent holes. If the score he or she gives you is different (higher or lower—some people assess themselves too many penalty strokes!), before he or she gives you the score for the hole, ask, "Jane (or Bob, or whatever the case may be), did you make a seven on that hole?" When you ask that question, use the number of strokes that you counted for the person at that hole. That way, you're giving the person a chance to be honest. He or she can agree with the score you gave and move on.

If he or she claims a score of six, give the person another chance to be honest. "Oh, I thought you took two shots out of that fairway bunker." By then, the person will most likely say, "You're right, I'm sorry." But if your opponent presses the issue, don't get angry, just say, "I had you down for a seven. But if you say it was a six, fine." Then turn around and walk away. The person will know that you know he or she fudged the score. If it happens again, call the bet off, or tell the person you won't sign the scorecard, and then forget about it.

Any kind of rule involving a judgment call (like where to drop after a shot that went in the water) is much tougher to enforce. You don't have the best perspective, because you're probably off playing your own shot. If someone is determined to cheat, they will be able to do it in these areas without you getting a good look at it—like finding and moving a ball in the woods to get a clear path out of the trees. You can suspect that they are bending the rules, but in these situations, it's often best just to keep your mouth shut. Or ask one of the other players in the group whether he or she noticed anything funny. Maybe you're the one who is mistaken. If everyone in the group agrees that the person is grossly breaking the rules, consider confronting him or her about it.

If you have to confront someone about bending the rules, the most important thing to remember is to not get angry. Keep a matter-of-fact, sympathetic tone. Treat it as a mistake, not a crime, and you won't get a blow-up. Remember that this is a civilized game.

The Least You Need to Know

♦ Never confront someone about cheating unless what he or she is doing affects you—like in a tournament or when money is being bet.

♦ The most common forms of rules-bending are bumping the ball to improve a lie, marking a ball on the green closer to the hole, dropping a new ball in the woods when the first one is lost, and fudging the score after a hole.

♦ Always give someone several chances to be honest before you confront him or her about cheating.

♦ In most cases involving scoring disputes, the person in question isn't trying to cheat. He or she just didn't compute the score correctly.

♦ If someone is cheating in a competition or a betting situation, give that person the benefit of the doubt the first time you see it happen. After the second offense, confront him or her as soon as possible.

♦ When you confront someone for cheating, don't do it in an angry or accusatory way. Try to stay as matter-of-fact as possible.

Chapter 24

Golf and Business

In This Chapter

- Making the most of a round of golf with the boss, clients, or colleagues
- Keeping the balance between business and pleasure
- Knowing your limitations

I bet a few of you reading this book have never picked up a golf club but are supposed to play in an outing with the boss in the spring. If good weather is a few months away, then there's some time to get your swing in order. If your outing is next week, you could be in big trouble!

Either way, even if you have no golf game by the time you're scheduled to play with the boss or in another business situation, at least you'll know how to behave after you read this chapter. Business golf is really an art form. I've had to master it as a professional because of my endorsement opportunities. Part of signing with a company to endorse its products is playing golf with some of the top executives in their company outings. The happier they are with me, both at the outing and in general, the more lucrative it can be. That endorsement money is just a part of being a professional golfer.

Hitting the Links Like You Mean Business

Many people take up golf because of the game's business possibilities. In fact, a recent National Golf Foundation Study found that 12 percent of all new golfers are taking up the game for business reasons.

Many executives play golf with a passion, and a round of golf equals five uninterrupted hours of access for a person looking to get ahead or make a deal. Because golf is such a social game, it really lends itself to business situations. It's tough to talk about mergers and acquisitions over a spirited game of basketball, but when you're waiting on the tee for a slow group to putt out on a par-three, you've got all the time in the world.

If you're playing with your boss or another important contact, the first thing you should do is a little reconnaissance—you know, a little research. If you work at a larger company, see whether you can find some co-workers who have played with the person before. If you work for a smaller place, you've probably heard firsthand about the boss's game. Ask whether the boss or contact takes his or her golf very seriously or likes to have a good time. Some people are very focused and don't like any extra chatter between shots, while others are very social. If a social player can't play with a group, he or she would rather not play.

If you're going to be playing at a private club, see whether you can get some information about it. Is it fancy, with a strict dress code and big tipping? Is it more laid back? Does the boss or other contact you'll be playing with like to bet? Is he or she going to be counting on you to be a partner in a match against some of his or her friends? Arm yourself with as much information as possible. You're less likely to be surprised on game day.

Take the information with you to the course. If you don't remember anything else, remember to be on time! Being late for a tee time with your boss, client, or another important colleague might be something you'll never recover from, either that day on the links or back at the office. Make sure to get good directions to the course and leave early. Aim to get to the course at least an hour before your tee time. If you've never been there before, count on at least 15 minutes of fooling around, figuring out where to park, where to leave your street shoes, and where to meet your playing partner.

CAUTION

Double Bogey

Make sure that you clean your equipment before you play with your boss. You wouldn't go into a staff meeting with chocolate on your tie, would you?

After you've made it there on time, the other main thing you need to remember is to be a pleasant partner. Not only is it nice to make a good impression on the business contact you're playing with, but it's nearly as important to make a good impression on his or her friends. If the person you played with talks you up after the round, that's worth more than anything you could come up with on your own. So do your best to be a charming partner and courteous golfer. That means no cursing after a bad shot and no sulking if you're having a bad day. My favorite playing partner for a pro-am round is a person who is as cheerful on the first hole as he is on tee 12, after missing a 3-footer for double-bogey on the 11th green.

Handicaps: This Is No Time for Delusions of Grandeur

Some time before the morning of your round with the boss or other business contact, he or she probably will ask you for your handicap. If you're a complete beginner, it's important to say so up front. Don't fudge on this point. You won't be able to hide your inexperience when you do get to the links, so it's much better to be honest. If nobody asks you before you get to the tee, again, this is no time for delusions of grandeur. Be honest about your skill level. Your playing partner won't look down on you, but he or she will appreciate your honesty. Nothing is worse than claiming to be a 12-handicap, and then shooting 120. It's much better to give your honest handicap, say 30, and shoot 98.

Because the scores are weighted by handicaps, it is less important how good a golfer you are and more important that you play to the level you are capable of. The best way to do that is to relax and try to treat it like any other round. I know that's easy to say and harder to do, but it's really the key to playing well and enjoying yourself with the boss.

One thing you have to take into consideration when you tell your boss or colleague your handicap is the difficulty of the course you will be playing. Ask around. Find out whether the course has long holes or is very tight off the tee. Most of the time, when you get to the first tee and announce your handicap, the members of your foursome will know how to adjust it to fit the course.

Double Bogey

Don't ever exaggerate your golf skills to your boss or another business associate. When you're out there on the course, the truth will be very easy to see.

The Clubhouse: No Business Done Here

You'll never recover from three things: being late for your tee time, having bad manners on the course, and discussing business at an inappropriate time. I've already talked about being late. I'll get to the part about good manners shortly. Right now, let's talk about the best times to discuss business.

Think of the clubhouse, all of it, as the no-fly zone. It's an unwritten rule at most private clubs that no business is to be discussed in the locker room. Extend this rule to the golf shop and the bar after the round. Actually, you might find the most productive of your golf outings with the boss or a business colleague to be the ones where you don't talk about business at all. Just go out and have a good time and talk about something other than business. That's how people become friends.

If you have to talk business, get into the round first. My advice is to wait until you're close to the back nine. If you start right off the bat talking about business and putting on the hard sell, it makes it look like that's all you're there to do—talk shop. Optimally, business talk should just come up naturally. You shouldn't even have to force the issue. Because you and your boss know each other mostly from work, that's the first thing you have in common, so it will be a natural topic of discussion. Waiting to bring up business talk lets both you and your boss get into the swing of things, so to speak. You'll get a feeling of what kind of player he or she is, and whether business conversation is something he or she would be open to. Maybe all the conversation is about basketball or the stock exchange. Participate in those discussions. Don't try to steer the subject back to business. Just like in any other social setting, go with the flow. Chances are, if your partners are in the middle of a conversation about the Academy Awards, your attempt to talk about next week's staff meeting won't go over so well anyway.

Keep It Casual

Follow your boss's or colleague's lead when it comes to the level of seriousness on the course. If he or she is a cutthroat competitor, you would be wise not to giggle after hitting a bad shot and say, "Oh, well, it's only a game." And if the boss is a fun-loving, laid-back player, it probably wouldn't be a good idea to be gung-ho, win-at-all-costs competitive, and make her putt out every 2-footer. Try to gauge the mood of the foursome early and do your best to match it.

I've found that the most invaluable tool in a high-pressure outing with the boss is a subtle sense of humor. A light-hearted joke or some self-deprecating remark does a lot to show off your self-assurance.

Mind Your Manners

Remember the three things I said were the most important to keep in mind when it comes to playing with the boss? Minding your manners on the course is the third. Even more important than being a good golfer is being a good partner. That means being courteous on the course.

I've already gone over in Chapter 15 some of the things that you should—and should not—do on the course to be a good partner. Just to make sure we're on the same page, let me go over a few of them again, because in this case, having good golf etiquette is especially important.

- ◆ **Avoid making any noise or other disruption when another player is hitting.** That includes but isn't limited to talking. The biggest problem I have with some of the amateur partners I play with isn't the chitchat. Most know that they shouldn't talk while I'm swinging. But that doesn't stop them from digging around in their golf bags while I'm setting up to hit a shot. Zippers are zipping; papers are crackling. I would almost rather have them talk, because I could get used to that sound.

  Be especially careful about jingling change in your pocket. At one tournament, I was standing next to the green waiting for my playing partner to finish putting out. About 10 feet from me was a marshal, someone designated by the tournament to keep fans quiet during play. He had a large sign in one hand that read "Quiet Please," and when my partner stood over her putt, he raised it in the air. His other hand was shoved deep in his pants pocket, and he must have had $10 worth of change he was jingling around, blissfully unaware that he was making more noise than any 10 people in the crowd.

- ◆ **Be especially careful about staying out of someone's peripheral vision during the swing.** A person's concentration is focused on the ball during the swing, but a sudden movement on one side or the other will cause the eyes to involuntarily register what is going on away from the ball. That split second of lapsed concentration can cause some ugly shots. Of course, an extension of this is to not move around during anyone else's backswing. You could be making some irritating noises, and if the person can see you out of the corner of his eye, that's a distraction.

- ◆ **Take care of the course, especially if you're a guest at someone else's club.** Not only is it bad manners not to pick up after yourself or replace your divots, it shows a lack of respect for your host. Would you like it if your boss came to your house and dropped cigarette ashes all over your new carpeting and didn't worry about cleaning up? Remember, you are a guest. If that's not enough, remember you are playing with your boss—a person who, like it or not, will be judging you by your behavior. If you want to come across as careless and sloppy, that's your decision, but I don't think it's a good one. Don't drop your garbage on the course. Use the trash cans that are located near most tees, or just leave it on the little shelf in the golf cart. When you get back to the clubhouse, you can throw it away.

♦ **Keep your temper in check.** It's perfectly acceptable to curse at yourself and show some frustration, but don't take it out on the course. Smashing your club into the dirt and ripping a big gash in the grass is extremely bad form, as is throwing clubs. Show your boss your grace under pressure. Don't act like a lunatic.

♦ **Be complimentary, but don't suck up.** If your boss hits a horrible shot that slices out of bounds and breaks a plate glass window, don't say, "Good shot!" Your boss will know you're trying to be ingratiating. Commiserate, but don't patronize.

♦ **Don't be a know-it-all.** Remember how good it feels to be right about something? Everyone enjoys that feeling as much as you do and dislikes being proven wrong just as much. Even if you know something one of your boss's partners is saying is totally wrong or misguided, it's probably better for you just to keep your mouth shut and nod politely, unless you're asked a direct question. Answer truthfully, but be delicate. You don't want to make anyone look like a fool, especially your boss. When in doubt, just keep quiet. Remember, silence is golden.

♦ **Remember that the person who makes the best score on the previous hole has "the honor," which means he or she hits first on the next hole.** Then the person who had the next-best score hits, and so on. Forgetting this will earn you some long looks from your playing partners.

Reciprocating

As in any social situation, if you and your boss or business contact have had a good time playing together, invite him or her to play with you again. It's good manners, good business, and good sense.

After all, if the person enjoys playing with you, the more times you play together, the more comfortable you become with each other. And that, my friends, is how good contacts are built.

Extra Swings

One of the best golf experiences you can have is playing in a Tuesday or Wednesday pro-am with a professional golfer. Some of these pro-ams can be very expensive, like the one at Pebble Beach. But many are very reasonable, especially at LPGA tournament stops. Should you ever get a chance to play with me in one of these tournaments, here are some tips to make your experience more enjoyable:

◆ **Be positive.** You're paying to play on a beautiful day, on a great course, with some of the best players in the world. You aren't out there trying to shoot 15-under par. Having a good time is the most important part of the pro-am experience. Sulking about your game is sort of like missing the forest for the trees.

◆ **Ask questions.** I go out of my way to make my pro-am partners feel comfortable, but I'm always amazed by how many are intimidated by me. I don't know why. I don't bite. Pro-am day is a practice round for the pros involved. We're out there to enjoy the day as well. I'm not saying a pro-am round should be an 18-hole walking lesson, but don't be afraid to ask for some advice on a shot you aren't comfortable with. A pro-am is a learning experience. It's your chance to be up-close and personal with a pro player. Isn't there something you've always been dying to ask? Ask.

◆ **Know your limitations.** Many of the courses on which professionals play in tournaments are more difficult than the courses amateurs are used to playing on. Play from the appropriate tees. You aren't out there to kill yourself, and you don't need to impress anyone, especially the pro. And don't worry about hitting some bad shots. Remember the old caddie's adage—as bad as you might be, I've seen worse.

◆ **Don't come in with preconceived notions.** When I was just starting out on the LPGA Tour, I played in as many pro-ams as I could, because at some of them, we got a little prize money for helping our amateur team finish first. As a struggling 19-year-old rookie, I was looking to make any money I could. But I wasn't as well known as Nancy Lopez or Pat Bradley. Invariably, some of the amateurs I played with were disappointed they didn't get to play with a name pro. Don't let that happen to you. Keep your mind open and enjoy yourself. I know some fringe LPGA and PGA Tour pros who are absolute riots in pro-ams. They kid around with their partners and really help make the day exciting. Amateurs who were initially disappointed about not being paired with a famous pro forgot all about their reservations and had a great time. I also know some people who got their wish and played with some of the most famous players we have in pro golf. And they hated every minute of it, because the big-time pro ignored them for 18 holes and didn't give them any tips or help read any putts. They might as well have been playing in different groups. Is that any fun?

◆ **Don't forget the camera.** You'll want to remember the occasion, and I don't carry a little one in my bag, so I can't help you there!

You don't have to belong to a private club to be able to host your boss or contact in the way he or she hosted you at his or her private club. The best thing to do is to find the highest-rated daily-fee or resort course in your area and book a tee time a couple of weeks in advance. Then tell your boss or contact you have it all set up and would really enjoy it if he or she could play with you again. Make sure to take care of both of your greens fees and cart expenses when you get to the course. After all, he or she took care of your tab the first time. Make it as easy as possible for him or her to agree to play.

Caddie's Advice

When you finish a round with your boss at his or her club, show your appreciation and extend an invitation to play again. Then follow it up later with a phone call or letter.

The Least You Need to Know

◆ If you forget everything else, always remember the three key rules of playing with your boss, client, or other business contact: Be on time, mind your manners, and wait for the appropriate time to discuss business.

◆ Wait until you've played a few holes before you even think about talking about business. And then, try to gauge whether it's appropriate before barging ahead.

◆ In the best golf-and-business outings, you don't even have to try to talk about work. Business will come up naturally, without any prodding from you.

◆ Remember your golf etiquette and be silent when another person is hitting. Don't stand in anyone's peripheral vision as they swing. Take care of the course and keep your temper under control.

◆ If you and your boss or business contact have enjoyed a good round, reciprocate. Invite him or her to play the next time and pick up the tab.

Chapter 25

Golf Organizations and Publications

In This Chapter

- ◆ Select company: Private courses
- ◆ Join the crowd: National golf organizations
- ◆ Ready to compete? Join a league
- ◆ Popular golf publications and websites

If you've decided that golf is going to be a regular hobby for you, or even an obsession, then you're probably going to want to find other people who enjoy the game for the same reasons you do. The United States has so many golfers, you can literally find just about any kind of group to join. In New York City, golfers have banded together to start their own club, even though they don't have their own course to play on. They just meet at different public courses around the city. They even have a club championship. You can spend $20,000 a year to play at a fancy private club, where golf is only one of dozens of social activities. You can play in a nine-hole, after-work league with a bunch of your friends. You name it, and you can probably find it. This chapter will make the finding part a little bit easier.

Is a Private Course for You?

If you're considering whether or not to join a private golf club, you need to ask your-self two questions—how much money do I have to spend, and what other alternatives are available?

Let's tackle the first question first. Just like public courses, you can find private clubs in many different price ranges, from $1,000 in initiation fees and $50 in monthly dues to $500,000 initiation fees and hundreds of dollars in dues. A lot of the difference is geographic. In the Midwest, which has plenty of open land, the average membership to a private club tends to be more affordable. In places like metropolitan New York City and San Francisco, not only is land far more expensive, but there are a lot more people and a lot fewer courses. Demand pushes the price up very high.

One thing to keep in mind about private clubs is that they usually have monthly mini-mums, a requirement that you spend a certain amount of money in the golf shop or restaurant every month. If you don't, the amount is charged to your bill anyway. That can add as little as $100 or as much as $500 to your monthly total. And if you want to bring one of your friends from work to play a round one Saturday, you're responsible for paying for that round as well.

Caddie's Advice

If you do join a private club, take advantage of the fact that you have a club pro who is ready and willing to give you a lesson. As a member, you can most likely get a discount rate.

If you decide to join a private club, shop around. Find out what the membership requirements are, what your initiation fee will be (most clubs have them), and how long, if any, the waiting list is. If you want to join Augusta National, for example, where they play the Masters golf tournament every year, don't hold your breath. Even if you're a billionaire, the only way to get in is by invitation. Many of the most expensive, most famous clubs in the United States are exceedingly selec-tive about new members. You probably shouldn't just walk into the clubhouse and say, "Hey, how do I join?"

If public golf is very expensive or inconvenient in the area where you live, perhaps you should consider joining a mid-level private club. Clubs like this thrive in the New York City area because there are so few public courses for such a large population of golfers. And if you can get a round on one of the city's overplayed tracks, which is no easy feat, the bill is a little more expensive than you would like to pay for a course of that quality. So many players decide to invest a little extra money and commuting time in a mid-range private club in one of New York City's surrounding areas.

You've got to decide for yourself if the public courses in your area offer what you're looking for at the right price. If you plan to play 50 or 60 rounds a year, for example, and a round at the public course you play at most frequently costs $20, then you know that any private club that costs you $1,200 or less and offers good facilities is a good bargain.

If money is really no object, you can think about buying or renting a house in a gated golf community. Often situated around resort golf courses, these places have lots that sit right on the course. Sometimes, your purchase price includes use of the course. Other times, it's an extra you have to purchase. But if you're just getting into the game, you've got some time before you have to worry about calling your real estate agent.

The USGA and Other National Organizations

National golf organizations represent large groups of golfers who are all interested in the same things. These groups can range from the very large (the United States Golf Association has three million members) to the very small (the Golf Writers Association of America has about 300 members). Usually, the dues you pay to these kinds of organizations go toward publications (magazines, books, or newspapers), the planning and staging of golf tournaments, and, in the case of the USGA, the maintenance of the *Rules of Golf*.

The first golf association in the United States, the USGA, was created in 1888 to promote the sport of golf in the United States. Modeled after the *Royal & Ancient Golf Association* in Great Britain, the USGA named as its goal to oversee national championships and create and administer the rules of the game in this country. It runs the

U.S. men's and women's Opens, the men's and women's U.S. Amateurs, men's and women's Senior Opens, and a host of other such tournaments. The USGA also regulates equipment, provides experts in agronomy for golf courses, and runs a comprehensive golf museum in Far Hills, New Jersey. Membership costs $50, and for that fee, you get a copy of the *Rules of Golf* and a USGA bag tag to identify your golf bag.

> **Par Primer**
>
> The **Royal & Ancient Golf Association** is Europe's version of the USGA. It is in charge of the rules in Europe and runs the men's and women's British Opens.

Extra Swings

The USGA has gotten a lot of extra attention lately over the issue of equipment regulation. Equipment manufacturers have been making bigger and bigger clubheads for drivers, with faces that make the ball fly faster than ever. The USGA has always regulated how fast the ball could travel. Now, they've put a limit on how "hot" the faces of drivers can be, and how big the clubhead can get. The USGA is worried that if drivers keep getting bigger and hotter, average-length courses would become obsolete. That might be true for professional players, who get the most benefit from the hot drivers, but the new rules don't have much impact on the average player—who needs all the help he or she can get!

The PGA of America, which is based in Palm Beach Gardens, Florida, represents club professionals, the people who run the pro shops and teach the lessons at public and private courses all across the country. The PGA, which runs nearly 30 tournaments a year for its members, is responsible for certifying those club pros in golf instruction, so that before you go for a lesson, you can judge a teacher on an objective set of credentials. It also represented the male tournament golfers until 1968, when a rift developed between the teaching pro and tournament pro divisions of the organization.

The tournament players separated and formed their own group, the PGA Tour, which is a non-profit corporation devoted to organizing and promoting the collection of tournaments that make up that tour. The PGA Tour, which is based in Ponte Vedra Beach, Florida, also runs the Champions Tour for pro golfers age 50 and over; the Nike Tour, which is the PGA Tour's minor league; and a collection of a dozen courses it owns.

The LPGA, or Ladies Professional Golf Association, is the PGA Tour's counterpart for female professionals. Based in Daytona Beach, Florida, it runs the collection of tournaments female pros play each week and coordinates education and training for female club professionals in teaching and golf promotion. The American Junior Golf Association also runs its own set of regional and national tournaments specifically for younger amateur golfers, broken down into age groups.

The National Golf Foundation, which was founded in 1936, is a non-profit organization dedicated to promoting the sport of golf. It commissions many different surveys and polls devoted to public participation in golf and the golf business and does consulting work for existing courses and developers who are interested in building courses. Based in Jupiter, Florida, it has 6,500 members. The Minority Golf Association of America, which is based in Westhampton, New York, promotes minority participation in the game, runs its own tournaments, and publishes a newsletter.

Extra Swings

The PGA and LPGA tours are the most prominent professional tours in the world, but they aren't the only ones. There are top-level men's and women's tours in Europe, Australia, South Africa, and Japan, and lower-level, minor league tours dot the American southeast. Men can play the Nationwide tour to get ready for the PGA Tour, and women can come up through the Futures Tour.

State and Local Golf Associations

Each state has its own golf association, and the collection of these groups is a sort of minor league to the USGA. The state golf associations run the state-wide open and amateur championships as well as regional tournaments whose winners feed into the USGA's system of national tournaments. Dues for state associations vary, and the main benefit for joining this kind of group is generally the discount you get on entrance fees for state and local tournaments.

Many cities and towns also have their own local golf associations, most of which are dedicated to organizing local tournaments. If you're interested in starting small and playing in some local tournaments before testing your luck on a larger scale, a local golf association might be for you. Check out Appendix B for a list of each state's golf association(s).

Leagues: Nine Holes and a Cloud of Dust

One of the most enjoyable ways to get involved with other golfers is to join a league. Leagues offer the most flexible means to play with a group of players of your own skill and interest level. In most metropolitan areas, you can choose from dozens of different leagues. Many companies organize their own after-work leagues.

Leagues are organized for men and women (or both), by day, time, and handicap. For example, you could play in a Monday league that starts at 4 P.M. and then play in a Saturday league that starts at the crack of dawn. After you're in any given league, players are sorted by their handicaps. Most leagues have either flight, open, or team systems. In a flight system, golfers are divided roughly into levels. The championship flight usually constitutes golfers with zero handicaps or better. Then comes the A flight, which is made up of players with handicaps from one to four. After that is the B flight, which has players with handicaps from five to ten. You move right on down the list. After you've determined your handicap, you join your flight and compete against other players of roughly the same skill level.

Other leagues are arranged in an open format. Everyone in the league submits a handicap and then adjusts his or her score according to that handicap. You turn in what's known as a *net score*, and your net score is compared to the net scores of everyone else. This enables everyone in the league to compete in one big tournament, as opposed to the flight system, which segments the field into five or six mini-tournaments. In open leagues, you're competing against everyone else, even the person with the zero handicap. In a flight league, you're only competing against the members of your flight. There's no real way to compare scores across flights. The good thing about flight leagues is that there are more chances to be a champion—instead of one overall winner, you'll have a winner in each individual flight. More individual champions means more gaudy trophies to put on the mantel.

> **Par Primer**
>
> A **net score** is the score you shot for nine or 18 holes with your handicap subtracted from it.

> **Caddie's Advice**
>
> At many town golf courses, league play fills up most weekday afternoons. If you aren't in a league, try to make your tee times for earlier in the day. Otherwise, you won't be able to get out. Unless you join the league!

In team leagues, you're most likely to play with one partner against the two other players in your foursome. There are many different formats, limited only by your imagination. In some leagues, the players with the lowest handicaps in each partnership compete against each other, as do the two with the higher handicaps. The team member who wins his or her match earns a point for the team. Then, at the end, the two teams compare their total score, adjusted by handicap, and the better team gets another point that way.

You can also play better-ball with your partner using scores adjusted by handicap. Whichever teammate gets the lowest adjusted score for the hole, the team uses that score. The team with the lowest aggregate score wins. In a team league, records of wins and losses are kept, just like in baseball or basketball. So if you play in a 15-week league, you're going to play with your partner against 15 other teams, and you can win, lose, or tie each one. The team with the best overall record at the end of the season wins the league.

After format, the biggest difference between leagues is whether they are played over 18 holes or 9 holes. This mostly has to do with time. If you're planning to play in an after-work league that starts at 4 P.M., unless you live somewhere with 24 hours of daylight, you're only going to get 9 holes in. Saturday or Sunday leagues are more likely to be played over 18 holes, as are many retiree leagues that are played weekday mornings. Choose whichever format and hole amount is best for your interests and schedule.

Extra Swings

Most leagues have handicap requirements and regulations that you should know about before you try to join. If you're playing in a 9-hole league, remember that your 9-hole handicap is half of your standard 18-hole handicap. Also, many leagues have upper limits on the handicap you can have to play. For example, if you have a 9-hole handicap of 15, you aren't eligible to play in a league that limits 9-hole handicaps to 10. That's okay, because you probably wouldn't want to play with a bunch of people with games that much more advanced than yours, anyway. It's much more fun to play with people close to your own skill level. If nothing else, at least you'll have someone to commiserate with!

Golf Publications

As any television network executive can tell you, what golfers lack in numbers, they make up for with spending power. Regardless of income level, golfers like to spend money on equipment and greens fees. Advertisers know this, so they like to tout their products wherever golfers congregate. The advertising base for pro-golf tournaments on television and in magazines is very strong. That means there are lots of programs and publications from which to choose. We're going to focus for a moment on golf publications.

The three most common monthly magazines devoted to the sport are *Golf Digest* (circulation of 1.55 million), *Golf Magazine* (1.4 million) and *Golf For Women* (500,000). All three are available at most newsstands for less than $4 per copy and by subscription for less than $20 per year. *Golf Digest* and *Golf Magazine* offer instructional stories with prominent teachers and players, along with travel and equipment stories. *Golf For Women* is the only national magazine devoted completely to instructions and features for female golfers.

Golf World (circulation 150,000), *Golf Week* (100,000) and *Sports Illustrated's Golf Plus* (400,000) are the three most common weekly golf magazines or supplements. *Golf World* focuses on game stories from the previous week's tournaments, player features, and international news. *Golf Week* is the most comprehensive statistical magazine in golf, with scores and updates from every major tour and many amateur tournaments around the United States. *Golf Plus* comes as a free news insert to 400,000 *of Sports Illustrated's* three million subscribers,

Caddie's Advice

Before you subscribe to a golf magazine, decide what facets of the sport are most interesting to you. Do you want to read more about professional players, or are you interested in instruction and equipment reviews?

based on the demographics of the area they live in. It focuses on game stories and in-depth professional player features. If you subscribe to *Sports Illustrated*, you can get the *Golf Plus* section added for no charge.

Golf on the Web

Golf websites have become one of the most popular ways to follow the professional game. The PGA, LPGA, and European tours all have their own sites (pgatour.com, lpga.com, and europeantour.com), and you can get real-time scoring updates at all three. If I make a birdie on the first hole of the McDonald's LPGA Championship, you'll know about it only a minute or two after I do, if you're logged on to lpga.com at the time. We've already talked about some of the websites you can visit to buy new and used equipment. Another website that comes in handy is ghin.com. It has a complete listing of every player with a USGA handicap. You can type in a player's last name and the state he or she lives in and get a listing of the last 20 scores he or she recorded. It comes in handy when your friend keeps trying to get you to give her extra shots in your next match!

The Least You Need to Know

- ◆ If money is no object or the public courses in your area are too crowded or too expensive, joining a private club might be for you.

- ◆ Remember that most private clubs have a minimum amount you must spend in their pro shop or restaurant each month. If you don't, you'll be charged that amount anyway.

- ◆ No matter what your focus or interest in golf happens to be, there likely is a golf organization, national or local, to fit you.

- ◆ Leagues are a great way to surround yourself with players of similar interests and skill levels. Look around until you find one that offers what you're looking for.

- ◆ Like golf organizations, you can find golf publications that cater to your interests. The national ones have a broader focus, while smaller, regional publications focus closely on one aspect of the game.

Appendix A

Par Primer Glossary

address Your body position (stance and setup) just before you start your swing.

alignment How you set up your body to hit the ball in a certain direction.

amateur A player who doesn't accept money winnings in tournaments. Opposite of a professional.

approach shot A shot played with the green as the target.

away The player farthest from the hole. Whoever is away plays first.

back nine The second half of an 18-hole round or golf course.

backspin Spin that is in the opposite direction of flight. It makes the ball land and stop, or roll slightly backward.

backswing The first part of the swing, which is moving the club away from the ball. *See* takeaway.

ball mark The dent left in the green when a ball lands.

ball marker A small, round piece of plastic or metal placed on the green on the spot where your ball was. It enables your fellow players to putt at the hole without any obstructions.

ball washer Instrument usually located by each tee-box that is used to clean golf balls.

baseball grip Grip that features all 10 fingers secured sequentially on the grip. Also known as the "10-finger grip."

best ball Taking the best individual score from a team of players on a given hole and using it as the team score.

birdie Playing a hole in one stroke less than par. For example, making a four on a par-5 would be making a birdie.

blade (1) To hit the ball in its center with the bottom edge of the club, instead of the clubface. (2) A type of putter with an elongated, cigar-shaped face.

block Hitting the ball on a straight line, but far right of the target.

bogey Playing a hole in one stroke above par (for example, making a four on a par-3).

bump and run A low shot from just off the green that flies for a short distance, lands, and then rolls toward the hole.

bunker Sand-filled hazard. Also known as a "sand trap."

caddie Person hired to carry clubs and provide advice about club selection.

carry How far a ball flies in the air. Added with roll to determine the full length of the shot.

cart Small motorized car used to drive around the course and carry clubs.

cast A method of manufacturing irons in which hot metal is poured into a series of dies. Most of these kinds of irons have perimeter weighting, which is mass around the edges of the club that make it more forgiving of off-center shots.

casual water A puddle or other incidental amount of water that is temporary and not part of the course. There is no penalty for hitting into it.

chili-dip Hitting the ground way before hitting the ball, causing a weak, popped-up shot or a grounder. Otherwise known as "chunking a shot" or "hitting it fat."

chip A short shot within 30 yards of the green.

chunk   Hitting the ground way before the ball, causing a weak, popped-up shot or a grounder. Otherwise known as "hitting it fat" or a "chili-dip."

closed clubface   When, on the downswing, the clubface is pointing left of the target, causing the ball to fly in that direction.

closed stance   Positioning the feet with the back foot pulled back from the ball. If you drew a line in front of your toes, that line would point to the right of the target.

clubface   The area of the front of the clubhead that should make contact with the ball.

clubhouse   The building at a course that houses the golf shop, restrooms, and a snack bar or restaurant.

collar   The strip of transitional grass surrounding the green that is shorter than the fairway, but not as short as the green. Also called the "fringe."

compression   How much the surface of a golf ball will give when it hits the clubface. The higher the compression number, the less the ball will give.

concede   To give your opponent credit for making a putt without having him or her attempt it. It is common for putts "inside the leather," or shorter than the length of a putter grip. You can also concede a hole—give your opponent credit for winning it—in match play.

course rating   A system that determines the relative difficulty of a course. The higher the number, the more difficult the course.

cross-handed   A putting grip in which the left hand is lower on the grip.

cup   Another name for the hole.

cut   Another name for a shot with slight left-to-right spin.

daily fee course   A privately owned course that is open to the public all or most of the time.

divot   A gouge of dirt and grass you take when you hit a shot.

divot repair tool   A two-pronged piece of plastic or metal used to fix a ball mark or other indentation on the green.

dogleg   A hole that isn't straight, but curves one way or another.

double bogey   Scoring two strokes above par on a hole.

double eagle   Scoring three strokes below par on a hole. Also known as an "albatross." This is the rarest score in golf. A hole in one on a par-4 is a kind of double eagle.

downswing   The part of the swing that comes directly after the backswing. The move of the club from the top of the backswing toward the ball.

draw   A shot that curves slightly from right to left.

drive   The first shot hit on a par-five or par-four hole, from the tee-box.

driver   The longest club in the bag, this club is usually made from steel or titanium and is designed to hit the ball from a tee.

driving range   A practice area where you can hit full shots.

drop   To put a new ball into play when the old one is lost or to replace the same ball into play after it ends up in an unplayable position.

eagle   To play a hole in two strokes below par.

etiquette   The standard of behavior and conduct on the golf course.

face   The front of a clubhead, where the grooves are.

fade   A shot with slight left-to-right curve.

fairway   The closely cut area of a hole that is usually on a straight path between the tee-box and the hole. The optimum landing area for a shot from the tee.

fat   Hitting the ground well before the ball on a shot. *See* chunk or chili-dip.

flagstick   The pole that stands in the hole as an aiming aid. Also called the "pin."

flex   The amount of "whip" in a shaft. More whip translates into more power and less control. Less whip means more control and less power.

flop   A kind of chip shot that is hit high into the air so that the ball will land on the green and stop quickly. Also called a "lob."

follow-through   The part of the swing that comes just after impact. The swing's "brake."

fore   The word you should shout if you think your shot will land near another golfer. A warning call.

forged   A method of manufacturing irons. These kind are made by hammering a piece of hot metal into shape. In general, they are less forgiving and more precise than cast clubs.

foursome   A standard group of players in golf.

fried egg   A ball that is stuck in its own divot in a bunker.

fringe   Another name for the collar. A transition strip of grass that is cut shorter than the fairway, but longer than the green.

glove   A leather or leatherlike cover for the hand that helps you grip. Left-handed players wear usually wear one on the right hand, and vice versa.

golf shop   Place at the course where you check in, pay for your round, and buy any equipment and accessories you might need, like balls or tees.

grain   On courses seeded with Bermuda grass, grain is the direction the blades of Bermuda grass are growing. Putts will drift in the direction of the grain.

graphite   A carbon-based substance used in golf club shafts. It is lighter and more flexible than steel, but more expensive.

green   The closely mown area that directly surrounds the hole, your ultimate objective. Where you putt.

greenie   On a par-three hole, hitting the tee shot on the green and closest to the hole.

greens fee   The charge for playing at a golf course.

grip   The leather or rubber strip at the top of the shaft where you hold the club.

groove   Scoring on the face of the club that helps create backspin on a shot.

ground   To put the club down (touching the ground) behind the ball. This is illegal in a hazard or bunker, but legal anywhere else.

ground under repair   Marked by white dotted lines painted on the grass, this is an area under construction by the golf course. You can drop from here without a penalty.

handicap   A method of adjusting your score in relation to par. This system helps golfers of any skill level compete on a level playing field.

hardpan   Densely packed dirt or grass.

hazard   Area made up of sand or water where you cannot ground your club.

head cover   Wool or synthetic sleeve that protects the clubhead.

heel   The area on the sole of the clubhead nearest to the point where the shaft connects to the clubhead.

hole   The ultimate goal in golf. Where you're trying to hit your ball. Each hole is surrounded by a green of closely cut grass. Also used as a verb: "I holed my chip."

hole in one   Hitting your tee shot into the hole. Drinks are on you!

honor   In order of play, the person who made the lowest score on the previous hole earns the right to play first on the next hole. Part of etiquette.

hood   To close the clubface during the swing.

hook   A shot with severe right-to-left spin.

hosel   The part of the club where the clubface connects to the shaft.

impediment   Loose items that you can move away from your ball without penalty (as long as your ball doesn't move), like twigs, stones, or garbage.

inside out   The proper path of the club on the downswing. The club comes from the body-side of an imaginary line through the ball to the target and finishes on the other side of that line, just past the ball.

interlocking grip   A type of grip that features the linking of the index finger of the left hand and the pinkie finger of the right hand.

iron   One of the collection of clubs in a set that runs from a 3-iron to a sand wedge, used to hit the ball from the rough or fairway.

kick   The direction a ball bounces.

lag   To putt a ball with the intent not to make it, but to leave an easy, short second putt.

lateral hazard   A water hazard to the side of the fairway or green. Set off by red stakes.

lay up   The practice of hitting a shorter shot if you decide you don't want to risk playing a longer one.

lie   What you should never do about your handicap. Also, the type of ground your ball sits on.

lift, clean, and place   Sometimes, when conditions are bad, local rules allow you to pick up your ball, clean it off, and set it down again within a clublength of the original spot.

line   The intended path of a shot.

lip   The edge of the cup or hole.

local rules   Special rules set up by individual courses to deal with special situations, such as a set of power lines located over a fairway.

loft   The amount of "lift" on a clubface. The more loft, the higher, and shorter, the club will hit the ball.

long irons   The 1-, 2-, 3-, and 4-irons. Named for the length of their shafts.

marker   The plastic or metal token placed at the exact spot where your ball is on the green, or the set of tees from which you play a hole.

match play   A contest between two players that is decided hole by hole instead of cumulatively over 18.

medal play   A contest between players decided by the best score for 18 holes.

metal wood   The longest clubs in the bag. Made with steel, aluminum, or titanium, these are designed to hit the ball a long way, with less premium on accuracy.

mulligan   A "do-over" on a tee shot. Usually only acceptable when playing a friendly round.

municipal course   A course owned by a city or town that is open to everyone in that town.

Nassau   The basic bet in golf. It is made in three parts—the front nine, the back nine, and the overall.

net   Your score, adjusted by your handicap.

open clubface   A swing with the clubface pointing right of the target at impact, which causes the ball to fly that way.

open stance   A stance where the front foot is pulled back from the ball. If you drew a line in front of your toes, it would point to the left of the target.

out of bounds Hitting the ball off the edge of the course. Marked by white stakes.

outside in Crossing the imaginary line drawn through the ball to the target from the side away from the body to the side closest to the body just after impact.

overlapping grip A grip that features the pinkie of the right hand resting in the groove between the index and middle fingers of the right hand.

par The score a good golfer should make on a given hole. Par is usually three for holes under 240 yards, four for holes from 240 to 470 yards, and five for holes longer than 470 yards. It is also the score a good golfer should make for a given golf course, usually 72.

perimeter weighting The distribution of mass around the edge of the clubface. It makes the club more forgiving on off-center shots.

pin The pole that sits in the hole as an aiming aid. *See* flagstick.

pitch A shot to the green from less than 80 yards away and longer than 40 yards away—longer than a chip, but shorter than a full shot.

pivot The weight transfer in the swing.

playing through A slower group allowing a faster one to pass on the golf course.

practice green An area, usually near the first tee, where you can practice putting before you start your round.

practice swing The rehearsal before a real swing.

primary rough As you leave the fairway toward the side of the hole, the first, shorter height of rough.

private club A course where only members and their guests can play.

pro-am A tournament, usually before the start of a professional event, where professionals play with amateur partners.

professional Someone who plays golf for money, or a person who is trained to teach golf.

pro shop The store at a course that sells equipment, clothes, and tee times; also called the "golf shop."

provisional   Playing a second ball if you aren't sure what happened to the first one. Then if the first one is lost or out of play, you don't have to go all the way back to the tee to play another.

public course   A course that is open to anyone who wants to play and pays the greens fee.

pull   A shot that doesn't curve but goes in a straight line significantly left of the target. The opposite of a push.

push   A shot that doesn't curve but goes in a straight line significantly right of the target.

putter   A club with a flat face used on the green.

range   The practice area. *See* driving range.

read   To decipher the line of a putt on the green.

release   Uncocking the wrists just before your club impacts with the ball during the downswing.

reverse overlap   A specialized putting grip in which the left index finger fits in the groove between the pinkie and ring fingers of the right hand.

rough   Grass that is grown longer than that of the fairway. It is designed to be harder to hit from than the fairway and as a penalty for inaccuracy.

round   Playing 9 or 18 holes.

run   The amount of roll on a shot. Added with carry to determine the full distance of a shot.

sandbag   To lie about your handicap and give yourself more strokes than you deserve.

sandie   To hit a shot out of a bunker onto the green and then make the ensuing putt for birdie or par.

score   How many strokes it takes for a hole or round.

scorecard   Where you keep track of your score. It also has hole, distance, and par information.

scramble   A form of competition where a team plays from the best shot from the tee through the green.

scratch   A handicap of zero, which means a player usually shoots around even-par.

secondary rough   Thicker rough that is further from the fairway than primary rough.

setup   The grip, stance, and alignment of a swing.

shaft   The engine of the club; it runs from the grip to the clubhead and is made of steel or graphite.

shank   To hit a shot off the hosel.

short game   Shots hit around and on the green—chipping and putting.

short irons   The 8- and 9-irons, pitching, and sand wedges. Named for the length of their shafts.

shut   Another term for "closed," it means that the clubface is pointed to the left of the target at impact.

skins   A form of competition where each hole is contested as a bet. If the hole is tied, the bet carries over to the next hole.

skull   To hit the ball above its equator, causing it to skid along the ground.

slice   A shot with severe left-to-right spin.

sole   The flat part of the club that rests on the ground. Clubs with flat soles slide along the ground, and clubs with angled soles dig into the turf.

spike   The metal, rubber, or plastic nipple that is screwed into a golf shoe to provide traction.

spike mark   An indentation in the putting green caused by a spike.

square   Returning the clubface to the ball pointed straight at the target at impact.

stance   How you place your feet in preparation for a swing.

starter   The person who is in charge of sending groups out on the golf course.

stick   The pole that sits in the hole as an aiming aid. Also called the "flagstick" or "pin."

stroke   A swing.

sweetspot   The best part of the clubface on which to hit the ball.

takeaway   The first part of the backswing, when the club is still on line with the ball.

tee   A wooden peg used to improve a lie in the tee-box. It can only be used in the tee-box.

tee-box   The area at the beginning of a hole, between the markers, where you can tee your ball and start.

tee time   The appointment you make to play a round of golf. Usually made at the golf shop several days in advance.

thin   Hitting a ball at its equator, causing a low shot; less severe than a skull.

top   Hitting the ball on its top half, which causes a grounder; more severe than hitting it thin.

trajectory   How high or low the ball flies.

trap   *See* bunker.

unplayable lie   A ball that is still in play, but in a spot where you can't make a swing on it.

Vardon grip   Another name for the overlapping grip.

water hazard   A hazard identified by yellow stakes. Drop behind the hazard at a point between where you hit it and the pin.

wedge   A short club with lots of loft.

winter rules   Because of less-than-average conditions, moving the ball to a better lie in the fairway.

yips   An affliction that affects the nerves in the hands and arms and causes the putter to jerk on short putts.

National and State Golf Organizations

In this section, you'll find a list of national and state golf organizations and associations that will help you get together with players who have the same interest and skill level.

National Golf Organizations

American Junior Golf Association (AJGA)
1980 Sportsclub Drive
Braselton, GA 30517
1-800-863-3669

Association of Disabled American Golfers
PO Box 280649
303-922-5228

College Golf Foundation
174 Tamarack Circle, Suite B
Skillman, NJ 08558
941-751-9746

The First Tee Program
425 South Legacy Trail
St. Augustine, FL 32092
904-940-4300

Ladies Professional Golf Association (LPGA)
100 International Golf Drive
Daytona Beach, FL 32114
386-274-6200

PGA of America
100 Avenue of the Champions
Palm Beach Gardens, FL 33418
561-624-8400

PGA Tour
112 PGA Tour Boulevard
Ponte Vedra, FL 32082
1-800-840-5628

United States Golf Association (USGA)
PO Box 708
Golf House
Far Hills, NJ 07931
1-800-222-8742

State Golf Associations

Alabama

Alabama Golf Association
PO Box 660149
Birmingham, AL 35266
205-979-1234

Alaska

Alaska Golf Association
1307 E. 74th Avenue
Anchorage, AK 99518
907-349-4653

Arizona

Arizona Golf Association
7226 North 16th St. #200
Phoenix, AZ 85020
602-944-3035

Arizona Women's Golf Association
141 E. Palm Lane, Suite 210
Phoenix, AZ 85020
602-944-3035

Arkansas

Arkansas State Golf Association
3 Eagle Hill Court, Suite B
Little Rock, AR 72210
501-455-2742

California

Northern California Golf Association
PO Box NCGA
3200 Lopez Rd.
Pebble Beach, CA 93953
408-625-4653

Southern California Golf Association
3740 Cahuenga Blvd.
North Hollywood, CA 91609
818-980-2709

Women's Golf Association of Northern California
5776 Stoneridge Mall Road, Suite 160
Pleasanton, CA 94588
925-737-0963

Women's Southern California Golf Association
402 W. Arrow Hwy. #10
San Dimas, CA 91773
714-592-1281

Colorado

Colorado Golf Association
5990 Greenwood Plaza Blvd. #130
Greenwood Village, CO 80111
303-366-4653

Connecticut

Connecticut State Golf Association
35 Cold Spring Rd. #212
Rocky Hill, CT 06067
203-257-4171

Connecticut Women's Golf Association
56 Buckingham Street
Naugatuck, CT 06779
203-729-3762

Delaware

Delaware State Golf Association
7234 Lancaster Pike #302-B
Hockessin, DE 19707
302-234-3365

Delaware Women's Golf Association
PO Box 15107
Newark, DE 19711
302-995-0955

Florida

Florida State Golf Association
8875 Hidden River Pkwy, Suite 110
Tampa, FL 33637
813-632-3742

Florida Women's State Golf Association
8875 Hidden River Pkwy, Suite 110
Tampa, FL 33637
813-632-2130

Georgia

Georgia State Golf Association
121 Village Pkwy., Bldg. 3
Marietta, GA 30067
404-955-4272

Georgia Women's Golf Association
5000 Harbour Ridge Drive
Alpharetta, GA 30005
770-751-1859

Hawaii

Hawaii State Golf Association
770 Kapiolani Blvd, Suite 701
Honolulu, HI 96813
808-589-2909

Hawaii State Women's Golf Association
770 Kapiolani Blvd, Suite 701
Honolulu, HI 96813
808-589-2046

Idaho

Idaho Golf Association
PO Box 9958
Boise, ID 83703
208-342-4442

Illinois

Western Golf Association
1 Briar Rd.
Golf, IL 60029
630-724-4600

Illinois Women's Golf Association
2213 Bristol Road
Champaign, IL 61821
217-352-9873

Indiana

Indiana Golf Association
PO Box 516
Franklin, IN 46131
317-738-9696

Indiana Women's Golf Association
9379 W. 600 South
Andrews, IN 46702

Iowa

Iowa Golf Association
8515 Douglas Avenue #25
Urbandale, IA 50322
515-331-3603

Iowa Women's Golf Association
152 Golf Lane
Burlington, IA 52601
319-754-7818

Kansas

Kansas Golf Association
3301 Clinton Pkwy. Ct. #4
Lawrence, KS 66047
913-842-4833

Kansas Women's Golf Association
2310 SW Mayfair Place
Topeka, KS 66611
785-266-0931

Kentucky

Kentucky Golf Association
PO Box 18396
Louisville, KY 40261
502-499-7255

Women's Kentucky State Golf Association
104 S. 9th Street
Murray, KY 42071
270-759-9949

Louisiana

Louisiana Golf Association
1003 Hugh Wallis Road, Suite G.
Lafayette, LA 70508
337-265-3938

Louisiana Women's Golf Association
1300 4th Street
Jonesville, LA 71343
318-339-7639

Maine

Maine State Golf Association
374 U.S. Route 1
Yarmouth, ME 04096
207-846-3800

Women's Maine State Golf Association
RR #10, 48 Rodrique Heights
Augusta, ME 04330
207-622-3570

Maryland

Maryland State Golf Association
Suite 395, Commercecenter East
1777 Reistertown Road
Baltimore, MD 21208
410-653-5300

Massachusetts

Massachusetts State Golf Association
300 Arnold Palmer Blvd.
Norton, MA 02766
774-430-9100

Women's Golf Association of Massachusetts
300 Arnold Palmer Blvd.
Norton, MA 02766
774-430-9010

Michigan

Golf Association of Michigan
24116 Research Drive
Farmington Hills, MI 48835
248-478-9242

Michigan Women's Golf Association
8520 Englewood Drive
Clarkston, MI 48346
248-625-8705

Minnesota

Minnesota Golf Association
6550 York Ave. South #211
Edina, MN 55434
612-927-4643

Minnesota Women's Public Golf Association
2915 Inwood Ave. North
Lake Elmo, MN 55042
651-773-3805

Mississippi

Mississippi Golf Association
400 Clubhouse Drive
Jackson, MS 39208
601-939-1131

Mississippi Women's Golf Association
530 Country Club Drive
Senatobia, MS 38668
662-562-7667

Missouri

Missouri Golf Association
PO Box 104164
Jefferson City, MO 65110
314-636-8994

Missouri Women's Golf Association
223 Whitmoor Forest Court
St. Charles, MO 63304
636-441-7092

Montana

Montana State Golf Association
PO Box 4308
Helena, MT 59604
406-458-3359

Montana State Women's Golf Association
PO Box 52
Sidney, MO 59270
406-488-5135

Nebraska

Nebraska Golf Association
6618 South 118th Street
Omaha, NE 68137
402-505-4653

Nebraska Women's Amateur Golf Association
5814 South 118th Plaza
Omaha, NE 68137
402-896-9597

Nevada

Nevada State Golf Association
PO Box 5630
Sparks, NV 89432
702-673-4653

Nevada State Women's Golf Association
1853 Chaise Drive
Carson City, NV 89703
775-883-6628

New Hampshire

New Hampshire Golf Association
PO Box 400
Canterbury, NH 03224
603-783-4554

New Hampshire Women's Golf Association
PO Box 16
20 Candia Road
Deerfield, NH 03037

New Jersey

New Jersey State Golf Association
1000 Broad St.
Bloomfield, NJ 07003
201-338-8334

Women's New Jersey Golf Association
16 Pennbrook Court
Boonton Township, NJ 07005
973-316-0716

New Mexico

Sun Country Amateur Golf Association
10035 Country Club Lane NW #5
Albuquerque, NM 87114
505-897-0864

Sun Country Amateur Golf Association–Women's Division
1835 Rita Drive NE
Albuquerque, NM 88201
505-844-6042

New York

New York State Golf Association
PO Box 15333
Syracuse, NY 13215
315-471-6979

Metropolitan Golf Association
49 Knollwood Rd.
Elmsford, NY 10523
914-347-4653

Women's Metropolitan Golf Association
49 Knollwood Rd.
Elmsford, NY 10523
914-592-7888

North Carolina

Carolinas Golf Association
PO Box 319
West End, NC 27376
910-673-1000

North Carolina Women's Golf Association
809 Mt. Vernon Avenue
Charlotte, NC 28203
704-332-4847

North Dakota

North Dakota State Golf Association
PO Box 452
Bismarck, ND 58502
701-223-2770

Ohio

Ohio Golf Association
4701 Olentangy River Road #200A
Columbus, OH 43214
614-457-8169

Women's Ohio State Golf Association
4221 High Pointe Drive
Medina, OH 44256
330-723-0598

Oklahoma

Oklahoma Golf Association
6217 N. Classen Blvd.
Oklahoma City, OK 73118
405-848-0042

Women's Oklahoma Golf Association
2224 Tanglewood Circle
Stillwater, OK 74074
405-372-6526

Oregon

Oregon Golf Association
2840 Hazelnut Drive
Woodburn, OR 97071
503-981-4653

Oregon Women's Golf Association
11910 SW Wildwood
Tigard, OR 97224

Pennsylvania

Golf Association of Philadelphia
PO Drawer 808
Southeastern, PA 19399
215-687-2340

Pennsylvania State Women's Golf Association
153 Skymeadow Lane
Leola, PA 17540

Rhode Island

Rhode Island Golf Association
One Button Hole Drive, Suite 2
Providence, RI 02909
401-272-1350

Ocean State Women's Golf Association
PO Box 597
Portsmouth, RI 02871

South Carolina

South Carolina Golf Association
PO Box 286
Irom, SC 29063
803-781-6992

Women's South Carolina Golf Association
PO Box 1759
Bluffton, SC 29910
803-757-4653

South Dakota

South Dakota Golf Association
307 W. 41st Street, Suite 8
Sioux Falls, SD 57105

Tennessee

Tennessee Golf Association
400 Franklin Rd.
Franklin, TN 37064
615-790-7600

Tennessee Golf Association–Women's Division
400 Franklin Rd.
Franklin, TN 37064
615-790-7600

Texas

Texas Golf Association
2611 Cedar Springs Suite 100
Dallas, TX 75201
214-468-8942

Women's Texas Golf Association
6234 Sugar Hill
Houston, TX 77057
713-467-4811

Utah

Utah Golf Association
PO Box 5601
Sandy, UT 84091
801-563-0400

Utah State Women's Golf Association
2054 Michigan Avenue
Salt Lake City, UT 84108
801-583-1785

Vermont

Vermont Golf Association
PO Box 1612, Station A
Rutland, VT 05701
802-773-7180

Vermont State Women's Golf Association
PO Box 352
Marlboro, VT 05344
802-464-5683

Virginia

Virginia State Golf Association
600 Founders Bridge Boulevard
Midlothian, VA 23113
804-378-2300

Virginia State Golf Association–Women's Division
600 Founders Bridge Boulevard
Midlothian, VA 23113
804-378-2300

Washington Metropolitan Golf Association
8012 Colorado Springs Dr.
Springfield, VA 22153
703-569-6311

Washington

Washington State Golf Association
355 118th SE, Suite 100
Seattle, WA 98005
206-526-1238

Washington State Women's Golf Association
1555 Parkside Drive E.
Seattle, WA 98112
206-325-1555

West Virginia

West Virginia Golf Association
PO Box 850
Hurricane, WV 25526
304-757-3444

Wisconsin

Wisconsin State Golf Association
PO Box 35
Elm Grove, WI 53122
414-786-4301

Wisconsin Women's State Golf Association
PO Box 724
Germantown, WI 53022
262-255-5188

Wyoming

Wyoming State Golf Association
500 Eighth Avenue North
Greybull, WY 82426
307-568-3670

Index

M

N

O

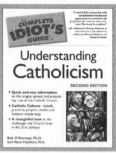

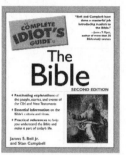

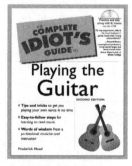

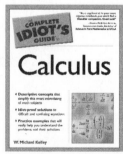